MW01623043

To Therese,

Thank you for your interest!

Gloria

Once there was and will never be again

by Gloria Siers

Published by:

AUTUMNBERRY HILL
941 W. Wing Road
Mount Pleasant, MI 48858

This book is based on a true story, but all characters, names, locations, and events have been fictionalized and are the product of the author's imagination.

ISBN 978-0-615-25733-4

Printed in the United States of America

First Edition

This book is dedicated to the memory of
the real Peter, who lived this story,
and to his dear ones,
Jane, Julie, Greg, Brian, and Kari.

Acknowledgments

Thanks most of all to my father, the real Peter of this story, who shared his recollections in wonderful detail.

Thanks to my mother, for her patience and help in translating my father's tapes and notes, and for her knowledge of the customs and traditions of their generation.

Thanks to my sister, Joanne, for her support, insights and encouragement throughout the years of preparation of this manuscript.

Special thanks to my initial readers, Linda Racine, Becky Kurtz, Father Joseph Favara, and Dr. Ronald Primeau, for their helpful comments along the way.

Special thanks to Dr. Paul H. Snyder, D.V.M., for his unwavering patience when answering so many questions about animal behavior and livestock in Eastern Europe, as well as his help with proper terminology and the understanding of health problems of farm animals in the book's historical time frame.

Thanks to Regina Somerfeld for her encouragement and assistance with the editorial evaluation.

Special thanks to the late Mrs. Georgina Grimard for her help in providing information that enhanced the chapters about Peter's time in western Canada. She was a gracious, kind woman. Although we never met face to face, we became friends over the years and I cherish the correspondence we shared.

Thanks to my children, Greg, Brian, and Kari, and my nieces, Jane and Julie, who were the inspiration for this work. This history is for them.

Very special thanks to my daughter, Kari, for the scores of hours she invested in the preparation of this manuscript for printing. Her help, talents and insights as a graphic designer are very precious to me and I appreciate every one.

Finally, heartfelt thanks to my dear husband, Paul, for his constant support, suggestions, encouragement and patience every step of the way, for years of listening to my ideas, and for his willingness to read and reread chapters over time.

Contents

Introduction

The words "Once upon a time" begin many English fairy tales. In the country called Ukraine, stories often began, "Once there was and will never be again." Those opening words in Ukrainian folklore introduced not only fairy tales and fables, but also true stories of heroic deeds and lives.

This story is about a boy named Peter, who lived and grew up through times of war, prejudice, sadness, joy, and hope. He never became a leader of a country or a great scientist, or rich or very famous, but he faced life with unique courage and determination. He was an immigrant. He was a dreamer, an idealist, and a lover of freedom. He was a common man whose life showed uncommon perception and hope.

In coming to know Peter, we can better understand our pioneer spirit. That adventurous drive built our land and came from the immigrants who brought their heritage and dreams to our shores throughout history. We are a nation entirely made up of immigrants and pilgrims. Even our native North Americans are thought to have migrated from Asia.

No one stands as a single point in history. Everyone is a part of the timeline of his or her ancestry. Somewhere on each and every timeline, someone with motivation and courage became an immigrant. Each was a seedling that was transplanted and had to find a place to take root before running out of life. Peter's story helps us understand how such a spirit grows and seeks fulfillment. He was part of the common people, and yet he was wonderfully unique. His tale is based on a true story.

Chapter 1

Fishes

Once there was and will never be again a little village boy named Peter. He was much like any other little farm boy, yet he was different because of the way life collided with his spirit. At first glance Peter and his village were seemingly unremarkable and ordinary, like common field flowers that bend in a summer wind. But on closer study, some so-called common flowers can be very special because of their sinewy stems, deep roots, and practical blossoms that enable them to endure and survive in a hostile world. Peter was definitely like a special field flower.

Peter's serious grey eyes were not a color that poets often praise, but they carefully watched the world around him and from an early age showed him many patterns in life. His wit was anything but common and his intelligence made him question what he saw because he wanted to understand everything. His rumpled clothes and tousled blond hair made him look unkempt, but he appeared that way because he spent hours exploring the underbrush or crawling through the hayloft watching tiny animals go about the business of life. He tried to absorb life the way lovingly tilled soil absorbs a gentle spring rain.

Peter's village, Opaka, was surrounded by low rolling hills, with fields that produced hardy crops like cabbages and potatoes or rye, oats and wheat. The carefully tended fields were interrupted in places by pockets of marshland or scattered forests of beech, oak, and pine. A narrow, lazy river wound past the northeastern boundary of the quiet settlement and gave the village geese a refreshing place to congregate in warm weather.

Peter often wished he could become one of the animals he loved to watch. He especially wanted to fly like a little bird, and in his daydreams he would swoop to the top of the ancient oak at the end of the common pasture at dawn to see Opaka waking in the gentle morning sun. The tall Lombardy poplars that lined the main road stood like quiet, loyal sentinels to watch for the approaching day. The weathered wooden houses and barns, with their thick, straw-covered roofs, and the bushy boughs of oak and beech trees in the farmyards softened the angular lines of the small, clustered farms. Here and there one could see geese flapping their wings to shake out the stiffness of a night's sleep and greet the morning light. People stirred in the farmyards, either heading to the barns to do chores or returning with heavy milk pails to the houses. Their clothes blended with the colors of unpainted buildings and fences and the tired soil that grew their crops. In contrast to the duller earthen tones were the long aprons of the farm women. The whiteness of the plain fabric rivaled that of the snowy geese and ducks.

In 1913, Opaka was a farming village of barely two hundred and fifty people, and it was located in Galicia, one of the crown colonies of the Austro-Hungarian Empire. The Ukrainians who populated much of it called the colony "Halychyna." Peter's father had once drawn him a little picture map of the area and of the tiny village that was home. Opaka looked like a little cross made up of its two intersecting roads. The main road ran through the village and led to the market city of Lubachiv about three kilometers to the north. The village school, the shoemaker's house, the roadside crucifix, the town hall, the blacksmith's shop, and the house of the old Jewish grain dealer were all located along the main road and were places that the villagers used when they gave directions or needed landmarks to guide their way.

The other village road served as the front border to most of Opaka's farmyards. The narrow rectangular properties looked like big banners unfurled on either side of the east-west road. The farmyards were only about fifteen to twenty meters wide and some eighty to one hundred meters deep. Each one had a straw-roofed house and barns, a chicken coop, an outhouse, a well that was usually shared by two neighbors through a common fence, and a door on the ground that covered the entrance to a root cellar. A muddy, rut-filled lane ran along the back of the farms and served as an access route for people and wagons as they headed out to work the fields beyond the village.

The village church, built of the same weathered, unpainted wood as the rest of the structures in Opaka, had a tin roof, and, in keeping with traditional Ukrainian style, featured three onion-shaped domes on top. It sat next to its little cemetery on a low hill in a grove of beech trees, just to the west and north of the crossroads. The church was Peter's favorite landmark because when he saw it, he knew he was only a few farmyards away from Ivan Soroka's house. Ivan, Peter's best friend, lived on the south side of the village road near the church.

Peter's family lived east of the main thoroughfare, past the blacksmith's shop and past the section of road that touched the riverbank and then curved to the right to let the land between the water and the road broaden out enough for farmyards to exist on both sides of the road. The farms in Opaka looked almost identical to a casual passerby, but from his babyhood Peter learned to note subtle differences among them, such as the pattern of the woven wooden gate that set his home apart from the rest.

One late afternoon Peter stood out in his farmyard near his mother while she scattered feed for the chickens. He asked her a question.

"Mama, where did I come from?"

Maria turned from feeding the chickens and looked down at her little son. She smiled at his earnest face and thought, *My little one, you're a farm boy and will understand soon enough. How should I explain now?* Peter stood there sucking his finger and looking up at her. She nodded slightly and mused, *Your legs seem suddenly longer and your face has begun to lose its baby-roundness. You're almost three and a half years old. My little Petrush, so full of questions, and you are waiting for an answer.*

Chapter 1

"Petrush," Maria began, "you know how I go down to the river to wash clothes?" He nodded, and she knelt down so that she could talk to him face-to-face. "Well, it was in the spring, on a cold, sunny day. While I was kneeling and rinsing the clothes, I saw a school of fish swimming by. One of the fish was a different color. The rest of them were silver, but one was golden and rosy-colored. I leaned over and caught the special one in my hands before it swam away. That special one wasn't a fish at all; it was you. Your skin was pink, and your hair was golden, just as it is now. I liked you so much that I decided to take you home, and Papa and I would keep you for our own little boy."

Maria smiled at her little son. He was always so serious and thoughtful. Peter's face brightened, and he hugged her tightly before he turned and ran off to the barn. Maria smiled, shook her head, and stood up slowly with effort. "You aren't a baby anymore," she murmured as she recalled his real birth. She had been taking dried towels off the fence that bright March day in 1910 when she felt the first twinge and knew that the time for the birth would come either that night or the next day. She had been to the river that morning with her next-door neighbor, Maresha Gont. Maresha was a kind, older woman who assisted village women as a midwife when the need came. Maria hadn't carried the heavy laundry but had gone along with Maresha for the short walk and some fresh air on the brilliantly sunny day. The first weeks of March had been bleak and grey, but that morning was clear and clean, and the sunlight had drawn her outside into its warm embrace. Maria couldn't recall any good omens attached to the beautiful weather, but she remembered feeling great joy when she had seen the gentle rays glittering on the rippled surface of the river and had noticed how even the tiny fish that darted near the shore caught and reflected the golden light. Living things and life itself always held her respect, and she felt very close to God at the time of the birth of each of her children. She felt it was a time to glimpse and touch and be a part of creation itself. *Ah! Such lofty thoughts!* She smiled once more. *Indeed, my "little fish," you were born the next morning, and even when you were a tiny baby, the sunlight reflected on your golden hair. You aren't a baby anymore. Another baby will come soon, Petrush,* she thought as she gently patted her faintly rounded stomach, *but you will always be my "little fish."*

Maria turned from the task of feeding the chickens and took a moment to feel the breeze that brushed her face. The heat of the day lessened as evening neared, and she wanted to enjoy the coolness before returning to the steamy kitchen to finish preparing supper. She looked toward the road to see if her husband, Myhailo, was coming back from his visit with old Baran. She didn't see him but stood a moment longer to enjoy the air. "Such daydreaming!" she said, chuckling. "You'd think I was a young maiden with time to dream, not a mama of hungry children!" She shook her head at her frivolous mood and took one more deep breath of the cool air before going into the house.

Peter, in the meantime, had run straight into the barn to the far stall where the cow stood near the calf pen. Pundyk, the family dog, was there too. He was the same color as the new wood Papa had used to build the pen. Pundyk raised his head as Peter approached, and the dog's tail tapped a friendly greeting on the side of the stall. Peter petted him before letting himself into the calf's pen. The calf had been born four days before, and Peter loved to pet it and feel its velvety coat. He loved the mother cow too. The whole family called her "Mama Cow." They had bought her that summer already pregnant with this, her first calf. Her baby was reddish-brown and white like she was, and Peter loved the feel of the calf's soft hair. It felt as fine as the velvet that rich people wore and was even more special because it was alive and warm. Peter sat on the floor of the pen and hugged the new baby.

"Mama," he said to the cow, "you have a fine baby."

Peter thought about what he had just asked his mother and then remembered how Papa had told Peter that the cow was going to have a calf. "See how the cow gets fatter, Petrush?" his father had said. "And see how the skin on her stomach bulges and twitches? The calf is growing inside her, and that movement you see is the calf stretching and moving its legs." Peter was fascinated. Four nights ago, the cow had begun to moo in that eerie way that meant the calf wanted to be born. Papa and Peter's half-sister, Daria, went to the barn to help in any way they could. Peter wanted to go with them, but Mama told him to go back to bed and wait until morning. "Papa will know what to do, and you know Daria will help him," Mama had said. Daria was thirteen years old, but Papa often said that she was of more help with a calving cow than most doctors he knew. The next morning Peter awoke, dressed, and ran straight out to the barn to see if he could help too, but when he arrived at the door, he saw Papa wiping off the wet, shaky newborn calf with straw. Daria was stroking the cow's neck and cooing soothing words to the weary animal. No one saw Peter stamp his foot in frustration. *I missed it!* he thought. *I wanted to see the calf come out of the cow's stomach!*

Now, four days later, the calf already had grown bigger. Peter stroked the warm, drowsy creature and hummed to it. He listened to the crunching sound that Mama Cow made as she ate her hay. Crunch, crunch. It was a nice sound.

"You know, little calf, my mama said she found me with the fishes. Papa told me about St. Peter in the icon at church. Papa says St. Peter was a fisherman. I wonder if Mama and Papa called me Peter because of my fishes."

Peter sighed and smiled. He thought about his own Mama. She seemed to be getting a little fatter around her middle, and Mrs. Gont kept talking about "when the baby comes."

"Mama Cow," he went on, "I think my mama is going to have a baby again. She's growing it in her tummy like you did." He suspected that he grew there too and smiled. "My mama said she found me swimming with the fishes." His smile widened, and he ran off to the house with Pundyk because his mama had called them to supper.

Chapter 2

Family

Peter stopped at the well to wash his hands before going in to his favorite supper. Mama had made varenyky, and the familiar mouth-watering smell of fried onions encircled the farmyard like an irresistible net to catch him and pull him steadily to the house. When Peter stepped inside, he saw his two brothers and Papa already standing near the big table, while Daria helped Mama serve the food.

"Petrushu, were you visiting the calf?" Daria asked.

"Yes!" Peter said brightly. "It looks like it's grown even bigger since this morning!"

The girl smiled and gently pointed him to his place at the table. Papa led them all in the sign of the cross three times, before saying the "Our Father." The prayer seemed so long, especially because Peter had eyes only for the big bowl of dumplings and the jar of sour cream on the table in front of him. Everyone made the sign of the cross again and sat down to begin the meal. Varenyky! Peter's eyes danced as he watched Daria put three on his plate, spoon the shimmering golden melted butter and minced onions over them, and then finish off the masterpiece with a big dollop of sour cream on the side.

"Want me to cut them up for you?"

"Umm!" Peter nodded. Somehow it seemed a shame to ruin the perfect dumplings by cutting them up, but at least she did it neatly. When Peter tried to do it, he made a mess. Varenyky were made from a noodle-type dough that was rolled out and cut into circles with a tin cup or a glass. A rounded teaspoonful of filling was put in the middle of each circle, and the dough was folded over and pinched together so that it looked like a creamy-white closed clamshell. The varenyky in front of him were filled with mashed potatoes flavored with minced fried onion, butter, and a bit of white farmer's cheese. In fall and winter Mama filled varenyky with sauerkraut too. Sometimes when fruit was in season, she even filled the dumplings with cherries and served them as a dessert. As he lifted a morsel of his favorite potato-filled ones to his mouth and tasted it, he felt wonderful. Life was perfect when there were good things to eat.

Because it was Sunday, the family sat around the big table, and everyone had individual plates. For simpler meals, the family often gathered around a large pot or bowl set on a smaller table. At those times, each family member had his or her own fork or spoon in one hand and a chunk of thick bread in the other, and they ate from a common container.

"Well, how does the calf look to you, Petrush?" Papa asked.

"It's perfect, Papa! I wish we could keep it."

Peter's father smiled, but said firmly, "It's a bullock, and we'll wait for a heifer."

Peter's brother, Oleksa, was seven and a half years old. He sat next to Peter and devoured the small pile of varenyky on his own plate. His full name was Oleksander, but in Ukrainian, as in so many languages, there are ways of shortening names or adding endings to show special affection. Peter's name in Ukrainian was Petro, but everyone at home usually called him Petrush. Oleksander was called Oleksa. Oleksa could eat twice as many dumplings as Peter but was usually hungry soon after supper was over. He wasn't fat or a glutton, just growing taller. Peter wished he could eat as many varenyky as Oleksa before he got full. More than that, he wished he could grow as fast as Oleksa seemed to. Oleksa, with his dark brown eyes and curly brown hair, seemed so worldly to Peter because Oleksa had already been in school for a whole six months. Peter didn't like being the littlest in the family and wished he could be as big as Papa, but Mama said Peter would grow up soon enough. That didn't comfort

Peter at all. He felt like he had been three forever and was always going to be younger and smaller and an easy target for Oleksa. Oleksa teased him incessantly and liked to bully him. In return, Peter gave Oleksa a terrible time. Still, no one else dared to bother Peter when Oleksa was around, so Peter always felt safe from local bullies. Some of the time, Peter considered Oleksa to be his hero, next to Papa of course. The rest of the time, he contemplated trading Oleksa to Mrs. Gont for a baby rabbit.

"I just finished my seventh dumpling," Oleksa muttered to Peter. "Want to have a contest?"

Peter looked at Oleksa and felt very little.

"What's the matter—can't the baby eat anymore?" Oleksa taunted quietly.

"Is something wrong, Petrush?" Myhal asked from across the table. Myhal was Peter's half-brother and was almost twelve. Because his real name was Myhailo, like his stepfather, everyone used the nickname Myhal or "Young Myhal" to avoid confusion. Confusion over names was not confined to Peter's family. It seemed that just about every family in Opaka had a Katerina, an Anna, an Ivan or Janush, and a Myhailo. The names were considered good ones because they honored favorite saints of the village, but it got so that when someone yelled "Hey Ivan!" about a quarter of the village men turned around to answer. Young Myhal had heavy dark brows that gave his angular face an almost fierce look if he frowned, but he usually smiled at Peter. "Petrush?"

"Hmm?" Peter was lost in his own thoughts and the taste of his supper. He slipped a piece of dumpling into the sour cream and carefully lifted it to his mouth with his fork.

"You look as if something is wrong," Myhal said, concerned. He liked his little brother and always tried to make sure that Oleksa didn't pick on him too much.

"No. But Myhal, will you tell me a story after supper?"

Myhal smiled and thought about Peter's love of all kinds of stories. He loved stories about epic heroes, animal fables, explanations of things he saw in nature, and tales of great moments in history. Everything seemed to interest him. If he couldn't find anyone to tell him stories because they were busy with chores, Peter would tell stories to Mama and try to make her laugh. Myhal remembered many times that he had seen Peter swing by his hands on the side of the stall while Mama milked the cow, entertaining her with little jokes and fables. Mama called him her little scholar. Myhal had only two more years left of school before he would be free to spend all his time farming. He couldn't wait for that. School was all right, but because he could read and write and knew how to add numbers, he felt he had enough education to be a good farmer. Myhal looked at his little brother and knew seven years of school would never be enough for Peter.

"Sure, Petrush. How about the story about the fox and the crane?"

"That would be very good!" Peter said happily and finished the last bit of food on his plate.

"Myhal, I need your help with night chores," Papa said between mouthfuls.

"Yes, Papa. Do you mind the story a little later?" Myhal asked his brother.

Peter's face showed his disappointment.

"Don't worry, Petrushu," Daria said. "If you stay in and help me with the dishes, I'll tell you the story while we work, and the time will go quickly for me too." Daria looked at Mama and saw how pale she was. "Mama, tonight why don't you go outside and rest and enjoy the cool air? I have a helper to clean up." She patted Peter on the head, and he smiled. "Oleksa will help too," she added and nudged him before he could protest. "The evening is so pretty. Please go out and rest!"

Mama smiled. She was tired. She always felt more than the usual weariness of a farmer's wife when she was expecting a child, and the offer was one she longed to take. Before she could decline politely, Peter piped up in a serious tone.

"I promise not to drop anything. I'm a big boy. I can help. If we take our time, Daria will have time for *three* stories!"

Mama laughed and Peter was happy that his words made her smile. She looked at the reluctantly helpful Oleksa and then at her daughter and littlest son and said, "All right, I shall be an empress and hold court over the geese and ducks. Thank you, I'd love to sit down."

Papa and Myhal followed her outside and then headed for the barn to do chores. She passed by the bench near the door and went around to the side of the house to sit on a bench there. The side bench offered a view of both the farmyard and the setting sun to the west. The busy sounds of stacking pottery and jostled forks drifted through the open window, and Maria heard the traditional beginning of all stories and epic tales.

"Once there was and will never be again …" Daria began, and the story of the fox and the crane and their strange dinner parties started to unfold.

Maria leaned back against the wall and sighed softly. She rubbed her stomach gently and thought, *It's a joyful thing to carry a child. I just wish I didn't get so tired.* Her thoughts began to wander. *My mind seems determined to daydream today and remember the past. Some Sunday evenings are like that. They give more time for a soul to think and pray.* She watched the sun as it hung low: a brilliant fiery-orange ball in the sky.

Strange. Strange how a breeze, a smell, or even the colors of the sunset bring back old times, thoughts long tucked away. What was it now? Sixteen years ago? That long? On a night like this, my parents greeted the village matchmakers who had come to arrange the wedding between young Jascko Mlodzinski and me. They were so excited. "A young man," they said, "Polish, yes, but he has his own farm!" "Oh," they told me, "you won't have to live with your mother-in-law! His own farm! You'll be well-off for life!" Mama and Papa were getting old and frail and were afraid I wouldn't be taken care of. The matchmakers came, my dowry was settled, and Mama tied the embroidered towel on the arm of old Mr. Koval to show that talks had reached a successful end. My fate was decided.

I didn't even know Jascko. I'd never been to his village. It is just on the other side of Lubachiv, yet we had never gone there. This farm was his inheritance from a bachelor uncle who lived here. So we met before the wedding. How nervous I was! With his heavy, dark brows and his wide shoulders and hairy arms, I thought I was betrothed to a bear.

Chapter 2

Maria gave a little laugh and continued thinking, *His look was so fierce, but he was kind to me and a just man. Still at seventeen, what did I know of being a wife? It didn't matter. Maria Flis became Maria Mlodzinski. At nineteen I was a mother. My little plump Daria with her dark hair and beautiful eyes. So dainty, so sweet. She was patient and let me learn how to be a mama. My little angel child.*

Maria listened to Daria's gentle voice as it drifted through the window: "And so Petrush, the crane thought she would repay the fox's rudeness and invited him to supper. She served soup in a tall thin jug with a narrow neck. 'It's all I have to serve it in,' the crane told the fox …"

Daria, Maria thought, *you taught me what it was to be a mama, and you are so much a little mama already. You're such a friend to all life. No creature on our land, whether it's one of our own or some wild thing, is afraid of you.*

Young Myhal stepped out of the barn to fetch a pitchfork, and Maria watched him return to his work. *You're so like your own Papa,* she thought. *Your broad shoulders and those heavy, brooding brows. You have his kindness and have learned Myhailo's patience as well.*

Little Myhal was born less than two years after Daria, she recalled, *in the autumn before Jascko died of the fever. The same winter my own Papa died. Such a fever. So many were sick. Jascko was so young. I hardly knew him, and yet he gave me two children and this farm. How great a mystery life is.*

She said a prayer for her first husband and her parents. Her meandering thoughts began again, and she smiled with more sparkle in her dark eyes. *How afraid I was. Alone, a widow, and with two babies. Only poor sick Mama and my sister Pashia to help me. I'd known Myhailo Fedyk all my life. I always knew him as grown-up. When I was a baby, he was already fifteen. I often wondered why a good man like Myhailo had never married. In my loss he came to help with the farmwork. He repaired the barn, plowed the fields, and helped me with the other heavy work. At the same time he did his own work on the farm that belonged to him and his half-sister. And he was gentle and distant and made no demands. How could I not come to love him? With his grey eyes and light coloring, he was so different from Jascko in his looks. So different from memories I had. He loved Myhal and Daria and was so kind to them. When I told him once that I was afraid all that work was too hard for one man to do, he simply said, "When you do it for people you love, it isn't hard."*

How untraditional we were! Tsk! I'm certain there was gossip! In Opaka, nothing goes without gossip! She laughed softly. *How rare indeed. We married for love. For practical reasons too. But for love as well. 1903. Twenty-three years old and twice married. My dear Mama lived to see it, but sadly enough she was gone when our little curly-haired Oleksa was born three years later. Then little Petrush was born four years after that, and now another one to come in the spring. God grant us all health and keep us safe.*

Maria was lost in her reverie, and the sun cast a golden light to soften her features. She looked every bit of her thirty-three years, but on his way back to the house after chores, her husband, Myhailo, saw her and thought she looked beautiful. She wasn't beautiful like some fine lady who might wear silks and live in a splendid city, but beautiful because of her brown eyes and wavy brown hair, the way her face was shaped, and beautiful too because of her strong spirit and her gentle, kind ways. She had a keen wit and a clear, pure laugh when she was happy. He loved her very much. He washed his hands and face at the well and walked over to join her on the bench.

"So, Maria, can I sit and help you to hold court over the farmyard in its golden light? You seem so far away in your thoughts. Can't little Opaka hold your interest, or are you off to Kiev in your daydreams?"

She laughed softly. "Kiev? I wouldn't know what to do there. Your papa was the one who wandered to our village from places so far away. I'm no wanderer. No, Opaka holds my thoughts and my life. Everyone and everything I love is here."

They smiled at each other and sat together in silence to share the evening and the sunset. The dishes and storytelling soon were done. Daria and Oleksa stayed inside to read lessons for school the next day, and Myhal finished chores in the barn. Peter came outside to lean against his father's knees and watch the sunset with his parents.

Peter looked up at his father and noticed that his light brown hair was thin on top.

"Papa?"

"Yes, Petrushu."

"Papa, why is your hair thin on top?"

"I'm not a young man anymore."

Peter studied his father's features and saw lines around his eyes and mouth but not as many as on really old people in the village, so Peter decided his father wasn't old yet. Mama watched his scrutiny and smiled at him. Peter liked to see her brown eyes soften like that and thought she was the most beautiful woman in the world. Peter adored both his parents. They were strict in the typical fashion of most parents in Eastern Europe, but their affection was never far below the surface. He crawled up into his father's lap and felt the strong arms hold him there. Mama took Peter's small hand and held it for a little while. Those simple actions let Peter know that he was loved more than words could have said. To Peter, the world seemed very beautiful.

But the world, beautiful or otherwise, did not end at the boundaries of the family farmyard or at the edge of the village. In time war would cast ugly shadows over the sunshine Peter felt in his young, happy world. His village was in the crown colony of Galicia in the Austro-Hungarian Empire. Some people contended that the region should someday be part of Poland, in spite of the fact that three-quarters of the people who lived there were Ukrainians like Peter's family. Governments, with their arguments and battles, become very involved with certain interests and goals. The sunny world of a child and his family is of little consequence when powers contemplate war.

Chapter 3

St. Nicholas

Winter had come. The work in the fields was finished. Potatoes had been dug and stored. Papa had everything secured, and Mama had more time now to sit beside the stove and spin combed flax into thread. Life began to slow down after the exhausting work of harvest time. The slowness of the pace was not what troubled Peter. What bothered him was a surprise that Mama said would come on a special day. Ever since she had told him that, time hadn't seemed to move at all.

The special day was the feast of St. Nicholas. Because it was a holy day, all of the family went to church that morning except Young Myhal. It was his turn to stay home to tend the livestock while everyone else went to Divine Liturgy.

Peter's family was Catholic and belonged to the Eastern Rite of the Church called the Byzantine or "Ukrainian" Rite. The Polish people in the area called them Greek Catholics to set them apart from Roman Catholics. The traditions and development of the Byzantine Rite are as ancient as those of the Roman Rite. The difference between them comes from the fact that one was influenced by the culture and traditions of Greece, eastern Europe, and western Asia, whereas the other was influenced by the western culture based in Rome. Eventually the eastern part of the Church broke with Rome in the schism that took place in 1054 and became the Orthodox Church that continues today. Several hundred years later, a portion of the Orthodox Christians returned to the Catholic Church to be under the authority of the Pope of Rome, but they still retained their rituals and theology and are now the Byzantine Rite of the Catholic Church. Peter had heard Papa explain the history to Oleksa, Myhal, and Daria, but Peter didn't understand it very well. He was too young to know what it all meant, but someday it would affect him greatly. At his young age, time in church seemed very long, but he enjoyed the heavy fragrance of the incense, the chanting of hymns, and the beauty of the ritual.

Peter and his family gathered with the other villagers in the small church and chanted responses to the priest's prayers. Their priest came out to Opaka from his parish in the nearby city of Lubachiv to celebrate holy days and almost all Sunday liturgies in the modest church that was dedicated to the Holy Trinity. The domes of wealthy, big churches in large Ukrainian cities were covered with gold leaf and shimmered in the sun. Peter's church had only tin to cover its domes, but golden sunbeams danced and gleamed on them just the same.

Peter stood next to Papa and leaned against him a little. Liturgy was long, and as the old priest droned on with the sermon, Peter became bored and began to study the benches he saw along the wall. *I wish I could go sit down,* he thought. *Papa said that only people who are very old or sick or lame can use the benches. Everyone else has to stand. Maybe I could say my foot feels like it's full of needles and I need to sit down. No, Papa would probably tell me to wiggle my toes, or he would just hold me and rub my foot.*

Peter leaned back against Papa, looked up at the ceiling, and continued to lose himself in his thoughts. *The walls and the ceiling are so pretty. I wonder why Mama and Papa don't want to paint the inside of our house a deep red like this. I like the gold trimming too. The colors make church feel warm even on a cold day.*

There's the icon of St. Peter up there in the corner near the ceiling. Good day to you, St. Peter! He always looks like he's staring right at me. Sometimes I feel like he watches me just to make sure I behave. Mama and Papa already do that.

Peter looked over at the high windows on both sides of the

church. He liked to watch the sunbeams come through the many tiny panes of clear glass to play with the smoke rising from the incense. Sometimes the smoke seemed to make shapes in the golden light. *I wonder if those shapes are really angels playing hiding games in the shadows and light,* he thought to himself.

In front of the altar where the priest stood, a wooden partition stretched from the floor to the ceiling and across the entire alcove that held the altar. This wall had three doors that opened through it. There were two side doors and one wide double door in the middle that opened for viewing the altar. Papa once told Peter that the structure was called an iconostas, and it separated the area around the altar from the rest of the church. For Peter, the wall held a different, special fascination. The iconostas was covered with wood-carved flowers and vines that served as decorative borders for large icons that were hung there. The large icons on the iconostas were of Christ, the Blessed Mother, and some of the venerable fathers of the early Church. Peter loved to let his eyes trace the meanderings and the smooth carved surfaces of the vines that curled around the icons like elegant frames.

Now where is he? Peter asked himself. *I follow the vine up and around the icon of the Blessed Mother … then that leaf near her shoulder. He isn't there! I wanted him to be there again. That little mouse. Where is he? Last time he sat there on that curly vine and blinked his little shiny, black eyes at all the people. I don't think anyone saw him but me. Everyone was watching the priest. Even Oleksa for once. By the time I got Oleksa to look, the mouse was gone and Oleksa never believed me that it was there. I hope that vine near her shoulder is one of his favorite places because I want to see him again. I hoped he would be back today.* Peter sighed, and his shoulders drooped.

Peter looked up at the priest. *Liturgy is so long today. Mama said there's going to be a surprise. I don't think it'll come at church.* Peter yawned and leaned heavily against Papa's knees. In a few moments he felt Papa's strong arms lift him up, and Peter rested against his father's shoulder. Peter could see everything easily now and soon lost himself in the repeated hymn that Papa and all the people were chanting. "Holy Father, Nicholas the saintly …"

Chapter 3

At home, the only work the family did was to tend to the animals. They spent the day so quietly that Peter became more restless than ever. *For a day that's supposed to have a surprise in it, this is a very boring one,* Peter thought.

Suppertime finally came, and Peter looked for a special cake or some other treat that could be the great surprise, but nothing came. While Mama and Daria cleared the dishes, Peter sat on the side bench along the wall with his elbows on his knees and his chin cupped in his hands. He swung his legs slowly and sighed once again. Peter looked under the main table and noticed some straw had been spread on the earthen floor. No one had said anything about it. *When did that get there?* he wondered. He had bothered Mama so many times with the question "When is the surprise?" that she had become annoyed and told Peter to wait and be patient. Peter continued to hold his chin and swing his legs, but he didn't know how much longer he could stand to be quiet. *What if it never comes at all?* he thought. Mama glanced at him and smiled to herself, but she said nothing.

Peter watched his mother finish wiping the table and saw that she looked wider across her middle. He was certain now that it was because of the baby growing inside because one day Mama had let him touch her stomach to see if he could feel the baby moving. "Come, Petrushu," she had said, "put your little hand here. Your sister is kicking." Peter had been a little afraid but had put his hand where Mama told him to, and his eyes had grown wide when he felt her tummy jump right under his fingers. He had felt the hard little kick, and his face had broken into a wide grin. "Mama, she said 'Hello' to me! As soon as I put my hand there, she touched it from inside you!" Peter smiled when he remembered this.

Peter watched his mother fold the drying towel and finally sit down to rest after the long day. The house stayed quiet. Daria and the other boys were reading near the big warm stove. Papa was lost in his thoughts, and Mama closed her eyes and must have thought about something happy because she smiled. Peter sat alone on the bench and wished he could yell or maybe cry because he felt so frustrated.

Suddenly they all heard the sound of horse's hooves outside. In a few moments a hard knock came at the door. It was not the muffled sound of a gloved hand. It was more like a stick hitting the wood. Peter sat up to see who would come at such an hour. Papa opened the door, and there in the doorway stood a tall man holding a wooden staff. He was dressed in a long elegant red robe, made of fine brocade like a priest's vestment. He had a white beard that reached his chest, and he wore the veiled hat of a Byzantine Rite bishop. Behind him, tied to the post, was a white horse. Peter stood up. He didn't realize it, but his eyes were open wide, and his mouth dropped open as he took in the sight of the night visitor.

"Welcome, Your Eminence," Papa said politely and motioned for the visitor to come inside. "Please come and sit down by the stove and warm yourself. It's such a cold evening. Please."

The stranger was greeted and welcomed as St. Nicholas! Peter stood rooted as if he were in a trance. St. Nicholas! Holy Father, Nicholas the saintly!

"Petrush, have you forgotten your manners?" Papa chided.

Peter couldn't move and forgot how to speak.

"It's all right, little one, we have not met before. At least not that you remember," St. Nicholas said to him gently. "Come here, my boy. Don't be afraid; I won't harm you."

Peter stepped forward. St. Nicholas placed his hand on Peter's head and blessed him.

"What is your name?"

"Peter."

"Ah, that's a strong name. Do you know who St. Peter is?"

"Yes, Your Eminence." Papa had called St. Nicholas "Your Eminence," so Peter repeated it and hoped it was the proper thing to say. The man seemed to be from another world. He wasn't anyone Peter recognized, and his voice sounded older and deeper than any Peter had ever heard.

"Are you Myhailo's young one who is the great lover of God's birds and beasts?"

Peter didn't understand.

"I have heard of you," the old man said with a knowing smile.

Chapter 3

"You're the one who sat for hours last summer watching the storks build their nest on your roof. You wept when one of the young ones fell from the nest and you found it dead on the ground the next morning. Isn't that so?"

"Yes, Your Eminence," Peter answered shakily. How did he know all that? Peter's eyes grew even wider.

"It is good to have respect for all God's creatures, my son. Treat all life gently, that life might treat you the same."

The old man looked intently at Peter as if he could see into him, and Peter felt himself blush. St. Nicholas began to talk with Mama and Papa. Peter watched and listened, but everything seemed to be happening in a haze. It was real, and yet it seemed unreal. St. Nicholas asked about the family and the farm and then spoke directly to young Myhal, Daria, and Oleksa, who were seated on the benches across the room.

Mama and Papa offered him something to drink and brought out a plate of sweet egg bread that had been baked for the visit. After he had finished, St. Nicholas thanked them for their kindness and stood up, preparing to leave.

"Thank you for your generous hospitality. This is a warm and loving home. May God's blessing rest on you all, now and always." He raised his hand in blessing, and everyone bowed and made the sign of the cross. He reached into a pouch on his belt and tossed a few handfuls of something into the straw under the table. He blessed them again and left.

Peter stood perfectly still and wondered if he was dreaming. Oleksa was certain it was all real and was already heading for the table when Mama stopped him.

"Petrush, St. Nicholas scattered treats for all of you under the table in the straw. Why don't you see what's there?"

Curiosity made Peter snap back into the real world. He and Oleksa scrambled under the table and found candies, nuts, and small coins in the straw. Peter grabbed as many candies as he could reach and then remembered to share some with Daria and Myhal. The boys also offered some politely to their parents.

"How did you like your surprise, Petrush?" Mama asked smiling.

"The last time St. Nicholas came, you were too small to remember."

"It was wonderful!" Peter answered, beaming.

That night, when Peter was tucked in and ready to sleep, he thought about everything that had happened and repeated the words from the hymn at church. "Holy Father, Nicholas the saintly …"

Chapter 4

Christmas Is Coming

Peter and Oleksa sat on a bench near the stove. They watched Mama pick up a wooden tube, wash it, and then dry it. The tube had one closed end that served as the bottom of the vessel when it stood on end. Mama poured in some kernels of wheat that had been soaked in water and handed the tube to Oleksa. She gave him a cylindrical piece of wood, which he slipped into the tube, and then he began to pound the kernels of wheat.

"Won't we end up grinding it into flour?"

"No, Petrush," Mama answered. "Just pound the wheat until the hulls come off. Then pour the wheat out, pick out the clean kernels, and put them in this bowl."

Oleksa pounded for a few minutes and poured the contents onto a cloth. Peter picked out the white pearls of wheat, put them in the bowl, and set the hulls aside. The wind was howling outside, and it was pleasant to sit by the stove and help Mama get ready for Christmas. The two boys were preparing hulled wheat for "kutia," one of the twelve special dishes Mama cooked for Holy Supper on Christmas Eve. There were some tasks, such as pounding the wheat, that could be done ahead of time.

"Petrush," Mama said, smiling, "you'll be four years old in the spring! Because you're getting to be such a big boy, you can help do more to prepare for Christmas."

Peter was pleased, but Oleksa had a smirk on his face. "This is a 'baby job,'" Oleksa whispered. "Mama's only trying to make you feel grown-up."

While Oleksa pounded, Peter watched the activity in the family's one-room house. Mama always kept a clean house, but for Christmas, she scoured everything twice as much. Papa had whitewashed the walls in the fall, so Mama simply mopped them to wipe down any dust or cobwebs. Myhal had dusted the open beams that held their straw roof before Mama began to cook that morning, and now he was washing the three windows of the house. Daria, wrapped in a woolen coat and a long warm scarf, lifted the small mountain of coverlets and pillows she intended to carry outside to drape over the fence. Mama liked sweet-smelling linens on the beds, and a day in the frosty air and sunshine seemed the perfect way to freshen bedding in the middle of winter.

Daria stumbled back into the house with icon towels and a tablecloth that were frozen stiff from their morning on the fence. She'd washed them and hung them there to freeze-dry and now intended to iron them. "The wind is so strong!" she exclaimed to help excuse her noisy entrance. "Look, Petru, the tablecloth could stand up like a wall!"

"Don't let it touch the floor," Mama warned. The floor was the last part of the ritual of cleaning. It was hard-packed earth and only needed a good sweeping. A few people in the village had wooden floors, but most had earthen ones. The soil had been packed down for so many years, it was very hard. Peter never thought much about the fact that the floor was earth rather than wood. It was the way he had always known it, and he couldn't understand why some people made a big fuss over how wonderful wooden floors were. Maybe they were a little warmer, but they were creaky.

"Stop daydreaming. My arms are sore, and it's your turn to pound since you're such a 'big boy,'" Oleksa teased.

Peter began the process while he watched Mama scrub the long benches that ran along two walls of the house. The benches were wide and served many purposes. Thick mats, part of the bedding being fluffed by the gusty wind outside, were laid on the benches at night to make beds for the children. A pillow and feather coverlet or woven blanket finished each cozy makeshift bed. During the day the bedding was either stacked up on overhead shelves or folded neatly on the bench in one corner. In daytime the benches served as places to sit or as extra work surfaces like a tabletop.

In one corner of the house stood Mama and Papa's big bed. Mama had already taken the decorative woven coverlet out of her storage trunk, and it was waiting on the high shelf. Peter loved to look at the pretty geometric designs and the deep red, black, and white colors. Mama used the coverlet on the bed as part of the holiday decorations. The other decorations were pretty embroidered pillows, towels, and table linens that were saved for only the most important holidays.

"Here, Oleksa," Peter said, "Would you pound for a while? My hands are wet from the wheat, and they're getting cold."

Oleksa took the cylinder from his little brother and for once didn't tease him about the short time he had worked. Peter turned toward the big friendly stove and rubbed his small hands near its radiant warmth. The stove was the dominant feature of the house. It harbored all the family's cooking and baking and was the only source of heat during cold weather. Stoves in the region where Peter's family lived were constructed in such a way that the wood fire was built in a large masonry box that rose almost a meter from the floor. Pots for cooking were set on top of its flat surface. There was another compartment for a second fire to make the oven hot enough for baking. The oven was a second smaller box that sat on top of the larger one. The very top of the oven was a flat ledge and extended behind the chimney to the wall of the house. This ledge was called the "peech."

When it was very cold in winter, grandparents or the youngest children of a family slept up on the peech to enjoy the extra warmth. Because Peter had no grandparents, he shared the peech with Oleksa and the family cat. Peter didn't mind his brother, but he wasn't very fond of cats. Peter watched the old black and white cat lick its fur, stretch, and then curl up on the peech.

I wish you'd go to sleep in the barn, you cat, he thought. *You don't like to listen like Pundyk or Mama Cow does. You act like you're so important that you don't need to show any manners. You're even worse than Oleksa!* Peter glanced at Oleksa and hoped his brother couldn't read his thoughts.

Daria adjusted the three wooden chairs near the big table the family used for special occasions and then came over to wipe off the smaller table near the stove where the two boys were working. Mama used the little table to knead bread and prepare all the family's food. It was also the table where everyone gathered for simple meals.

Peter looked into the bowl to see how much wheat still had to be pounded. "Looks like we're almost done." Peter liked helping, but he was getting bored.

"Good! You take the cylinder again," Oleksa told him.

Mama dusted her cherished icons. For as long as Peter could remember, the icons had been hung in their special place on the eastern wall. They were only printed paper, not the real paintings on wood that you could find in churches or in the homes of wealthy people, but they were treated with reverence. While Peter watched, Mama draped the clean, freshly ironed towels over the top and sides of each picture.

"Why do you put those on the holy icons, Mama?"

"To decorate them. The same way we use special linens at church to decorate the altar or the tetrapod. I also put them on to protect the icons from becoming dusty."

Peter looked at the icons of Christ and the Blessed Mother and two smaller ones of St. Michael the Archangel and St. Nicholas. "They look pretty," he told his mother sincerely. The faces of the holy people stared back at him with round eyes and stark features. "Sometimes I feel like their eyes follow me," Peter murmured half to himself.

"Maybe they do," Mama told him. "Once, at church, Father Ivan told us that icons are windows of heaven. We can see into heaven through them. So, I guess, the saints might look at us through the same windows. What do you think?"

Peter didn't know what to say, so his eyes just grew larger, and he shrugged his shoulders. He looked at the icons and thought about the windows.

Chapter 4

"We have to hurry to get done! Papa will be ready to leave soon!" Oleksa urged.

"Oleksa, while you're waiting for him to finish, would you please go out to the komora and bring me a small sack of flour? I need to start supper soon."

Oleksa put on his hat and woolen coat and ran out into the cold air. The "komora" was a room that was attached to the house but could only be entered through its own outside door. It was a pantry, and much of the family's food was stored there.

Foods that could be ruined if they were allowed to freeze and thaw, such as potatoes and carrots, were stored in a root cellar or sometimes buried in the ground in one of the family's fields. The storage spots were topped with big, wide, bound-straw cones that spread from one to two meters across and about a meter tall in the middle. The straw cones kept whatever was buried well insulated against very cold and hot temperatures.

Peter watched his mother dust the cupboard that held the family's dishes and extra pots. She polished the two storage chests on the floor that contained linens, and finally, she dusted the single wardrobe that held the family's clothing. No one had many clothes. Each had one set of good clothes for special occasions and then some older work clothes.

Mama is always cleaning, Peter thought. *The house looks clean to me, but she always finds another "speck" of something. If I weren't pounding wheat, I'd be hiding in the barn with Pundyk. If I sit around here very long when Mama is finding specks, she tells me to go clean my boots.* He glanced at the small entry cove where coats were hung and where boots stood in neat rows. *Cleaning isn't fun,* he thought, *but Christmas is wonderful! All the good things to eat!* He watched his mother scrub the windowsills. *One of the best things about Christmas is that the cleaning is finished!*

Oleksa let the wind carry him into the house, and then he slammed the door against the cold with a satisfying bang. Before Mama could scold him for being rough, Peter called out, "Look, Oleksa, the wheat is done! Look how much we did!"

Before Oleksa could answer, the boys heard Papa's yell from the farmyard. "Get ready, boys! We'll be leaving now!"

"Can we go now, Mama?" the boys asked together.

She smiled and nodded. "You did a fine job. Thank you!"

Both boys ran to get ready to leave. Papa was going to take them to the city to buy some herring and spices for Holy Supper on Christmas Eve. Peter and Oleksa loved to go to see all the marvelous things that the old Jewish shopkeeper kept in barrels of brine and in deep bins along the walls. It was a real adventure!

"Thank you, boys," Mama said again. "You were a great help." The door closed before she could add, "Behave yourselves." Christmas was coming, and everyone was in a hurry.

Chapter 5

Christmas Eve

Peter and Oleksa leaned into the bitter wind that blew that last day before Christmas Eve. They squinted to see through the swirling snow and tried to run the last few steps to their house and to the warmth they knew would be inside. The two boys stumbled through the door together and stamped snow off their boots.

"Ohhhhh!" Peter wailed. "Mama, it is sooo cold out there!"

"I know! I'm glad both of you had your mittens on and were bundled up," she said sympathetically while she unwound the long scarves the boys had around their necks and halfway up their faces. "There's milk heating for you on the stove."

Peter and Oleksa hung their coats by the door above their boots and still shivered after they sat down near the stove. Peter rubbed his pink hands and stuck his stocking feet toward the radiant heat. He and Oleksa wiggled their toes inches away from the stove as if to beckon the warmth to hurry and come to thaw them. Daria poured the milk into cups, and the boys gratefully took the warm drinks.

"So how was the practice?" Daria asked. It was Advent, and Oleksa had let Peter come with him to practice singing Christmas carols with some of the other boys in the village.

"Good!" Oleksa said proudly. "We went to Bohdan Soroka's house. We were supposed to go to Ihor's, but his sister has a fever, so we all went to Bohdan's. Peter was happy. He and Ivan got to sit there together and make faces at us the whole time we tried to sing the serious words."

"That's not so," Peter defended himself. "We only did it once or twice. Ivan and I learned all the words to 'God Eternal.' It's my favorite. I wish I could carol this year."

"You're too little," Oleksa insisted. "So is Ivan. It's too cold for three-year-olds."

"I'm almost four."

"That's enough," Mama said. "Oleksa is right this time, Petrushu. Wait another year or two. Besides, Ivan would be sad if you went caroling without him. He's even younger than you, and he catches cold so easily his mama would never let him go."

"Yes, Mama," Peter murmured. Giving up caroling for Ivan was easier than giving it up because Oleksa told him that he was still a baby.

Mama stirred the soup that was almost ready. Myhailo and Myhal weren't back yet from chores, so she had a few minutes to sit down and rest before the evening meal.

"Ivan and I were talking about Christmas tonight," Peter began, "and I was telling him about all the things you and Daria told me. He said his mama told him about the prayers and fasting before Christmas too. He knew that we don't have to follow the same rules about giving up meat and milk until we're seven years old."

"That's right. This is the first year that Oleksa will be following the fasting laws," Mama said, and then she smiled at how Oleksa suddenly sat up straight and looked very important. "Some people call it 'Black Fast.' That means we have no meat, dairy products, or eggs. On the whole day of Christmas Eve we have such a fast."

Peter replied, "I told Ivan what Daria said about why we have it on Christmas Eve. About how it is to honor the memory of the Blessed Mother as she traveled to Bethlehem on a donkey and how she suffered before Jesus was born. He thought that was nice to think of her."

Maria smiled at her youngest son.

"We talked about how Mary and Joseph couldn't find a place to stay and how Jesus was born in a stable with animals all around. You know, that really wasn't so bad. Some people don't like strangers and aren't friendly to them, but Ivan and I think that animals are nice even to strangers if they are kind and friendly. I like barns, anyway.

"We talked about Holy Supper too. He knew all about having twelve different foods, but he didn't know why. I told him it was for the twelve apostles. Was that right?"

"Yes. You have a good memory, Petrushu. That reminds me—tomorrow I begin to cook early in the morning, and I have to build a hot fire in the oven before it's time for you to get up. So tonight you and Oleksa can't sleep on the peech. Let's make up your beds on the benches before Papa and Myhal come in for supper."

Supper was simple that night and was finished quickly. The cold weather and the anticipation of the important day to come made even the children eager to go to sleep.

Maria awoke in the middle of the night and began the cooking and baking. She bent over the stove to add more wood to the fire and felt the baby kick inside her. She gently rubbed her stomach. "I see I have someone to keep me company even at this time of night," she said to herself. She had been awake and working for about three hours when Myhailo awoke to go to the stable for early morning chores.

"Maria, it's so early! You'll be exhausted by the time supper is ready."

She smiled at him and lightly shrugged her shoulders as she kneaded the soft dough. "It won't hurt me to have a longer day today. My fast isn't as strict this year because of the baby. I'll rest while the dough rises and some of the other foods cook."

Myhailo doubted that she would rest much at all, but he was happy that the priest had told her that she was not to follow the strict fasting laws.

"Still, Maria, it could be a simpler Christmas this year. No one expects extra treats."

"Myhailo, you know the children would be disappointed if there were no pampushky." She stopped a moment, and her face lost its sparkle. "Who knows what next Christmas will bring?" she said in part to herself. "Somehow I feel I have to do all I can this holiday. Our tomorrows are so uncertain. There's so much talk of war." She looked at the sleeping children.

Myhailo saw her face and quietly went over to her. He put his hand behind her neck to gently rub the tight muscles there. "Everything will be all right. Don't worry. Next year we'll have a new child to share our holiday, and it will be even more wonderful."

She looked at her husband and smiled. "I promise to eat something later and to rest more today," she said, seeing his concern. In years past she had tasted nothing of what she had prepared until the evening meal was ready. If she needed to know if the food was seasoned enough, she had asked the younger children to taste and give their opinions.

"See to it that you do. I'll ask Petrush for a full report on what you do today. He tells me everything," he said, grinning.

Later that day, Maria glanced at the window and saw the beautiful royal blue light that only snowy winter twilights possess. "All right, Oleksa, there are a few thin clouds in the sky, but I want you to watch for the first star. Holy Supper will begin after it appears."

Oleksa knelt on the bench near the side window and wiped away the condensation on one corner of the windowpane so that he could peer out. A veil of clouds finally blew past, and the brilliant evening star showed its clear light. "It's there, Mama!"

Maria peeked through the glass and smiled. She smiled at the beauty of it—and also because the cooking was finished right on schedule. It was time to start preparing the table for supper, but first she and Daria helped the boys bundle up in their coats and scarves to run out to the barn to meet Papa and Myhal. Papa and his three sons were about to begin another portion of the Christmas Eve tradition.

After chores were finished, Papa gave Myhal a sheath of rye. Oleksa was given a bundle of rye straw, and Peter carried a little bundle of hay. Papa carried a large bundle of wheat that he had tied securely around the middle. The boys followed their father back to the house and joined him in greeting Mama and Daria with the joyful exclamation, "Christ is born!"

Chapter 5

"Glorify Him!" Mama and Daria answered.

The straw was spread on the earthen floor under the table. The rye and hay were spread on the large table that was used for special meals. Papa's bundle of wheat stood leaning against the wall in a corner. All these things were done to remind the family that Christ was born in a stable and was placed in a manger instead of a cradle.

A braided wreath of garlic was placed in the middle of the table. Mama spread her embroidered linen tablecloth over the garlic, rye, and hay and placed the serving bowl on the garlic wreath. The wreath had a symbolic purpose of warding off illness as well as the practical purpose of holding the bowl securely so that it would not tip on the surface of the table, which was now bumpy because of the rye and hay.

Everyone gathered around the table and began the meal with prayers. Papa took a small bun called a Kolada. It was made and baked in the same fashion as the bread used in communion in church. One bun was given to each family just before the holiday by the "diak" from the parish. The diak was the layman who helped the priest in all liturgical functions and who chanted responses to the priest's prayers. Papa broke off a piece of the Kolada and passed the rest of the bun around the table until each family member had some. Then they all ate their portions.

The meal began with the herring Papa had bought in town. He and Mama had pickled it with vinegar and spices, and it was delicious. Beet soup, called "borscht," followed. The soup was flavored with shredded sweet cabbage and dried mushrooms.

As a special treat, Mama made little dumplings called "vooshka" which means "ears." They were made of a noodle dough that was rolled out thinly, cut into little squares, and wrapped around a filling made of minced mushrooms and onions fried in oil. The little dumplings were triangular in shape. Mama pinched two of the corners together and when she did, the dumplings looked like the cute little ears of a piglet. Peter loved the vooshka and has happy to find that Mama had slipped an extra two into his borscht.

Baked kasha (buckwheat) was served next and was followed by

stuffed cabbage, called "holubchi." The cabbage leaves were filled with either rice or kasha seasoned with onions, mushrooms, salt, and pepper. Varenyky counted as another of the dishes, and Mama made both potato-filled ones and some filled with sauerkraut. For the holubchi, varenyky, and kasha, there was a mushroom gravy that could be poured on top.

Mama filled out the meal with dishes of beans, shredded cabbage, and stewed dried fruit. After all the main dishes were finished, they had the soft, fresh pampushky buns with a special prune filling. Mama also served a special holiday bread called a "Knesh."

The final dish was "kutia." It was served cold and was made from the boiled, hulled wheat that Peter had pounded. It had been mixed with ground poppy seeds, honey, and chopped nuts. Sometimes raisins were added, but they were a rare treat.

In various regions of Ukraine, the order of the dishes of Holy Supper varied, but basically, the assortment was the same. In some places kutia was served first, but in Peter's family it was last. The children were delighted by an old superstition about kutia: if you took a spoonful of the sticky mixture and flipped it at the ceiling, and a few kernels of wheat stuck there, the next year's harvest would be a good one.

"I know what you're thinking, Oleksa," Mama said, watching her son eye the overhead beams while he held a spoonful of sweetened wheat. "We all know that Papa is the only one in this family who should even think of flipping any kutia up there. He has the best aim, and if he did do it, I'm sure the harvest would be good." Her brown eyes flashed a warning at her husband, but she couldn't suppress her smile.

"No, Mama, this year I will not tempt fate," Papa said while he looked at Oleksa. "All this good kutia is going right into my stomach to ensure a good feeling at the end of this perfect meal. I think it best that everyone do the same."

Myhal's eyes danced, but he didn't laugh out loud. He watched his parents send messages across the table with their eyes and was more than pleased that the family prankster, Oleksa, had been stopped once again. "A very good idea, Papa," he agreed.

Chapter 5

This last course was eaten out of a common bowl, and everyone was careful to leave a portion at the bottom. After they were finished, their spoons were tied together with a cord woven from field grasses and put into the bowl. The bowl and spoons were left on the table when the family went to sleep. The kutia was left out in that way so that in the night, all the spirits of deceased family members could come and share the Holy Supper.

"Wake up, Petru," Papa whispered while he gently shook Peter's shoulder. It was after midnight, and everyone had to get up to go to church. Peter's head felt as if it were filled with fog, but the walk through the frosty night, with the stars overhead and the snow crunching under his feet, helped him to wake up completely. He was on a great adventure. He was going to Liturgy at night for the very first time!

The church was so beautiful! The pretty decorations, the carols, and the incense all swam through Peter's thoughts. He prided himself on being a big boy and staying awake, so when he blinked, he was very surprised to find himself on the peech the next morning. He saw Mama fixing breakfast and singing carols softly to herself. He mumbled something, and Mama looked up.

"What did you say?" she asked smiling.

"What happened to the church?"

She laughed softly. "Ah, little fish, Papa picked you up toward the end of liturgy because you were falling asleep on your feet. He held you, and you fell asleep on his shoulder. Papa carried you all the way home, and he and Myhal lifted you up there to put you to bed. It's all right. He didn't mind."

Peter's clouded thoughts began to clear. He was embarrassed that he fell asleep at his first night liturgy, but the warmth of the stove and the feather coverlet tucked around him felt wonderful. Then his eyes opened wide.

Today is Christmas! he thought. "Christ is born, Mama!" he said happily and climbed down from his warm ledge.

Chapter 6

"What Is War?"

Borders and boundaries mean little in time of war, little more than a painted line or a thin wire fence. Trouble and sorrow have no problem seeping through and changing lives. Although the hint of future sadness was present, Peter did not know it in the early years of his life. Who cared about governments or nationalism or hate when the world was a peaceful summer afternoon nap on the edge of a field where the cows grazed? The need to care came. There was talk of war. Children younger than Peter were playing games and calling each other Muscovites and Austrians. *War.* What was war? Whenever Peter had a question, he ran to either his Papa or his Mama, and he did the same this time.

It was nearly suppertime. Mama was in the house cooking the evening meal and tending to baby Katerina. Everyone called her Kashia. She was only a few months old, was very sweet, and had already begun to smile. She always gave Peter her most special toothless grin whenever he stopped by her cradle to tickle her or play with her fingers. He told her what the animals in the barn were doing each day and how the storks or swallows were progressing with their nests and hatching their babies. She listened to him with wide eyes and would make baby noises and smile as if she understood everything. Peter decided she was very intelligent. He just wished she would hurry up and learn to walk. Mama said that would take almost a year, and that seemed so long.

Peter knew that his Papa was back from the fields because he saw the caked work boots standing outside the door. He pictured his father's tired face, red from the heat of the day. *At least,* Peter thought, *if the boots are by the door, that means Papa has already put the horses in the barn, has washed at the well, and is resting.* Every day after Myhailo came home, he sat and told his wife about the fields and the news he had heard.

His father looked up as Peter ran in.

"Petrush," Mama said gently, "that's no way to enter the house."

He slowed to a walk and came and stood in front of his father. Myhailo looked down at his littlest son and saw the solemn expression. *Ah,* he thought with weary pleasure, *Petru has that look again. He has a question. Probably something about some mouse or weasel he saw today.* His mind wandered for a moment. *I wish life held more restful times like this when I can sit here near my wife and children and feel peace. If I had known married life could be this good, I wouldn't have waited until I was thirty-seven years old to begin it. But if I'd married sooner, it couldn't have been to Maria. Never found a good woman until her. That's why I waited.* He watched her stir the soup while she made funny faces and cooed to the baby. Myhailo glanced back to the little boy in front of him. *Those serious grey eyes like some old professor. Petrush must have a question.* Peter stood waiting for permission to speak as he had been taught.

"What is it, Petrush?"

Now that he was free to talk, Peter hesitated. He never wanted to talk of foolish things and hoped that his question was a good one. "Papa, what is war?"

His parents looked at him. Mama's eyes glistened with quick tears. Papa's face turned ashen. *It has begun,* they both thought. *It has already begun to touch our children.* His father said nothing, so Peter went on with his questions.

"Who's going to fight? Are the Muscovites going to fight the emperor? Will they kill lots of people and ruin things?"

Myhailo's chest grew tight, and he felt as if the room had been drained of air. Images of his wife and children seemed to fade. He only wanted his hard but good life to continue. He and Maria spoke just yesterday of their fears of the coming war and the changes it would bring. The war. It was going to come. He looked at his wife and the room around him once more to make certain everything had not already vanished. His eyes came to rest again on his little son.

"What's a Muscovite, Papa? What's an Austrian? Who are the Prussians? Will they fight us or help our emperor?"

Myhailo felt sickened by the thought of what could be lost when war came. *The world is so fragile,* he thought, *like a pane of glass before a hideous storm. One blow, and it will shatter. I feel so cold.* He had to speak and stop the long stream of questions.

"Wait, son, be patient. There will be time enough for you to know everything. You're still little. You don't understand. I can't tell you. Not now."

Peter looked at Papa. His father stood and looked down at him with eyes that were filled with pain. *Oh, son,* he thought, *I hope someday to answer you. To be alive and at least talk of it.* He touched Peter's blond hair and then dropped his calloused hand down to the upturned face and touched it gently. Papa walked out of the house. Peter watched him leave and then looked up at his mother. She saw Peter's face and held out her arms to him. Peter ran over to her and wrapped his arms around her waist. The two of them hugged each other. Peter knew that he should say nothing more. Not now.

War officially began on August 1, 1914. An order came from Emperor Franz Josef that all men had to serve the army. Peter's father was thought to be too old for the infantry and instead would drive a supply wagon for the troops. It also was determined that their farm wagon and the family's two horses would serve the army too.

Peter's brain grew numb. The endless flow of questions ceased. It seemed as though life was a weird sort of dream and everyone around him moved mechanically. The only thought was, "Papa has to leave." It seemed only an instant between the arrival of the notice and the morning of the parting. Mama packed some warm clothes in a cloth sack and prepared a lunch that she wrapped in clean cloths and put in a box. There was a flask of something to drink. Peter watched his father pack his old work boots and his good, newer boots too. When he saw the new boots were packed, a new thought registered in his young brain. "Papa will be gone a long time."

Farewells and last embraces came. Myhailo held Maria for a long time before he hugged the children. He held Kashia with one arm, and she nestled against his neck. He hugged Oleksa and then Daria and Myhal. Petrush. Little Petrush stood miserably off to one side near the wagon. He didn't know yet what war was, but he was beginning to find out. War took Papa away and made everyone cry. Papa saw him. He looked even smaller than usual. His little shoulders drooped, and his face seemed too small for the big, tearful eyes. Papa went over to him and knelt down. Peter, baby Kashia, and Papa hugged each other tightly. When Papa stood up, he touched Peter's head in a slow gesture of love and farewell. Myhailo turned back to Maria, embraced her again, and handed little Kashia to her. He stumbled as he stepped up onto the wagon because his eyes were filled with tears. He wiped them with his sleeve and picked up the light whip. He sat there for a moment and looked at the house and the ones he loved so much standing there in front of it. The two older boys stood close to each other. Daria picked up Peter and hugged him because he was crying now. Maria held the baby. He lightly tapped the backs of the horses with the whip and clicked his tongue. The animals reluctantly moved out of the yard. Myhailo turned several times to see his home and family before the wagon disappeared around the bend in the road.

Time stopped for Peter. The shock of watching Papa leave and the sense of fear shared by everyone in the family seemed to stop thought for a while. Each day seemed like the one before, but as time went by, each day provided a little less in the way of food and wood for the fire. So much of what they had was necessary for the war effort. The first sacrifice was to let Papa go to serve. The second was the loss of the wagon and horses. The Austrians wanted men and horses. Then the Russians came. The villagers called them Muscovites. They took over the village by autumn and confiscated cows, pigs, sheep, geese, and chickens for their own use. The peasants were told to harvest the fields quickly in spite of the fact that all the able-bodied men and horses and decent farm wagons were gone from the village. The Muscovites wanted a share of the crops too.

Just after Papa left, Mama told the children that they were more fortunate than most. The family had Mama Cow and a second cow that was a calm, gentle creature named Midnight. There were no pets like families might have in the city. All the animals, including their brown mongrel, Pundyk, had certain jobs to perform, and they were loved and respected by the family. There were also some pigs, sheep, chickens, and geese that meant a winter free from hunger. Until the Muscovites came.

Myhal ran into the house on a bleak autumn day and called out, "Mama, soldiers are coming! They've already finished with the western half of the village. They're taking animals and food and blankets! What are we going to do?" His young voice cracked. He was afraid and needed to hear his mother tell him that everything would be all right.

"What can we do? We have to let them have what they want. They have guns. I don't want any of you to be hurt. Remember what Papa always says: 'If we have each other, that's all that is important.' Papa is right. If they take some of our stock, we'll still have what is important." She said these things to calm her children, but thought, *They could very well empty the barn and the house and the komora too. God, watch over us and give us strength! I'm glad Myhailo isn't seeing this. He would do what he'd have to do, but he would be so angry. Now is not the time to antagonize men with guns in their hands.* She saw the soldiers through the window at the same instant that the sound of their marching reached the house. "Come, children, let's go outside to wait for them. I don't want to feel like they are coming to drag us out of our house."

Peter stood near his mother in the middle of the farmyard when three soldiers and their officer came into the yard. He expected big, monstrous-looking men with evil faces and gruff voices, but the young men who walked past them looked like they could be any one of their neighbors who had been called away to the war. The ones in front of him were strangers. Their dull green uniforms and the big guns they carried made them look important and dangerous, but Peter noticed that none of them looked straight at Mama or the children. They acted tough, but Peter wondered if they didn't look a little bit like big boys who were about to do something naughty—tough and sassy, but a little ashamed. Or were they afraid? The soldiers headed straight for the barn, and Mama sent Myhal to help them open the pens. He went not so much to help, but to try to see that they didn't do extra damage or steal things. Maria wondered if really it would make any difference. They would take what they wanted, and no one had better say anything about it.

The young officer, a man no more than twenty, came up to her and started to speak to her. He spoke Russian, but she understood him because the words were similar to Ukrainian. He said the soldiers needed food, and it was the privilege of the villagers to provide them with livestock and bread. He also ordered her to show him the house, the komora, and the stable. While he was inspecting the property, Maria and her children watched the Muscovites drag off the family's sheep, pigs, and some very unhappy, vocal chickens. They took sacks of flour and sugar from the komora and made it understood that they would be back for more food when it was needed.

Peter's head swam. Once again, the numbness set in. Even if he could have thought of questions, he was sure this was not a time to ask any. He watched people talking—soldiers talking to Mama and his family. They weren't really talking though. The men in the green uniforms were giving orders, and Peter's family was expected to carry them out. Strangers came into their farmyard and into their buildings and told them what to do, and they had to do it. Peter felt numb, but even through his numbness, he was terribly afraid.

When the soldiers left, all the pigs were gone. Only three chickens remained. The sheep and all the geese were taken too. The last soldier took Midnight with him. Mama led the children back into the house and tried to comfort them.

"We're fortunate," she told them. "They left Mama Cow for us. She's like a part of our family. Midnight was still new to us. The officer said Mama Cow looked too thin for beef, and when I told him she lost her calf this spring, he said they didn't want such a scrawny animal. And we have chickens! We can get three eggs a day when they're laying well. Yes, we're very lucky. They also left the pantry almost untouched." She thought of the precious sugar and flour they had taken. "And remember, they took nothing from the house. We have our quilts and blankets to keep us warm in the winter."

No one said anything. Mama started supper, and they all went about their little chores mechanically. Peter's thoughts began to form once again. He'd seen the officer directing his men and how the officer seemed to like using the power he possessed, but the young man still talked to Mama with some respect.

Peter didn't know how lucky the family really was. All the livestock could have been taken. Peter would never know that Mama and the children clustered around her reminded the Russian of his own family. In a fleeting nostalgic moment, the officer decided to leave them a cow and a few chickens and then think himself a generous fellow so that he could rest well with his conscience. Before he left, he told Mama that from time to time the soldiers would be using the stable, the komora, or even the house for sleeping quarters.

"They took nothing from inside the house," Mama had said. *That's because Mama is smart,* Peter thought. *Two nights before the troops came, Mama and Daria went through the cupboards and gathered all the best towels and pottery. Mama packed everything so carefully in a small wooden trunk Papa had kept in the barn. Then she took her very favorite thing: the fine woolen shawl Papa had given her when they were married, so pretty and trimmed in that long fringe.* Peter remembered how she looked when she would fold it in half into a big triangle and wrap it around her shoulders to wear at special times. He remembered the white background and the pretty red and pink roses and thought, *She hugged it and kissed it and wrapped it in linen and put it so gently, like she would put down a baby, into the trunk. Then when it was very dark, she and Myhal went out and buried the trunk under the big oak tree on the edge of the farmyard. Mama said it would be protected there—more than it would be out in a field or a damp forest. She showed Myhal how to cut out the sod and carefully lift it off in big pieces. They dug the hole, buried the chest, covered it up again with dirt, and put the sod pieces back in place. Myhal told me they even scattered the extra dirt around the yard and stamped it down so it wouldn't look like anyone was digging. "In a few days," Mama had said, "no one will see any sign of what we did here." When the soldiers came, they didn't know it, but their tramping around helped to cover all the tiniest signs of fresh digging, and Mama breathed easily. Mama is a smart woman.*

Peter missed Papa terribly. Having soldiers near the village made him nervous, and although Mama and his brothers and sisters were with him, he felt afraid. Peter wanted to be brave and help Mama, so he said nothing about his fear. Sometimes, though, he would fall and bump his knee, and when he cried, instead of simply wailing, he heard himself sobbing, "Papa come home," as he rocked back and forth and rubbed his hurt spot. He didn't think about what he was saying until he heard the words come from his mouth. At night he had bad dreams of being lost and trying to find his father, and he would cry. He'd dream that Papa found him, and suddenly he'd be sitting on his father's knee and watching the sunset with Mama. He'd feel strong arms around him and stop crying, but then he'd hear Mama or Myhal tell him softly to wake from his dream, to pray, and then to go back to sleep. He wanted the arms to be Papa's, but they never were.

No word came about Papa's whereabouts. He had never learned to write, and the only hope they had of hearing of him was news brought back to the village by someone who had seen him. Because the war had just begun, no one expected to hear about anyone very soon.

War had truly begun, and no one escaped its effects. There was no fighting in the area surrounding Opaka, but the soldiers were there. The farm chores still had to be done. The soldiers wouldn't help, but they told the villagers to hurry with their harvest. They wanted to be certain that there would be plenty of food available for the troops. Mama worked with Daria and Myhal to harvest the crops. Peter and Oleksa tried to help carry things in handcarts, but most of the time, Mama told them to watch Kashia and keep her out of mischief so that Mama and the older children could do the heavier work.

Harvesting was more difficult that year because they didn’t have the help of the wagon and horses. Most of the families in the village were in the same predicament. Mama’s married sister, Pashia Zuravel, watched her own husband, Stepko, go off to the Austrian infantry and had to harvest her fields with only her three daughters to help. Little Ivan felt very lucky. His papa did not go to war. He was a strong, hard worker but was blind in one eye, so the army didn’t want him. Vasyl Soroka had often cursed fate because as a boy he had gone riding and collided with a tree branch that destroyed his eye. When the war began, the affliction he hated so much kept him home to help his wife and children and his neighbors as well. The Sorokas had to sacrifice horses and a wagon to the war effort, but Vasyl helped build small carts and organized schedules using the few old horses left in the village to help his neighbors bring in their crops. Once the harvest was in and stored, the villagers felt a little more secure as winter approached. The army could demand more food at any time, but at least there was the hope that there would be enough to keep the village families fed until the spring.

Peter was running home one late autumn morning. Mama had borrowed some millet from Mrs. Kucharski and had sent Peter with a new sack to repay the kind neighbor. As he ran, he saw old Mrs. Baran hanging wet towels on her fence. She was singing a sad song that she thought no one heard. No Muscovites were around—they were on maneuvers—but Peter was there, hidden by the woven-wood fence. He slowed to a walk past her fence and listened intently.

> The country is weeping in 1914,
> So our lord mayor has told us.
> Saturday morning preparations were made,
> On Sunday there were the farewells.
> Said farewell to his wife,
> Said farewell to his children,
> Said farewell to his family and so he went.
> When will you return, dear father of ours?

Chapter 6

Will you find us still here and alive?

Peter felt a tingling chill run through his body. Yes, he was finding out what war was. He had heard other songs too, and he found it easy to remember the words. This one reminded him of Papa, and his eyes began to sting. He began to run. Running helped to take his mind off crying, so he ran as fast as he could all the way home.

He opened the long front gate and ran straight into the house. He didn't bother to check to see if soldiers were anywhere around because he knew they were away for a few days. Muscovites had been everywhere lately, it seemed. The week before, they had used the barn for sleeping quarters. There wasn't room for many in the house, but the officer of the patrol slept inside on one of the benches. There was nothing Mama could do to stop them, but whenever a soldier slept in the house, she sat up to watch her children sleep.

The house was open because of the warm weather, but Peter bumped the edge of the door on his way inside, and the clatter made Mama jump. She had been very nervous since the soldiers came to the village. They made everyone nervous.

"Mama! I'm back!"

"Good boy! Was Mrs. Kucharski there?"

"Yes. She said 'Thank you.' "

Mama stood at the stove and started to make soup for that day's supper. She smiled at him and watched him sit down on the side bench to begin one of his "visits" with her. Peter began to sing.

The Emperor sat at his desk one night,
Thinking of how to defeat the Russian menace.
He wrote a letter to the Prussian King.
"Oh illustrious Prussian leader, come to our aid!"
The reply came:
"I will come to the aid of my beloved Emperor,
And we shall defeat the Russians easily,
One fine morning between breakfast and lunch."

Mama had turned and watched him sing in horror.

"Petrush, be quiet!" she whispered. "Have you lost your senses? The Muscovites will hear you, and there'll be trouble! Where did you hear such a thing?"

"I heard old man Kazhanko singing it on the other side of town. All us boys sing it when we play."

"Never sing it again."

"Oh, we'll fight the Muscovites ourselves!" Peter said, swinging his fist.

"And what army do you have that can do that?"

"All us boys. Ivan, Myhal, Stephan, Maxim, Bohdan, and the others. We'll show them that we'll defend our emperor. I'm not afraid of them. I'm five years old!"

"Not quite. You're only four and a half."

Peter didn't like to be reminded of his age.

"Petrush."

"Yes, Mama?"

"Petrush, promise me you won't sing those songs anymore. You boys play games and feel very brave. You play your games and think you'll play more tomorrow. The Muscovites don't play games. Don't think that they'll play any with you."

Peter looked at her face and felt a tingling along his spine. When she looked that serious, she scared him.

"You've begun to see what war does. Don't be foolish. We must take care of each other and wait for Papa to come home. Give me your word, Petrush."

"I promise, Mama," he said softly. Peter would keep his word.

Chapter 7

Bubbles and Battles

Winter came and passed, and the spring brought the succession of days that led to an important one for Peter.

"Hey, Pundyk, ol' fella," Peter cooed while he patted the dog gently on the head. "Guess what? I'm five! I'm not four anymore!" The dog sat next to the bench where Peter rested in the farmyard and cocked his head to one side while he listened. "Two weeks ago! You weren't feeling so good, so I'll bet you didn't notice. Hah! Now Oleksa can't call me a baby." Peter made a face while another thought occurred to him, and he stared off into space. "The trouble is, everyone else gets older too, and I'll never catch up." He looked back at the dog. "It isn't fair. I wish I could catch up to Oleksa. Then he couldn't bully me." Pundyk looked up and licked his young master's face with his long pink tongue.

Because it was wartime, Peter wasn't allowed to go far from home to play. He saw Ivan only at church or once in a while when he came with his father to help Mama with some heavy work in the barn. Peter had to spend almost all of his time with his own brothers and sisters or Pundyk. Myhal was thirteen years old and became the man of the family when Papa went off to war. Still, it was Oleksa whom Peter idolized. Oleksa was only nine and delighted in teasing Peter, but that didn't shake Peter's special admiration of him. Oleksa didn't go to school each day because he was needed at home to help while Mama worked in the fields. On the days he was at home, Peter was left with him.

Bubbles and Battles

With Muscovites camped in or near Opaka, and strangers wandering through the village, Mama was afraid for her children. "When I'm away from the house, you must always keep the door barred. Open it to no one until I come back," she warned, and the children were expected to do as they were told.

Oleksa did not always obey his mother. He did obey, however, when it was to his advantage. Peter was old enough to be trusted not to leave the farmyard, and because he found it boring to sit in the house all day, Mama told him he could play outside with Pundyk. When he was outside, he had the responsibility of tending to the cow and chickens. The only problem was that when Oleksa let Peter out in the morning, he would bolt the door after him and wouldn't let him in again until just before Mama came home. Peter protested, but Oleksa simply said, "Mama said not to open the door to anyone." Peter knew that if he told Mama about it, Oleksa would dream up some revenge when she wasn't home.

One grey day, Peter was playing outside. Pundyk had tired quickly of a game of fetch, and Peter was not surprised. The dog had always had the reputation of being the village scrapper. From most of his battles, he had come home the victor. But the last time, he had barely dragged himself back to the front gate. Peter had found him there and called Myhal to help carry the poor dog to the house. No one knew what had happened. He was so badly torn and hurt that Mama took one look at him and gave him little hope. The dog was in great pain but let Mama wash his wounds and even cleanse one very badly swollen eye. Mama let him sleep in the house near the stove and fed him soft porridge. She rubbed his cuts with ointment and gently scolded him when he weakly licked off all of the ointment he could reach. For three days and nights, Mama, Daria, and Peter soothed the dog with soft words and tried to get him to eat and drink. He barely moved, and the rumbling in his throat when he breathed kept Peter awake at night. Finally on the fourth day a cart pulled into the yard, and Pundyk sat up to make a weak attempt to bark. They were all so happy that they forgot to run out to see who had come. Pundyk had come through his crisis. He became more docile after that and never again went out to pick fights.

Chapter 7

Pundyk had been sleeping in the barn for three nights and seemed happy to be back on duty as guardian of the animals. Peter liked having the dog outside again during the day. After a game of fetch, Peter checked to see how the dog's wounds were healing.

"Your eye looks pretty good," he said softly, "but I still can't scratch you behind the ears. Don't want to rip open those cuts again." The dog licked Peter's hand. "Let's go to the barn." The two of them went inside and Peter began discussing the war with Mama Cow. She had had another calf, a young bullock, and it was growing nicely. The family hoped to sell it to the Jewish dealer before the soldiers took it. Peter swept out the barn, carried water for the animals, and encouraged the chickens to keep laying eggs. After those duties were finished, he and Pundyk checked the outside fences and gates to make certain no Muscovites had invaded their property. He casually walked by the place where Mama had buried the wooden chest and saw that nothing betrayed her secret.

"Chores are done, Pundyk, and our borders are secure," Peter said, mimicking a soldier. "Let's go back in the barn and watch the swallows. They've built more nests and are raising babies." They went in through the small side door, and a swooping bird almost collided with Peter. The bird twittered and chirped to scold Peter for getting in the way. He and Pundyk dove for a pile of clean straw near one of the stalls and sat there out of the way of the angry mother bird. After she was satisfied that they weren't going to bother her, she resumed her task. Peter loved to watch all creatures at the business of living, so he quietly snuggled up to Pundyk and watched the swallow feed her babies.

"Look at the funny little nests, Pundyk. They're made from mud and grass and twigs, and they're like little pockets glued to the wall. You know, this mother bird is a lot like the storks when they were feeding their babies," he whispered to the dog. Pundyk watched the swallow and appeared to understand what Peter said. "The storks didn't come back this year. Maybe the soldiers scared them away. Those birds worked so hard to feed their hungry babies. It seemed like the young ones just never got full. Listen to these babies! They no sooner take the bugs, and they're cheeping again." Peter thought a moment and hugged the dog. "I think all good mamas work too hard, and no one seems to notice. Mama works so much since Papa's gone that she doesn't have much time to talk anymore. She's so tired all the time." He sighed. Pundyk wagged his tail in sympathy, and the tapping noise on the side of the stall sent the mother swallow into another tirade. She began to swoop at them again, so Peter grabbed a piece of straw, put it in his pocket, and then fled the barn with the dog.

Peter sat down on a bench near the well, and in a cup he mixed some rainwater from a pan with some soft soap Mama had made. Peter stirred it well and then took the piece of straw from his pocket. Pundyk watched Peter dip the straw into the soapy water and then blow into the straw. A large shimmering bubble appeared at the other end, flew off the straw, floated in the air, and broke right in front of Pundyk's nose. The dog sneezed and shook his head.

"Don't be so nervous," Peter laughed. "You lost a fight, and now you're afraid of bubbles!"

Peter blew bubbles as fast as he could. He wanted to see how many he could float around the yard at one time. The bubbles cheered up the dreary day, and Peter was enjoying himself. He split one end of the straw and blew steadily into the soap solution until it overflowed with froth. Pundyk watched the bubbles with his head tilted to one side. After a while Pundyk began to chase the single bubbles that Peter began to blow again. Peter gazed at the silent, fragile balls floating on the breeze. Pundyk ignored his stiff muscles and ran after them like a puppy.

"You know, Pundyk," Peter murmured, "I wish I were a sorcerer. I wish I knew magic. I would stand in a battlefield and change all the flying bullets into bubbles. Then no one would get hurt. A war fought with bubbles wouldn't last long. Bubbles are so pretty that the soldiers would watch them and forget to fight. A war fought with bubbles wouldn't hurt Papa either, and then we could be sure he'd come home to us."

Peter put down the cup and sat quietly. He was sad and didn't feel like playing anymore. Pundyk came over to him and nudged Peter's hand so that the boy would pet him. Peter sighed and hugged the dog tightly.

"Let's see if Oleksa will give us something to eat."

The two companions headed for the house. There was no bright sun to tell the time, but Peter's stomach rumbled and told him that it was time for lunch. Oleksa was left in charge of the house and little Katerina. She was still in diapers and was beginning to walk, so she needed constant supervision. Oleksa was gentle and good with her, and Mama trusted him. Peter tapped on the front window.

"Oleksa, give me some bread and butter. I'm hungry."

True to form, Oleksa decided to give Peter a difficult time. "Hop on one foot like an old man. If you don't, I won't give you any bread," Oleksa sneered at him through the window.

"What?" Peter asked.

"You heard me. Hop on the prespa two times in each direction."

The prespa was a wide board placed on the ground next to the house and running across the entire front of it. The board helped to deflect the rain that trickled off the straw roof, so that it wouldn't wash ruts into the soil around the house. Peter did as he was told because he knew his brother. Oleksa was good to his word, and Peter got his lunch.

Oleksa usually thought up little things for Peter to do just to show him who was in charge. One day when Mama was expected home soon, Oleksa let Peter into the house to help make porridge for supper. He began to order him around, but Peter refused to take any more bullying. Oleksa caught Peter by the arm and hit him. Peter managed to squirm loose and kicked Oleksa in the knee. Both were shouting and swinging fists at one another, so neither noticed when Mama and Pundyk came in. She was furious. When they saw her, they both stopped shrieking and were still. Oleksa stopped rocking back and forth on the floor where he was holding his knee and stood up to face his mother.

"What is going on in here?" she said in a low tone. Her anger was unmistakable. "I was halfway down the road when I heard screaming. Pundyk was outside barking. I thought half the Russian army was in here beating my children! Now tell me what is going on!"

Oleksa was silent, so Peter took his chance. He began to tell all about Oleksa's bullying. He listed all the pranks he could recall, as well as the commands he had to follow before he was allowed to get food or come into the house. Mama listened and stared at Oleksa. Peter then gave details of how Oleksa was beating him up just before she came home. There, he was finished. Peter was relieved. He told her everything and felt safe from Oleksa's revenge. Oleksa looked frightened but then glared at Peter with a look that could have withered the most confident spirit. Mama noticed the look.

"And Oleksa, why were you on the floor just now? What's wrong with your knee?"

"Peter kicked me."

"Peter, is that true?"

"Yes, Mama. I was just trying to get away and he was hurting me, so I ..."

"That's enough from both of you! If anyone is going to give beatings around here, it will be me! Do both of you understand?"

Both boys stood silent.

"Do you understand?" she shouted.

"Yes, Mama," they answered together.

"Oleksa, the bullying stops now. If you ever do any of those things to Peter again, I will skin you alive."

"Yes, Mama."

"Come here."

Oleksa stepped forward. He was almost as big as Mama, but she still managed to give him quite a thrashing. Peter felt avenged. Oleksa finally was sent to sit in the corner and rub whatever was especially sore. Peter watched him walk over and sit down and was suddenly jolted by the sound of his mother's voice.

"Peter! You come here!"

Peter looked up and saw her anger aimed at him. He didn't expect that. She picked him up and spanked him soundly.

"That is for kicking your brother in the knee. You could have hurt him badly. Don't you ever do that again!"

Peter was sent off to another corner to rub his behind and think about his evilness.

"There is enough fighting in this world," she said, glaring at them both. "It will not enter this house because of my own sons. I don't care what the rest of the world is doing. We will keep peace in our own family! I never want to see or hear fighting between you again. Do you understand?" They both nodded. Mama turned and almost tripped over Pundyk. "And you! You'd better learn to stop your fighting too, or the next time you won't recover!"

The dog's head hung down, and he whimpered.

Mama went to Kashia and picked her up to cuddle her. The baby was frightened by her mother's anger. Neither the boys nor Pundyk became perfect angels after that, but they thought twice about most of the things they would have liked to do. Mama meant what she said, and they never wanted to test any of her threats.

Chapter 8

The Frozen Coat

Winter was cold whether you enjoyed the snowy weather or not. It was cozy to be inside near the stove and help Mama spin or prepare the loom for weaving cloth, but Peter quickly grew restless. Sometimes Mama told him that he could go and play in the snow, and when she did, he would be off in an instant in spite of the frigid weather.

One clear, cold day when the soldiers were away from the village, Mama told Peter to go outside and play with his brothers. Daria was content to care for Kashia, and Mama had weaving to do. Myhal and Oleksa repaired two sleds from the barn, and Oleksa told Peter he would take him sledding on the road. There weren't any hills in Opaka, except for the banks near the river. The only hills were those out near the common pasture and some of the farthest farm fields, but they weren't allowed to play that far from home.

The tools essential for sledding on the flat terrain were short sturdy sticks. Myhal taught the boys to lie on their stomachs on the sleds and then push along the ground with the sticks. The packed snow on the roads would get an icy crust after a mild day in the sun, and if there was the slightest slope at all, pushing with the sticks would help the sleds move very fast. Peter loved to tell Mama about the sensation of speeding along.

"It must be what it's like to fly like a bird," he told her with his face glowing from excitement and the cold. Then he swooped around the room to show her.

Chapter 8

"So, I see. Just remember that when baby storks are taught to fly, they must also learn to land. Try to find a soft snow bank for your landings, my little fledgling." She smiled and gave him a gentle pat on his bottom before going back to her work.

A few weeks later, Oleksa took Peter and their sleds to the riverbank. Because of the steeper slope, they achieved incredible speeds and ended up streaking across the ice-covered river to the other side. Oleksa watched over his little brother and taught him to steer. After a while Oleksa noticed that the bank was getting crowded and was worried that some of the bigger, rougher boys would collide with Peter.

"Hey, Petru, let's get out of here! Too many sleds. We'll go farther down the bank." The two brothers pulled their sleds about a hundred meters farther downriver.

"Oh look, Oleksa, the bank is even steeper here. I'll bet we can go all the way across the river without even trying!" Peter cried happily. No one was nearby, so they had only to throw themselves onto the sleds and set their sights for the far side of the ice. Peter savored the sense of flying, and the wind whistled past his scarf-bound little face. What heaven it was! He shut his eyes to dream that he was a bird and then opened them an instant after reaching the river's edge. There was a sickening cracking sound, and he screamed when he felt the sled break through the ice!

"Oleksa!" he shrieked, and tried to turn his head to see his brother, but all he saw was the broken edge of the ice and then the grey-green water of the river when it splashed over him. One instant his body was warm and excited, and the next he felt the shock of painful cold as his woolen clothing absorbed the frigid water like a sponge. He panicked. Peter had heard of people drowning, and his brain screamed, "I'm underwater!" Peter's mouth filled with water, and he realized he couldn't breathe. He tried to move his arms and legs, but they were so heavy he felt like he was tied up with rope. He saw light above him and felt weight on his back. The next thing he knew, he was lifted through sloshing water and chunks of ice and thrown to the bank two meters away. His mittens were soaked and were starting to freeze on his fingers, but he grasped and clutched at the dried grass along the bank to keep from sliding back in. His heart pounded in his ears, and he felt like his throat would never open for air. He tried to shout, but nothing came out. *Oleksa. Where are you?* he wondered. Then through the stinging cold of his hat and scarf, he heard Oleksa shouting to him.

"Are you all right, Petru? I'm here. I hope I didn't hurt you. I had to throw you like that. You're so heavy!"

Peter turned his head. Oleksa was standing waist deep in the water, throwing sleds back onto the bank, and then he stumbled out of the broken ice and water himself.

"Come on, Petru, get up! Our coats are freezing. We have to get home now!"

Peter had never felt so cold in his life. His skin ached so much it felt like it was on fire. Other boys from farther down the river saw what happened and came running. One boy shouted that he would bring the sleds, so Oleksa took Peter by the arm. His teeth were chattering so hard he didn't know if he could form words to speak, so he just pulled his little brother down the road. Peter's body hurt everywhere from the icy water. His bones ached, and his legs wobbled so badly he wondered if he could walk all the way home.

Oleksa saw him shake and felt sorry for him. Through gritted teeth he mumbled, "Don't be a baby. You're too heavy to carry, so move, or you'll freeze to death!"

The word "death" frightened Peter and he moved quickly past the few farms between the river and home. Myhal saw them come into the yard and ran to help. He pushed them into the house and shouted, "I'll go get the sleds and find out what happened!"

Once inside and safe at home, the boys were frankly a little excited about their adventure. Mama was excited too, but not in the same way. Daria helped to strip off their stiff, frozen clothes, and Mama wrapped the boys in soft feather quilts that were warm from sitting on the peech.

"Oleksa," Mama said tightly, betraying her mixed fright and relief, "I thought you were supposed to watch out for Peter's safety."

"I was, Mama!" he wailed in frustration. "That's why …"

"I can't see that you were very careful. Look at you!"

Chapter 8

"But Oleksa saved my life," Peter said in his defense. "He picked me up and threw me out of the water."

Mama listened and yet was preoccupied. She scolded them, and after Myhal returned with the sleds and the story of what he discovered, Mama was silent for a while.

"Mama, I know why they went through! There's a spring that feeds into the river there, not far before it widens into the lake. I couldn't believe that there'd be thin ice now—not after all the cold weather we've had. But with the spring, the moving water kept the ice thinner there."

"Why were you sledding there, Oleksa?" Mama asked.

"I thought it would be safer," he said. Seeing his mother's expression, he went on quickly. "There were so many big boys, rough ones, coming to the usual place, so I thought we'd move. I didn't think to test the ice first." His voice trailed off into a squeak, and he thought he'd better be quiet.

Mama sighed. "Look," she said, trying to be calm, "there are so many dangers now. The ones we can avoid we must avoid. We must take care of ourselves until Papa ..." She wanted to say "until Papa comes home," and the thought cut like a knife into her heart. There had been no word for months. She didn't even know if he was alive. She looked at the boys. "You cannot go sledding on the river again this winter. It isn't safe, and you can't afford to get sick either." Mama trembled and turned to the stove to heat some milk to warm the boys and help them avoid some of the bad effects of their chill.

The boys pulled the quilts around them more tightly and were unhappy about the new rule. She had already told them that they couldn't go sliding on foot on the frozen river. No one could afford ice skates, but when the ice was slick, plain boots did very nicely. Mama objected because the patches of rough ice on the river tore up the leather soles of their precious boots. Boots were expensive, and the boys were not to tear them up sliding around like fools on the ice.

A few weeks later, after a brief thaw, the weather turned very cold again. Mama and Oleksa took advantage of the sunny weather and went to market in Lubachiv. Myhal was doing some chores for a neighbor, and Daria was at home with Kashia. Peter was free to play. He stepped outside and immediately heard laughter and shouting coming from the river. Some of the village boys were on the ice and playing loud and happy games while the soldiers were away. Peter could not resist temptation.

What could a little sliding hurt? he thought. *I'll pick the smoothest sections of the ice and take care not to tear my boots.*

He ran down to where the backwaters reached the crossroads. Some boys were having contests to see who could slide the farthest, and others were just running, twirling, and showing off. Peter would not be outdone. He joined in the games, and when his turn came, he went into a running leap. An instant later he found himself up to his belt in water. "Oh, no!" he wailed. "Not again. But at least this time my head stayed dry," he told himself philosophically. He floundered in the shallow water and was thoroughly wet before he crawled out. He felt very cold, but in a moment his coat and pants froze, and the ice cut the wind so much he felt warmer. He could hardly walk. He couldn't move his arms at all because the sleeves of his coat were frozen. It felt as if his clothes were made of wood rather than wool. Some of the boys were laughing, but Peter hardly heard them.

"Now what do I do?" he muttered to himself. "Mama will spank me so hard my seat won't be cold for the rest of the winter."

He kept walking so that he wouldn't turn into a statue. His teeth chattered both from fear and from the cold. As he headed for home, he heard a voice calling to him. It was Natalia Soroka, Daria's best friend.

"Petrush!" she laughed. "What happened?" Before he could answer, she saw the pinched expression on his face and felt sorry for him. "Listen," she said softly, "Why don't you come to our house? We'll dry your clothes, and then you can go home, and no one will know what happened."

Peter nodded, and she took hold of one stiff sleeve to help lead him to her home. Peter could barely turn his head, but he looked up at her from the corner of his eye. *Mama talks of angels sometimes,* he thought, *I'll bet they're like Natalia.*

When they neared her house, little Ivan ran out to greet them.

Chapter 8

Ivan was Natalia's little brother and held the door open for them. Ivan helped Peter to get out of his clothes and wrap up in a warm blanket while Natalia laid the wet things over the stove. The smell of steamy wool filled the house. She stuffed his boots with dry rags and then turned her attention to boiling water for some herb tea to warm Peter's insides.

"Your Mama will be upset if she hears about this," Natalia said as she took out a tin of tea. "Daria told me about the sledding accident with Oleksa. Promise me you'll stay out of the river for the rest of the winter. If you want to swim with fishes, wait until summer."

Peter blushed and felt his face turn hot. He quietly drank the tea when it was ready and let Ivan try to cheer him with the latest village gossip. Before his clothes were dry, there was a knock on the door. Natalia opened it, and Daria came running in.

"Is Petrush still here?" she asked and ran over to him. "Some boys came to the house and told me you fell through the ice. They said they saw you stumbling down the road after Natalia. Petrush, you should be glad Mama wasn't home!" Peter shrank down into the folds of the heavy blanket that curled around him like a cocoon. "Don't worry, I won't tell. I left Myhal with Kashia and promised I would come right back after I saw you were all right. Come home when you are dry, but don't be late for supper." She felt his forehead with her hand and gave him a little smile while she shook her head. Peter felt better immediately.

For the next few days Peter was especially well-behaved and helpful, in spite of a slight fever and runny nose. He spent hours helping Mama spin and never asked to go out to play. There are no real secrets in a village as small as Opaka, especially when there are as many witnesses as Peter had that day. Mama heard about his mishap and the help he received, but she decided to say nothing and just took advantage of a few days of very helpful behavior.

Chapter 9

Fears

By the spring of 1916, Muscovites had occupied the territory around Peter's village for almost eighteen months. Fate spared Opaka from actual battles during that time, but shooting was often heard in the distance because soldiers practiced maneuvers in the nearby forests and fields. The areas around Opaka and neighboring Felzendorf were used mainly for training and for housing and feeding soldiers who were on their way to the front. Because the farmers had to share so much of their harvest and livestock, the villagers existed on thin soups and porridge.

"The weather soon will be warm enough for us to begin planting, Mama," Daria said brightly. She sat on the side bench and clapped her hands to get the attention of little Kashia, who was playing with wooden spoons on the floor. Her brothers were out in the barn doing chores, and Daria enjoyed the quiet time in the house with Mama and the baby.

Maria smiled. "Yes, it will," she agreed as she sat at her loom. *It'll be good to be out in the sunshine again,* she thought. *Good to have warm weather lessen the need for so much wood for the stove. The woodpile has dwindled after the long winter. Food is dwindling too.* She shook her head slowly while she worked and frowned. *The root cellar still has some potatoes and carrots and onions. There's still some flour and millet. Not much wheat though. So many soldiers have passed through. I didn't know how we'd get through till spring. At least there've been fewer in the last few weeks. I hate it when they sleep in the barns and here in the house! Forgive me, Lord, for my thoughts. I hope some villagers somewhere are kind to my Myhailo wherever he is.* Maria wiped her eyes quickly so that Daria wouldn't see her tears. *It's been so long,* she thought. *Over seven months since we last had news. Someone told Vasyl that Myhailo sent word from the front. He sent his love and his prayers. Those words. They touched my heart like warm bright sunshine. To know he was alive! Dear God, let him be all right.* She prayed silently and let the rhythm of her weaving calm her.

Daria and Kashia were playing a clapping and singing game, and the baby giggled at a face Daria made. Maria glanced at them and briefly stopped her rhythmic movements. *Daria,* she thought. *Another worry. At the beginning of the war, she was still a child and safe from the hungry looks of the soldiers. Young Russians seem to have some respect for old women and mothers like me, but I've seen them leer at some of the young maidens in the village. There've been rumors. About soldiers and girls. Daria has begun to blossom into womanhood. I've kept her with me whenever soldiers are around. We have to be so careful. And I have to be careful with my sons too. Soldiers. Strangers. Stories about soldiers and young boys! How can I watch them all? We have a bar on our door, but what good is that against soldiers with guns? Stop this, Maria! God will watch over us. He will send us nothing we cannot bear. Nothing!* Maria felt the familiar spiraling fear begin and struggled to fight it off with prayers and thoughts of how she had to keep the family safe until Myhailo came home.

When warm spring weather finally came, Maria put aside her weaving for work in the fields. Oleksa stayed at home once more and cared for Kashia while the two older children went to work with their mother. Peter was six years old, and while the rest of the family returned to a familiar routine, he was about to begin a great new adventure.

"Petrush," Maria told him, "When the soldiers aren't in our area, you will take Mama Cow to pasture. She needs the sweet grasses, and you're big enough now to be a cowherd."

Peter stood very straight and felt especially important. "Yes, Mama! I'll try very hard to be a good one."

"Mama Cow knows the way to and from the farm, so let her

help you learn your new responsibility."

Peter was overjoyed. He dearly loved the gentle red and white cow and had enjoyed a good rapport with her since she first became part of the family. Oleksa had been the cowherd before Kashia was born, but after Papa went away, Oleksa was needed at home to take care of his little sister so that Mama could go to the fields. Mama Cow's trips to the pasture were infrequent unless one of the neighbor children took her. Now Peter would do it.

Late one morning, on the way home from the pasture, Peter saw a woven basket lying out in the middle of a field. He left Mama Cow by the side of the road and ran to fetch it. It was heavy and well made with a hinged lid and clasp like a suitcase.

Mama would like this, he thought. *She could use it to store things. It's been a long time since Mama had a present, and I'll be the one to give her this!*

Because Peter was allowed to take out the cow only in the morning, he was always home in time for lunch. He took the cow to the stable and gave her water before he ran to the house to show Oleksa the basket.

"I've seen these baskets before, Petrush. The soldiers use them for carrying bullets."

"But they just left it in the field. It was empty! They must have thrown it away. Do you think Mama will like it?"

Oleksa had lessened his teasing of Peter, but he still could not resist a chance to frighten him a little. He hunched over his little brother and spoke in a rough whisper, close to Peter's ear. "Muscovites never throw anything away," he rasped. His face was solemn. "They know exactly where they leave everything!" He paused to give his words time to create the desired effect. Peter's eyes widened, and he started to tremble. "One of them was probably watching you and will come to get you now for stealing their property!"

Peter felt his hair stand on end. Grown-ups told horrible stories about what Muscovites did to children that they didn't like. The adults told the stories to frighten their children and keep them from having anything to do with the soldiers, but Peter didn't know this. His mind raced with terrible images of what was going to happen to him.

"If I were you," Oleksa murmured, "I'd go and hide."

"Should I put it back?"

"No, they already know you have it."

Peter ran to put the basket in the hayloft. Then he ran and hid behind a grain sack in the komora. He lost all desire for lunch and cowered there until Mama came home for supper. He was so quiet, she wondered what was wrong with him. There didn't seem to be any trouble between Peter and Oleksa, and she was too tired to ask for explanations.

No Muscovites came after Peter that day, that week, or ever. After a few days, Peter suspected Oleksa was up to his old tricks. Peter didn't like being made a fool but was relieved that he would not be arrested. After a few weeks he gave the basket to Mama, and she was very happy with it. Mama had her present, and Peter was not in trouble. Everything turned out all right, but Peter vowed never again to pick up or take anything he found lying around. Just in case.

Fears haunted everyone. Some grew from the frightful visions in one's own mind, some came with the strangers who marched through the village, and some even came from the heavens above. Villagers were people of faith, but their faith was also mingled with superstition. They believed in evil spirits, curses, and omens. To most of the tales and folklore, Maria listened with interest, but she always turned to prayer for any strength she needed. Visual signs and dreams, however, were another matter. Something one could actually see was taken seriously.

Summer arrived with several weeks of hot, humid weather, and sometimes Peter was allowed to spend some of the uncomfortable nights sleeping in the hayloft where it was cooler. He loved the chance to be by himself at those times and think.

The house was dark and quiet when Peter awoke in the night. He was in the loft and had left the loading door open to whatever stray breeze might wander in. He listened for what sound might have awoken him—maybe an owl or some other night creature scurrying away—but he heard only Pundyk's steady breathing. The dog slept up in the loft when Peter did, and the two of them had a nice view of the farmyard and the night sky. Peter was lying on his back with a mound of hay under his head. He looked up and saw that the hazy blanket of clouds that had held in the sticky heat in the early part of the night had cleared away, and the stars twinkled clearly. The moon was a crescent. Peter stared at it and suddenly realized that there was something odd about the way it looked. A line of stars extended from the lower end of the crescent in such a way that it appeared to be a perfect shape of a sickle. He stared at it for some time, and it troubled him. Finally he sat up. Pundyk lifted his head and growled to let Peter know he was there and ready to protect him.

"It's all right, Pundyk," Peter whispered. "I'm going to get Mama." The dog started to follow him. "Stay!" he ordered, and climbed down from the loft. He ran across the empty, dark farmyard and let himself into the house. He crept over to Mama's bed and touched her shoulder.

"Mama," he whispered. "I see something in the sky. Please come out and look at it."

"What is it, Petru?" she said half-asleep. "Are you sick?"

"No, Mama. Please come outside with me. I want to show you something."

"Are soldiers here?" she whispered as she got out of bed.

"No, Mama. Something is in the sky." He took her hand and led her out into the middle of the farmyard. He pointed at the moon. "Is that a sickle, Mama?"

His mother looked up and gasped softly.

"Well, Mama?"

"I think you better get back to bed, Petrushu."

"Is it a sickle?"

"Yes, it looks like one."

"What does it mean, Mama?"

She didn't answer him, but her mind told her, *It means a lot of things. None good. A sickle, a sign of danger. A sign that threads of life as we know them may be cut. A sign. A sign of death? God help us! A sign of an oppression to come?*

Peter watched her stand very still. She shivered in spite of the warm night. "Please, Mama, tell me."

Chapter 9

"I'm afraid it doesn't mean anything good."

"I don't understand."

"I think it's a sign of something that will come upon us."

"Like what?"

"It's a symbol."

"I don't understand"

"Go to bed, Petrush, and don't worry. Just say your prayers again and ask God to watch over us." She kissed his cheek and hugged him before she sent him back to the loft.

Peter climbed up to his bed near Pundyk. The dog licked Peter's hand, and his wagging tail whipped a few pieces of straw into the air. Peter looked down at his mother and watched her stand in the yard for a long time with her face turned up to the sky. She stood perfectly still and then quietly made the sign of the cross before she turned and went inside the house. He looked back at the sickle, and it continued to trouble him. Someday he would know what the symbol meant, but that night he did not. He said his prayers, made the sign of the cross too, and went to sleep.

Chapter 10

Wandering

"You know, Mama Cow, you're such a good mother." Peter stood in the barn and spoke fondly to the gentle beast. "Your baby is what? Three weeks old? Anyone can see you love all the babies you've had. You lick them and moo to them and watch that they're safe. Your new baby daughter's name is a good one, I think. Myhal came up with it. Bura. Do you know what it means?" The cow looked at him intently and blinked. "It means two things: stormy and ruddy. She's so frisky and such a pretty reddish-brown color! Her name fits her, don't you think?"

The only other calf the cow had had since the war began was a bullock. Peter's mother had feared that the army would take it for meat, so one time when the soldiers were away from town, she had arranged to have the Jewish livestock dealer come to see the calf. He couldn't offer Mama much money, but he was able to give her some supplies like flour, sugar, and other things the family needed in exchange for the calf. When the Muscovites returned, they raided the family's komora again, so the family lost in the bargain anyway.

"My Mama hopes that somehow we can keep Bura. She'll grow to be a good milk cow." The calf began to suckle. "Wouldn't you be happy to have your daughter near you? Your other babies were bullocks and were traded to dealers. I know it made you sad. Maybe this time we can keep Bura away from the soldiers and the dealers too!"

Peter remembered Mama saying that Bura was very small, and

no one would be interested in her as food for a few months. But then winter would come, and the soldiers would be very hungry. The idea frightened Peter. He lifted his head and listened. Someone was calling him.

Mama called Peter from the door of the house. Daria, Myhal, and Oleksa were already inside collecting food and other things and stuffing them into sacks. Peter ran over to his mother and saw the frightened look in her eyes.

"We have so much to do, Petrush! Go inside and help!" she said and turned to run out the front gate and down the road.

Daria wrapped a bread in cloth and saw Peter's puzzled look. She came over and hugged him, saying, "Petrush, you have to be a brave boy for Mama. An order came from the Muscovites. The front—the fighting—will soon be in our village. It'll be dangerous. We have to leave for a while until the fighting stops."

Peter began to cry, and she hugged him again. "Petrush," she whispered, "we're all afraid. Mama is afraid too. I saw her crying when she heard the order. She said to me, 'Daria, what will we do now? We have no wagon, no horses!' We have to help Mama and be brave. She went to find a neighbor who will share a wagon with us. We have to take Mama Cow, Bura, the chickens, and the new filly. They have to be safe too!"

Daria looked at her little brother's face. He stopped crying and wiped his eyes and nose in his sleeve. His mouth was set in a tight line, and his lower lip stopped trembling. He was only six, but he was not going to add to Mama's burden. "Good, brave boy," Daria said and kissed his cheek. She went back to packing what little food was in the house.

Mama came back with news that old Mr. Janko had a rickety wagon that the army hadn't wanted. He planned to hitch old Dusty to it, and in spite of the mare's age, if the wagon wasn't overloaded, she could still pull it. Mama saw the serious faces of her children and tried to ease their worry.

"It's summer! It'll be easier to travel now that winter's gone. Take your warm coats, though; we may have to sleep out under the sky if the fighting goes on for long. If you catch cold while we travel, it could be very bad. I want you all to be careful and help me by being good."

Her voice was supposed to be light and matter-of-fact, but the fear she felt crept in to make her words waver. No one seemed to notice. They silently collected clothing, food, and blankets. Kashia was walking very well now. She was excited by the packing. She thought they were going for a picnic again, like the last time when the family did spring planting.

Within the hour, old Mr. Janko was there with his horse and wagon. Dusty looked tired but otherwise undisturbed by all the activity. She nibbled at the grass near the front gate as if she were in the pasture and not hitched to a broken-down wagon. The family's parcels were set in place next to Mr. Janko's few belongings. Their chickens soon were perched on the slatted sides of the wagon near Mr. Janko's old rooster and prized hen.

Myhal led the family cow to the back of the wagon and securely tied her there. Little Bura followed her mother and made frightened, bleating noises. Myhal didn't tie the calf to the wagon because she would follow her mother naturally. If a calf as young as she was tied to the wagon, she might stumble and be dragged. He packed a short rope to use if someone did have to lead the calf along. Oleksa brought out the little red-brown filly that the family had found and stood ready with Pundyk to follow the wagon.

Kashia sat on a low bench inside the wagon, and Peter was told to sit next to her to watch that she didn't fall. He did as he was told but wished he could walk with the grown-ups. His little sister's excitement soon faded into whimpers when the clucking chickens, barking dogs, and crying babies in other carts and wagons on the road began to frighten her. Peter tried to hug her and tell her a story, but she wouldn't listen. He soon forgot what he was trying to say when he heard his mother arguing with Mr. Chorney.

On the way out of town, Mr. Janko stopped the wagon in front of the house of old Mr. and Mrs. Chorney. Mama wanted to make certain that they were going with the rest of the villagers. The old people were in their house and refused to leave.

"Please," Maria pleaded, "You have to come with us! There'll be fighting here. You can't stay. Come, ride with us if you're afraid to go on foot. There's room."

"You go ahead," Mr. Chorney said. "We'll stay behind and die inside our own fences if we have to. We'll stay here and face what comes!"

"No!" Maria shouted. Then she lowered her voice to a gentler level. "That's foolishness! You can't choose your own time to die. If you stay here, you'll surely be killed. You have to come!"

"You go ahead and save yourself because you're young," the old woman said. "You have to worry about your children!"

Maria wouldn't listen. She took their coats, two blankets, and what meager food she found in the cupboard. Mr. Janko pushed the old couple to the wagon. Maria came out with their things and sent Oleksa to their barn.

"Here are some things you'll need," she said turning to the Chorneys. "If there's anything else you want, I'll fetch it. I won't let you go back to the house. I sent Oleksa to bring your animals. My parents are dead now, God rest their souls," she said, crossing herself. "Your children are gone from this village, so for now, we're one family. You're coming with us if we have to tie you to the wagon! No time to argue. Come on!"

The old couple looked at Maria and then at each other. They finally nodded and stepped onto the wagon. The old woman lifted Kashia onto her lap, and Mr. Chorney took the reins. Peter jumped off to join those who walked.

The procession consisted of a long caravan of wagons, carts, wheelbarrows, people on foot, and livestock. Children and the bewildered beasts of the farms both cried together because they didn't understand what was happening. Some of the old women wept openly out of fear. Others marched silently, already weary from the preparations to leave. Peter looked around him and saw the confusion and sadness and was afraid.

What will happen now? he thought as they left the village behind them. *Where will we sleep? What will we see?*

Hours passed, and the wanderers continued on. Peter was tired and sat on the back of the wagon with his feet dangling over the edge. The wagons came to open fields where a bloody battle had been fought. Peter smelled the smoke from the gunfire and small brush fires that had burned themselves out along the edge of the forest and road. At first Peter didn't understand what he saw.

All the young crops look trampled, he thought briefly. *What is all that heaped in the field?* The answer came to him with painful speed, and his eyes widened with horror. *Soldiers!* He shuddered. *They look like piles of dirty, muddy rags,* he thought. His eyes saw the dark stains on the bodies and the patches on the ground and tender plants. Confused thoughts thudded through his brain with the same rhythm as the sound of his heart pounding in his ears. He heard a soft gasp and realized that Daria was walking near his side of the wagon.

"Those plants have been watered with human blood," she murmured.

Peter shuddered as he looked back at the fields and then knew what the dark patches were on the soil. A sick smell invaded his nose. He had heard the expression "the smell of death," and now he wondered if that was what he smelled. Peter wanted to shut his eyes, but he kept looking and hoping it was not real.

Maria saw the faces of her children and didn't try to explain or comfort them. There were no words to say.

Peter's senses were overloaded by the terrible things he saw and smelled. Then he became aware of the moaning and weeping from the wounded and dying soldiers in the fields.

"Give me water," one cried out as the procession passed. A few of the villagers tried to help, but the wagons moved on. The villagers had to keep moving because no one was safe in an area so close to battle.

"Please … end my pain … my life," another man pleaded near the edge of the field.

Peter looked at the poor soldier who had just said that. The wagon was passing by the place where he was lying on the ground. The man was so badly wounded that his entire uniform was saturated with blood and caked with mud. Peter saw that he had a terrible open wound near his waist and lower back. The man's eyes stood out white and wild against his blackened face, and he looked right at Peter. Peter felt sick, and his stomach churned. He couldn't look away. His mother ran up to Peter and tried to comfort him with her arms.

"End my pain …" the man weakly pleaded again.

Peter saw one of the villagers run over to the soldier and place something on the ground. The wounded soldier reached for it, and as a shot rang out, the man's mangled body lurched. The moaning ceased. Peter began to shake. He felt he couldn't breathe. He couldn't say anything out loud, but his brain screamed over and over, *He killed himself! He killed himself! The man killed himself! Oh God, the poor man killed himself!*

His mother held Peter in her arms now, as if he were a baby again. She hugged him tightly and whispered, "Son, try to pray. Pray for him." Peter wondered if God really could hear prayers over the sounds of all the horrible cries and moans.

The villagers moved on, and there were more soldiers along the road and in the fields. Some called for water, while others said nothing because they were too weak. Many could be heard weeping or murmuring in delirium. Some looked twisted and ugly, and others looked as if they were asleep, but Peter knew they must be dead.

Maria looked at the fields and silently wept for the dead and wounded. *Some of their families will never know what happened to them or where they died,* she thought in anguish. *There are so few records. No tributes—only wives and mothers somewhere weeping for husbands and sons who will never come home.* She didn't allow herself to think about Myhailo and instead concentrated on seeing that her children were all right.

Peter thought about Papa and began to cry. Once, weeks before the wandering began, he had asked Mama why Papa didn't come home. She said she had heard nothing of him in almost a year and didn't know if he would ever come home. She wept bitterly then, and Peter never asked again. Now, he cried harder, and his mother put him back in the wagon. He leaned on the sidewall where Pundyk was napping and cried into his sleeves. Finally, after a while, he fell asleep with his arms wrapped around the faithful dog.

Wandering

Whatever dream eased his thoughts, it was gone as soon as he awoke. The creaking wheels, crying children, animal sounds, and distant thundering of guns brought him miserably back to the present. Peter shut his eyes again but could not sleep anymore to close out the horrible sounds.

They passed another area where a battle had been fought, and the soldiers' bodies were being carried off the field to army wagons. The murmured decision among the wanderers was that they would head for the forest. Everyone agreed it probably would be a little safer there. As they entered the forest, they heard shouts of "Zuruck! Zuruck!" Austrian troops were shouting at them to go back. The Russians were coming, and the battle would soon be there. The villagers turned and took another road. They walked as long as they could before night came. Near the outskirts of a small village, in a grove of trees, they bedded down for the night. Mama Cow managed to let down her milk in spite of all that was happening, and it seemed that her warm, frothy milk was the most exquisite supper they ever had.

Everyone slept lightly and with fear. The sounds of guns in the distance finally lessened in the darkness, but the night sounds of a woodlot further frightened young and old alike. Bura pressed close to Mama Cow, and Pundyk stood guard over both of them and the young filly. He didn't have the stable there to enclose him and the animals he guarded, but Pundyk knew his job well and never shirked his duties, even in the dark, strange forest.

Peter couldn't sleep, and his curious eyes searched the darkness. On the far edge of the small clearing where his family huddled together, he saw two bobbing points of light. Years later, perhaps he would tell himself that they were only the eyes of an owl reflecting pale light. But that night they might have been the eyes of Satan himself, out stalking his realm. The world had become Hell, full of violence, hate, pain, and torment. The pale points of light were sinister eyes to Peter, and they bothered him. He said nothing to Mama or the others, but he watched to make certain that they came no closer. If he slept at all that night, he could not remember any rest or dreams.

Chapter 11

The Spy

The next morning the caravan of wanderers organized again, and the sunlight seemed to give a little hope to the new day. At least it reminded everyone that they had lived through the night. After a breakfast of fresh milk and bread, Peter and his family set out on the road with the other villagers. As they neared a town called Lukavich, they saw troops camped on the edge of town. Their uniforms were neither Austrian nor Russian. Their helmets had sharp peaks on them, and when Peter was close enough to hear them talking, he wondered what language they spoke.

They sound like geese honking, he thought. *But that can't be so.* He listened as Mr. Janko spoke to Mama and the Chorneys, and Peter's eyes widened. "They're Prussians?" he said to himself in amazement. "So that's what Prussians look like!"

The Prussian soldiers stared at the wandering villagers intently, and the villagers cautiously stared back, including Peter, who eyed the soldiers warily. *Please, God, if they see Bura, let them see how little she is so they won't take her,* he pleaded silently.

As soon as they passed the encampment, a commotion began near the back of the caravan. People began screaming, and the Prussians were shouting back at them. Everyone stopped to see what was wrong. The shouting moved up the line from the back. "Maria! The Prussians have Oleksa!"

Peter saw his mother clutch her throat. "What?" she called back. "He's just a boy!" She started to run toward the back of the line.

The Spy

Old Mrs. Chorney held Kashia on her lap, so Peter was free to run after his mother. *Why would soldiers even notice Oleksa?* he wondered.

Maria reached the end of the caravan and saw some Prussian officers, a few troops, and her ten-year-old son. Oleksa looked very confused and scared. "Oleksa!" she shouted.

"Mama! I didn't do anything! One of the officers called to me. He said, 'Kommen Sie hier!' and motioned that I should come to the side of the road. He grabbed me and then …" One of the Prussians clamped his hand over Oleksa's mouth and shouted at him.

"Don't move, Oleksa. Be still. I'll do what I can." Maria tried to sound as if everything would be all right, but she had no idea what to do.

Peter watched his mother try to talk to the Prussians. He heard her ask if they spoke Ukrainian, but they gestured that they didn't. They talked to her, but she kept saying she didn't speak German. She began to wring her hands, and she bit her lip to keep from crying.

Now what? she thought. *I want to sit down and cry or scream. What do I do? Oleksa looks like he is going to faint. These men don't understand a thing I say.* She suddenly got an idea. When she turned around, she saw Peter and her two older children. "Petrush, stay with Daria. I have to go get someone. Don't talk to Oleksa." She ran back along the caravan.

Daria put her arm around him. Peter saw that Natalia and Ivan were there too. Ivan had big tears in his eyes, and he grabbed on to Peter's arm.

"Oh, Petru," Ivan whimpered. "Oleksa was near us in the caravan. Then one of those men over there started talking to him, and then they grabbed him! What are they going to do?"

Peter didn't say anything and just shrugged his shoulders. Maria came running back toward them with an old villager, Mykola Bula. She had once said that Mr. Bula worked for a German landowner and knew how to speak his employer's language very well. Bula walked straight up to one of the Prussian officers and began to talk to him. They talked and gestured for a few minutes, and then

Chapter 11

Bula turned to Maria with a grim look on his face.

"They say Oleksa is a Russian spy."

"What?" she cried. "He's a boy! We're loyal to Austria! Myhailo is in their army! How could they think such a thing?"

"They say he's wearing a Russian cap and a red sash, and he was the only one in the caravan who rode a young, healthy horse. He rides 'like a Cossack,' they say. They say he's a spy and has received special favors."

Maria looked at Oleksa. He did have on a cap, and she noticed, for the first time, that he wore a gaudy red belt. "But he found that cap on the road and asked me if he could play with it. There was no insignia on it. I didn't think it was a military cap. He *found* it and picked it up. No one gave it to him. Boys like to play. As for the belt, I don't know where that came from. He must have found that too! I haven't seen him since we began the march this morning. He wanted to ride the young horse near the Sorokas because they were at the back of the procession. Don't they see he's just a little boy?"

Bula tried to translate everything Maria said to the Prussians. The raised voices and the language again reminded Peter of geese, but the gaggling sound wasn't funny anymore. Now they were pointing at the horse. Maria was gesturing toward the animal and trying not to cry. Peter couldn't hear what she was saying, but everyone was looking at the horse.

"What do they want with your young filly?" Ivan asked. "Oleksa told us how you got her."

Peter thought back to that spring. The young filly had come to them by luck. One evening Mama and the children were on their way back from planting in the fields when they saw the young horse off in the distance. She was limping badly, and when the boys ran to her, they saw she was crippled. There were cuts and sores all over her legs. They caught her and brought her home where Mama took warm water and bathed the sores. She rubbed ointment into the filly's wounds and wrapped the thin legs with soft bandages.

"One of the army horses must have foaled," Mama had said. "This young one can't be more than six or eight months old. Maybe it ran off from the others and got tangled in brambles or was attacked by some wild animals. The army doesn't want crippled horses, so maybe she was left behind. Or maybe she ran off."

I think she ran off, Peter had thought. *She was probably afraid the soldiers would shoot her for meat.*

Now he watched the Prussian officers walking around the yearling, looking at her. Peter remembered, *So we found our little filly, and Mama said if her wounds healed, we'd have a good horse. By the time we had to leave for this march, the filly was all better.*

Bula translated for Maria again as the Prussian officers continued speaking. "When they saw the boy riding skillfully on the yearling's back, with his dark, curly hair, Muscovite cap, and sash, they concluded that he had to be a Russian spy. They said no mere peasant boy would ride a fine young horse and carry himself so proudly in a …" Bula gestured to the group of curious onlookers before continuing, "common band of wanderers." Mykola Bula put his hand on Maria's shoulder. "I'm so sorry, Maria. I want to help, but I don't know how. I only tell you what they say."

Ivan tugged at Peter's sleeve and pointed to the Prussian officer who was bending near the colt to look at the scars on her legs. Maria stood nearby and began to gesture at the horse and explain once again. Bula translated for her. The officer in charge said something, and then everyone was quiet. Maria looked at the faces of the officers and then at Mr. Bula. Their silence frightened her.

"What is it, Mykola? What are they going to do?"

"Trouble," Bula answered slowly. His face was white. "They say they are going to shoot the boy."

"No!" she cried. "Oh my God! No!"

Ivan gripped Peter's arm and wailed, "Oh, Petru!"

Peter looked up at Daria and Myhal. Daria reached for Peter, but he felt an arm come around from behind him to comfort him. Ivan's mother had been standing behind them, and she hugged both Peter and little Ivan. A murmur swept through the crowd, and then everyone was quiet. Everyone except Maria.

She walked up to one of the Prussian officers and began to gesture and plead all over again, and Bula tried to keep up with her in his translation. Other officers were called over to the group. Each listened in turn to what Bula told them. Maria told her story over and over again and insisted that they had made a terrible mistake. Negotiations went on for most of the day.

Peter and Ivan sat huddled on the ground together near Ivan's parents. Mrs. Soroka tried to get Peter to eat something and to have a drink of water. Peter took his cup to his mother and offered it to her. The look in her eyes frightened him.

The villagers were fascinated by the drama. No one moved on. They all decided to wait for Maria and Oleksa. Peter looked at his brother's pale face. Oleksa looked like he was going to be very sick. Peter wanted to cry but tried not to and hoped Mama could set things right again. Whenever he felt like he wanted to cry, he would run back to Mr. Janko's wagon to tell the others what was happening. He ran back and forth between the wagon and the place where Oleksa was held many times that day.

The arguments and pleas stretched from late morning into early evening. Finally the Prussians decided to let Oleksa go free. They confiscated his cap, sash, and jacket. The jacket was Oleksa's, but they took it anyway. Bula translated that Maria could keep the yearling and that she was to take her son and leave, but before she was free to go back to the wagon, Bula had to translate a very long lecture from one of the officers to Oleksa. Peter couldn't hear much of it, but what he did hear was about never picking up things that didn't belong to him. *Just like the basket,* Peter thought.

Mama put her arms around Oleksa, hugged him, and finally let her tears come. She looked up at Mr. Bula and was grateful for what he had done. "Thank you, Mykola," she said shakily. "Without your help this day could have ended in tragedy. You're a good man. Thank you for my son's life."

Mykola Bula said nothing. He tried to smile, but the strain of the long day showed on his face. He ruffled Oleksa's curly hair, but when he tried to speak, no words came. He nodded quietly to Maria and walked back to his cart.

Oleksa and Mama led the young filly back to Janko's wagon. Peter left Ivan with his family and followed Daria and Myhal back to the wagon too. No one said anything. There had been enough words that day.

The wanderers began to move again. After about an hour, they met a Russian patrol that commanded them to stop.

"Stop! You Austrians!!" they shrieked.

Peter looked at the shouting Russians and thought, *The Prussians thought maybe some of us were Russian spies, and now the Russians call us Austrians. No one knows who anyone is anymore.*

After the caravan halted, the Muscovites told the villagers to take another road. It was getting dark, so the weary wanderers took refuge in a large forest. Everyone settled down for another restless night of woodland noises, glowing lights, and creaking sounds. Pundyk took watch over the animals once again, and Peter slept a little more that night. The last thing he thought of as he leaned against Daria and Oleksa before he fell asleep was, *I hate this endless walking and never going home. I never want to be a gypsy.*

Chapter 12

Home Fires Burning

The next morning, news spread through the caravan that the Muscovites had pushed back the Austrians and the Prussians. The peasants could return to Opaka. On the way home they were stopped twice and asked for their papers and destination. By the afternoon the wanderers had reached home. There were no signs of warfare or looting in the village. Only the fields showed signs of battle. There were a few black patches left from small brush fires started by the shelling, but that was all. Peter saw his house and wanted to clap his hands and laugh and sing.

Home is so beautiful! he thought. *So beautiful!*

The older boys put the animals in the barn, and Pundyk went straight to his favorite spot by the door. The old dog stretched and yawned and curled up for a nap. Myhal looked at him on the way out of the barn and gently patted his head. Pundyk didn't answer with his usual wagging tail. He knew he was home and safe and was already asleep.

Mama started a fire in the stove while Daria and Peter unpacked. When the older boys came in from the barn, she called everyone together and prayed, "Thank you, dear Lord, for bringing us home again. Thank you for our lives, our safety, and this warm house that gives us shelter." Each made the sign of the cross. "All right. Let's get the beds made and take a nap. It'll be so good to sleep cozy and warm again!" She smiled as all of them eagerly obeyed.

When they were all bedded down, she sat in a chair near the

stove and watched them sleep. "You brought us all home safely," she prayed quietly and looked at her dear icons. "What other words are there than just 'Thank you'? They seem so simple, so small. My heart has been breaking with fear since all this began. Thank you for my children, for our lives, for our coming home."

She added more wood to the stove and looked up at the icon of the Blessed Mother. "With so much to be thankful for, I am afraid to ask for more," she prayed softly, and tears began to fall. "We saw so much suffering in those fields. I know each of those men had someone praying for him. I don't know why such torment must exist. I must ask. If Myhailo is still alive, please keep him safe and let him come home to us. Please."

She sat down intending to pray, but soon fell asleep. A few hours later, she awoke to the pale light of early evening. She went over to Peter and gently shook him to wake him.

"Petrush," she whispered, "It's time for supper."

"Mama," he mumbled sleepily, "let's eat supper tomorrow morning."

She laughed softly and hugged him. "I love you, Petrushu." She looked at the others deep in sleeps of exhaustion. "Go back to sleep. I'll tend to barn chores tonight. You're right. We'll have supper in the morning."

Peter's family could not stay home very long. In a few weeks the Russians came again and told everyone to leave. This time the villagers didn't go far. They went out of the village and hid under the trees near the river. The weather was terrible. Rain fell, and everyone got wet. The villagers clung to the embankment and each other and waited three days and three nights. Finally the distant fighting ceased, and they returned home.

A few days passed, and again the order came to leave. The villagers formed a caravan once more. They wandered far from Opaka, hiding in forests or finding shelter near other villages. Days, nights, sounds of travel, sun, rain, battlefields full of death and horror—everything became a blur to Peter and to everyone else. They felt like gypsies but without the happy songs and laughter that those bands of people were known to have. Not being home made soft summer showers feel like numbing winter cold. Food was tasteless. Time lost meaning. Being awake was a nightmare. Sleep was fitful. Dreams gave no escape. Maria tried to comfort her children and keep them to their prayers and chores. Peter longed to sleep again in the loft or to have the great joy of sitting in the kitchen while Mama baked bread.

Finally one morning word came that they could go back to Opaka, and everyone was happy. Even if they could be home for only a week or two, they would cherish the days. It was rumored that the Austrians had pushed back the Muscovites, and Opaka was Austrian soil again. No one really cared. Home was what everyone wanted. Home and a dry bed to sleep on.

As they neared Opaka, a murmur began to move through the group. There was a heavy, stale smell of smoke in the air.

"There must have been some burning," Myhal said to Mama.

The wagons and the wanderers turned onto the village road. Everyone became quiet. Then Peter heard some muffled weeping. He stood up on the wagon and looked in the direction of Opaka. Sad wisps of smoke still rose from what was once his dear village. The buildings were charred heaps of wood and straw. Opaka had been burned to the ground. There was nothing left except the church with its little three-barred cross on top. Even the Muscovites couldn't bring themselves to burn that. No other building was left as it had been. Everything was gone. Peter sat down on the wagon.

Home. Home is gone, he thought miserably. *No benches, no warm stove, no loft, no barn.* He wanted to cry but found he couldn't. He didn't want to be held. He didn't want anything. He didn't know what to do. It seemed there was nothing left to say. Nothing left to feel.

Maria and her children led the cow and filly into the farmyard. Little Bura followed Mama Cow and made little sounds that echoed through the stillness. Daria and Myhal held the chickens. Even the chickens were quiet. Pundyk sniffed at the blackened patches of ground. There were no fences anymore between the farmyards. There were just charred lines of crumbled wood. Even the weeds and grasses were burned into a fragile black lace that covered the ground.

Peter and his family stood in the middle of their farmyard and looked around them. Everything was leveled. The house was now an ugly black pile of smoldering, twisted beams and clumps of charred wood. A few of the blankets they had left behind were burned but still in a neat pile near what used to be the corner where the bedding was stored. The benches they had dreamed of sleeping on were black, brittle boards that crumbled when touched. Maria hugged Kashia to her, and all the children gathered around her. They held each other tightly and began to cry, but not for long.

"The Russians have retreated, children. I've heard that they leave nothing behind. This may be the sign that they're gone now for good. We have to begin again."

The older boys picked through the rubble to find beams and boards that hadn't burned through completely. Maria found some bricks from the old stove, and Peter helped her stack them on the ground. He found a metal plate from the stove too and put that over the bricks. Maria built a small fire on the ground under the metal plate and soon began to cook some porridge for supper. The bucket in the well hadn't burned, nor had the rope used to pull it up, so they could draw water.

The Gonts were in their farmyard trying to put whatever could be found in some order. After Maria had fed her children, Maresha Gont came across the burned fencerow with news.

"Word is spreading through the village that most of the crops in the fields have been burned too. Some plants are still left, so I guess we should be glad of that. That rain we cursed two nights ago probably saved at least a little. Old Koval said for me to tell you that Oleksa and Myhal can come and get some hay for your cow from his north field. The calf can still have her mother's milk, and probably the young filly would do all right on the cuttings from Koval's field too."

"Are you going to be all right?" the old neighbor went on. "My Ivan and I are going to stay at my sister's farm in Felzendorf." Felzendorf was a village on the other side of the river, about a kilometer and a half northeast of Opaka. "Her barn isn't completely gone, so we'll have at least part of a roof for a while. My old Ivan and I are too old for sleeping out under the stars." The woman chuckled but became serious again. "If you need us, send word to Felzendorf, will you?"

"Yes, I will," Maria promised. "You take care of yourselves. I'll miss you."

"Ivan says that you can pick through our rubble for wood if you need it. Oh, and some good news. Our dear neighbors from the other side of your property will also be gone for a while. They went on to Sinyava to stay with relatives there. With the Komars gone, you won't have all that fighting and bickering to listen to." She and Maria shared a smile and shook their heads at the thought of the bothersome neighbors who would be away for a time. "I know, I know," Maresha went on. "God sends little blessings in the midst of all this." The woman tried to be lighthearted, but the tears were very close. "Take care of yourselves. Remember where we are. When my old Ivan gets underfoot, I'll send him over here to check on you." The plump, motherly woman hugged Maria and wiped her eyes while she walked back to her farmyard to take some of the bags she and her husband would carry on their trek to Felzendorf.

That night Peter and his family slept out under the sky again, but this time it was not in some unknown woods. They were on their own land. They were home again. The Muscovites had left, and Mama said the family would be all right.

How can all this be? Peter thought as he tried to fall asleep. *How could men do this to my village? I asked Papa once to tell me about war. Now I know why he didn't answer. There was no answer. No answer could tell what all this would be like.*

The days that followed were spent foraging for food. The Muscovites had scavenged most of the food that had been stored in the komora. Now there wasn't even a komora left. There were some buried stores of root crops. Onions and some potatoes would still be harvested in the fields, so there would be a little food for the coming winter.

Each family in the village searched through the rubble for usable lumber or tin to build shanties against the coming cold weather. There wasn't much time. Fall had arrived, and already they felt the promise of cold winter winds. Peter and his family found some boards and pieces of tin in their own ruins and built a shanty for Mama Cow, Bura, and the yearling. It served as a family shelter too. It was pleasant to feel how much warmth a cow and other animals added to the small enclosed space.

Then that special morning came. Mama was busy stirring a pot of porridge, and Kashia was sitting on a little bench Myhal had made from three boards. Peter was near the road looking for pieces of burnable wood for the fire. He collected the chunks and bits in his arms and was straightening up, trying not to drop his little treasures, when he heard something. He turned to see what had made the sound and heard someone speak to him.

"Are you my Petrush?"

Peter spun around to look in the direction of the voice and saw a man silhouetted against the morning sun. The bright sun blinded Peter, but when the man stepped forward, throwing his shadow over Peter's face, Peter dropped his wood and shouted, "Papa!"

He hugged his father's legs and felt strong arms lift him up. Peter hugged his father's neck and laughed and just kept saying, "Papa!" over and over again. Maria looked up when Peter shouted and knew instantly what had happened. She ran across the yard with Kashia and Pundyk following her and tightly hugged both her husband and son. Tears were streaming down her smiling face, and she murmured his name mixed with a prayer of thanksgiving. Pundyk yelped at the sight of his master. After more than two years, he remembered Papa and jumped and yipped like a puppy.

Papa and Mama embraced again and kept kissing each other's cheeks. They both laughed and cried softly. Peter was so excited that he kept dancing around them and hugging them both. Kashia stood to one side and giggled at the sight of them, but when Papa picked her up, she started to cry because she didn't remember him.

They led Papa to the bench near the fire and sat him down. Peter kept hugging his father, and then Papa lifted him up on his lap and put his arms around his son. Mama stood by looking at him and wiping her eyes. Pundyk sat at his master's feet and raised his head now and then to nudge Papa's elbow so he would pet him.

"Papa," Peter said, "you look so tired. Have you been traveling long?"

"For over a week now, Petru. I've been walking mostly."

Peter noticed that Papa wore different boots than he had taken. They were too big, and when he slipped them off, his feet were wrapped in dirty rags.

"Sometimes I met someone with a horse and wagon and could ride for a while."

"What happened to our horses, Papa?"

His father picked up the light riding whip that he'd been carrying when he came home. "Do you remember all the things I took with me? This is the only thing left." The lines on his haggard face deepened while he stopped for a moment and remembered something, but then he smiled when he saw the sympathetic look on Peter's face and exclaimed, "But all I need now is here!" He hugged Peter again and looked up at his wife. "How is everyone?"

"We're all fine. We've been careful with our food and have stayed well. All the children have grown so much! Wait until you see them all together! Daria, Myhal, and Oleksa are helping Pashia and her girls with their shanty this morning. They'll be home soon for breakfast."

She handed him a cup of warm, frothy milk. Mama Cow was still giving her sweet milk on schedule, although the amount was small because fodder was scarce. Papa saw little Bura and the yearling near the shanty, but was too weary to ask about them. He took a long drink and wiped his mouth with his cuff. "Umm. A heavenly drink," he murmured.

"Papa," Peter said sadly, "you said that all you need is here. There's nothing. We couldn't save the house for you." Tears overflowed onto his cheeks.

"Petrush! Son! See this bench?" Smiling, he pointed to the three charred boards that held him. "To me this is as elegant as a throne. I don't need a roof or wall of wood. What I need is my family.

I have Mama and all my precious children! You don't know how I feared ..." He stopped for a moment at looked at his wife. "Even after all that has happened, we're all alive! Petru, I feel I'm as wealthy as a tsar! And right now," he winked, "I'm happy I'm me and not the tsar. I have all I need. The rest, my son, will come in time."

He hugged Peter tightly and looked up at Mama who returned his smile. They heard some happy shrieks off in the distance. Papa stood up. Oleksa, Myhal and Daria had seen him and were running home. He stood smiling, waiting to greet them.

Chapter 13

Winter

Everything seemed better with Papa home again. There wasn't much food, and they needed better shelter, but now things were more filled with hope. Mama began to sing again while she worked. Her voice was genuinely lighthearted, and her brown eyes flashed once more with laughter and wit because she found the world to be happier.

Papa decided to build a bigger shanty. He made a cook stove out of bricks and scrap metal, secured a stovepipe to it, and then built a new shelter around it with what lumber he could find. Everyone gathered inside when it was finished and had visions of being warm for the first time in weeks. Papa started a fire in the stove. Fierce winter winds blew so strongly that day that air backed up in the pipe, filled the shanty with heavy smoke, and sent everyone out coughing and sputtering into the cold. Papa frowned and muttered, "We could use it as a smokehouse."

Scavenging for food was a major occupation. It was an adventure to dig in frozen fields to find beets or carrots that had been overlooked. If potatoes were found, they were either roasted or made into soup. Usually everyone had a small portion of something everyday, but no one was well fed. As time passed, food became scarcer, and there were days when there was no food at all, only a cup of hot water or a half-cup of milk. Twice Papa came home with a wild rabbit, and then the family had meat. The animals felt hunger each day too and grew thin because fodder was in short supply, but Papa said they were strong and would survive on what little they could find until spring. After a time, one of the chickens was chosen for the soup pot. Mama had hoped to save them all until spring when they would lay eggs again and raise some chicks, but their feed was scarce too, so she said she'd use one in soup before it was too thin for even that.

Peter daydreamed about the smell of baking bread or sausage. The thought of sitting in a warm, dry kitchen during a storm was equal to a vision of heaven itself. Numbness, hunger, and chronic colds plagued everyone, but there was little anyone could do. It seemed to Peter that his nose was always running. He used an old handkerchief when Mama was looking, but the rest of the time, he just wiped his nose on his sleeve. He was secretly happy to come back from somewhere and have Pundyk greet him and lick his face because then the dog saved him the trouble.

No one had lumber or money to begin to build new houses right away. Mrs. Kucharski had a brother who lived on the other side of the district in a village that had escaped the destruction Opaka suffered. He dismantled one of his farm buildings and sent the wood and straw to his sister so that she could build herself a house. Hers was the first to be built in the village after the burning. Families left their small children with her for the day while parents and older sons and daughters either scavenged for food or went to work in the forests of the landowners who could hire help. Peter and Kashia were left there often. They liked the games and songs the old woman used to amuse the children, but what they liked most was the chance to be in a cozy house near a big warm stove.

By the middle of winter, some villagers had earned enough lumber and supplies to build small houses or barns. Papa chose to build a small barn first to house both his family and the animals. A barn didn't need the extra expenses or detail that a house normally called for, so it seemed the best choice. By late winter, the family and the cow, calf, horse, and chickens felt lucky to be sleeping in a new straw-roofed barn.

Chapter 13

With the animals and a small stove, the family began to remember how it was to feel warm. The stove had a small oven, and when she could get flour, Mama began to bake bread again. There wasn't much food, but the warmth and fresh bread eased hunger pangs.

In milder weather, Mama did some cooking outside. It was safer to cook on the metal plate over an open fire in the farmyard. She could use a bigger pot and leave it unattended for a short time and not worry about the barn catching fire. A shipment of cornmeal came from a place called America. It was very cheap, and Mama cooked it into a golden porridge. "If a man has cornmeal and some salt and milk to mix with it," Papa would say, "he has a meal fit for a king." It was filling and hot and had a good taste. Sometimes Mama topped the cornmeal mush with sour cream and fried onions. Peter thought it was delicious. All good things were cherished because everything was so scarce.

One day Peter's mouth watered as he watched a big pot of cornmeal bubbling on the fire out in the yard. It was all they had to eat for the day because they were out of money, and it was all but impossible to find any forgotten potatoes in the fields. He looked forward to the golden supper. He went to help Mama and Kashia clean out stalls in the barn, and they were almost finished when they heard a commotion outside. Pundyk barked and ran out into the yard. Mama and Peter followed just in time to see their big pot rolling over the muddy ground, spilling the last of the cornmeal porridge in broad thin pools. The Komars had come back to Opaka the week before, and their pigs were happily grunting and eating all the porridge in sight. There wasn't enough lumber yet to begin to build fences, and their neighbor let his small livestock roam at will. Peter felt the ache in his stomach and knew it wouldn't be soothed that day. Kashia began to cry, and Mama tried to comfort them both.

"Shhh. Quiet down now. I know how bad you feel. I want to cry too. There's nothing we can do about it now. You know how hard winter has been on our own animals. Those pigs didn't do this hurt us. They were hungry too."

Peter didn't understand how Mama could accept things calmly like that. She ran to quiet Pundyk and chase the pigs back to their own yard. Later when she was cleaning up the pot and the stove, Peter saw tears on her thin cheeks and knew that Mama hurt too. Pundyk cleaned up the last morsels of cornmeal on the ground. Hunger was painful for everyone and everything. It was another part of war, a part that lasted long after the shooting was over.

Chapter 14

The Sprouting of a Scholar

In the spring of 1917 Peter was approaching his seventh birthday with mixed feelings. When a child in Opaka was seven years old, he or she entered school. Villagers didn't wait for the beginning of a new school year in order to enroll an eligible child. When the birthday came, the child began formal education.

Neither Papa nor Mama had had the opportunity to learn to read or write, but they were determined that none of their children would be illiterate. Mama took Peter by the hand on the appointed day and walked with him to school. Like so many buildings in Opaka, the school was still under construction, but it was almost finished and provided a roof and walls for the young scholars of the village. Mama put her "X" mark on the papers that were needed for enrollment, and after that was finished, the teacher took Peter by the hand.

"Now he's mine. He must be in school," she said firmly.

Peter was frightened and pulled his hand back. Mama smiled when she saw his eyes widen.

"Everything will be all right, little fish. It's time to learn to swim in new waters."

He looked at Mama and pulled her down so that he could whisper in her ear. "I don't like anyone saying I'm hers except for you, Mama," he said so that the teacher wouldn't hear. He'd been with Mama and his brothers and sisters all his life, and now this teacher, this stranger, said he belonged to her! His lower lip began to tremble.

"Don't cry," the teacher told him. "There are many more here just like you."

That was no comfort to Peter. Mama looked at him and nodded her head while she gave him a little smile.

"Go, Petru, follow your teacher. I'll see you after school. Oleksa will bring you home." She kissed him on the cheek, let go of his little hand, and left to return home.

The teacher led Peter to a low bench. "This is your place. I want you to sit here each school day."

The teacher, a young Ukrainian woman, was rather pretty and very kind.

I don't like her, Peter decided immediately. *There has to be a way to learn to read and write at home,* he thought. *Mama says there isn't. I don't like it here.* He was so nervous he started to shake. The other children looked at him and laughed.

"Be quiet!" the teacher shouted.

Peter looked up at her. *When she shouts like that,* he thought, *she sounds just like Mama when she's angry.* The room became still. Peter felt oddly comforted by her shout, and he stopped shaking.

The first day he simply sat and looked around the room and listened to all that was taking place. The school was one of the first buildings that the village as a whole tried to replace after the burning. The one big rectangular room had whitewashed walls and tall windows that let sunlight fall on the rows of desks. The desks were nothing more than high benches with low bench seats behind them. They stretched across the width of the room. Wide aisles were on each side of the room near the windows, and of course there was an open space at the front for the teacher's table and a small blackboard. The stove that heated the school stood in the middle toward the back of the room.

On one wall was a huge map. Even on his first day at school, Peter knew what maps were because Papa had shown him some once when they were in Lubachiv. They had passed a store window that displayed a huge map of the colony of Halychyna. Peter had thought the map was pretty with all the colored lines and symbols. The map in the classroom was even more colorful. It was of the Austro-Hungarian Empire, and it showed the different regions. With all the dull tones of the benches, the walls, and even the drab clothes of the children and the teacher, the map was the only brightly colored object in the entire school.

Oleksa sat with children in a higher grade on the other side of the room. After school he walked home with Peter, and although he could have teased him, they made their way home in silence.

As the days passed, Peter was introduced to the entire routine in school. After he arrived in the morning, he and Oleksa put their coats on the proper pegs by the door and took their seats. When the teacher entered the room, all the children stood and recited the usual polite greeting that was traditional among Ukrainians. They all said, "Glory to Jesus Christ." The teacher answered, "Glory Forever." During the Christmas and Easter seasons the greeting changed to suit the holiday. The children continued to stand to recite the "Our Father" and then sat down to begin their schoolwork.

On Peter's second day at school, the teacher gave him a writing tablet and a pencil and showed him how to practice making lines, circles, and symbols that looked like little canes. He was to copy the shapes over and over again in preparation for learning how to draw numbers and the thirty-three letters of the Ukrainian alphabet. Peter began practicing, and before long the children were given a few moments to play outside. In the first days, Peter was so enthralled by all the things he was learning that he didn't want to take time to play or even have lunch. The teacher was patient and kind to him, and he began to think she was rather nice; he no longer feared that she would kidnap him. After the newness of his lessons wore off, he enjoyed recess almost as much as time in school.

Peter began to love school. He still could not read, but he had mastered the Ukrainian alphabet with its Cyrillic letters. While he practiced printing, he listened to the reading lessons the older children did aloud. The readings covered the subjects of history, geography, nature study, and even some folktales. Peter, "the questioning one," was beginning to get some answers, and his appetite was whetted for more and more. He watched the older students recite their lessons and answer the teacher's questions. When called upon each would stand respectfully, give the response, and then sit down. Peter's eyes were on his notebook, but he was aware of every move and every word that was said.

His teacher noticed his interest and how seriously he approached his lessons and would smile quietly to herself. In months to come, she would see him running breathlessly into school, pulling his notebooks from under his shirt. At first it seemed odd, but later she found out that he was sneaking off to school on those days instead of staying home to help with seasonal farm chores. He hid his notebooks under his shirt so that no one would know where he was going. What a change that was from so many of her students who sneaked off to go fishing or to play in the forests when they were supposed to be in school. Mama and Myhal lectured Peter about neglecting his duties at home. The lectures didn't do much good. He continued to come as faithfully as he could, regardless of the season. He was in love with learning.

At the end of each day, the students would rise and pray before the class was dismissed. For Peter, though, the school day wasn't over. He went over everything he had learned with whomever he could. Sometimes he would tell Mama or Papa about what he had learned, and if no one else was interested, Mama Cow would get a good portion of history or geography lessons while she chomped away at her evening meal.

The class routine and the use of the Ukrainian language continued for the first few years of Peter's formal education. He dearly loved the hours spent as a student. He loved his life with his family on the farm, but he found out very soon that books and ideas were his greatest love. His teacher saw this and encouraged it, and with her help his fascination with all subjects flowered and grew. He dreamed that the discovery of new worlds and ideas would never end for him. He hoped to go on to school for many years. What he could not foresee was that the world would change again for him. Another war would come, and the results of it would make his hopes as futile as those of a flower trying to thrive and bloom in a tangled bed of weeds.

Chapter 15

Spring

The greening of the distant forests and the feathery yellow-green haze of soft grasses reappearing over the fields and roadsides gave new hope to the village. Spring always meant rebirth, and that year it took on even greater meaning. Not only did tender green seedlings push through the soil to reach for the sun, but even more, the entire village seemed to grow once again from its roots. The charred remains of fences and buildings seemed to sprout new foundations and walls. Houses were beginning to appear, and small barns were already standing on most of the farms. What horses were left were at work helping to prepare the fields for planting. Life resumed a sense of normality after the insanity of war. Great powers were negotiating. There was rumor on the warming breezes that the Austro-Hungarian Empire would soon fall, but that was not a thing to fear. It was said that if it fell, all the nationalities it held would be given independence. "Independence" was a nice word to follow other words like siege, occupation, and war.

The human spirit also lightened and reached for the sunshine. During the long, bitter winter, it had become a fearful thing to look up and see the threatening clouds. The dark leaden sky seemed to drop its weight directly onto the shoulders of the hungry, cold villagers. Now the sky was blue and clear and far above their heads. The burden had lifted. There still wasn't much to eat, but there was now hope of a future crop.

Life began to renew itself everywhere one looked. Mrs. Gont

and her husband returned with their animals, and soon their yard was overrun with baby rabbits. Little furry balls of fluff hopped about, happily nibbling on tender green plants. In spite of a marked shortage of roosters, there were hens all over the village who proudly taught downy chicks where to scratch for food. Mr. Janko had a skinny "good-for-nothing" vagabond rooster who never spent much time in his own farmyard. That habit saved the bird from being made into soup by the Muscovites. They never could find him at home. In years past, he had been chased away by anyone who saw him in their yard, but that spring, no one gave him any trouble. He took advantage of his freedom and inspired the village hens to produce plenty of new life. With the new generation, there would be lots of eggs and chickens for cooking in seasons to come.

Peter was glad that Bura had been spared from butchering. She was still small, but sturdy, and Papa said she would grow into a good milk cow for the family. Now, with fresh grass beginning to grow, there would be enough food for both cows.

After sweeping out the barn one day, Peter sat down near Mama Cow's stall to tell her his latest news. "Papa says I'm going to be the one who takes you and Bura to pasture. Just me!" He smiled to himself. Being the family cowherd was a very responsible job. Mama Cow looked at him intently. She appeared to understand every word and tossed her head a bit as if to remind him that he still had a few things to learn. Peter took no notice. His thoughts were already on other things. He knew that tending cows could be hard work, but there would be quiet times too when he could sit on the edge of the meadow and think. Peter loved to watch little creatures scurry about, and he cherished the times he had been in the forest with his parents or Mrs. Gont when they went hunting for mushrooms. Cows were not allowed in private woodlots, but the pasture bordered on one, and he longed for the chance to study the animals at the forest's edge. Peter also looked forward to the chance to play with other boys who tended cows. Ivan was old enough to begin to be a cowherd too, and their work would give them more time to play together. Because Ivan was still too young for school, Peter hadn't seen him much during the spring.

Chapter 15

"Petrush! Come quickly! You have to see this!" Daria called excitedly, bringing Peter's attention back to the present, where he was sitting with Mama Cow in the barn. Peter ran out to Daria. Her face was beaming as she looked up at the barn roof. "Look! We're blessed this year! During the war they stopped coming. What a wonderful omen!"

She hugged Peter and pointed at the straw roof. There on the peak stood a tall stately bird with a long red beak and thin legs. Snowy feathers gleamed in the sun, and the black tips of the wings gave the bird a very handsome appearance. The storks had returned to the village! More importantly, one had come to their barn roof. Storks were a sign of good luck, and the villagers needed all the good omens they could find.

Peter gazed at the bird and met the look of the round, black eye that stared at him. The bird showed no fear of humans. Peter thought that the proud, elegant bird seemed almost condescending toward the humans who lived beneath the roof it had chosen for its nest. Peter's every spare moment in the weeks that followed was spent sitting and watching the birds carefully construct their nest.

Papa had told him once that the birds took great care not to damage the roof they chose to hold their nest. "Look," Papa told him, "all the village roofs are made mostly of straw, and straw and twigs are what storks use for nesting. But the birds never touch any of the straw on the roofs. They fly far to gather each little twig and piece of straw from cuttings in the fields and marshes."

Soon the broad, flat nest took shape, and curiosity nagged at Peter until he finally gave in to it. He had to get up on the roof to get a better look. He climbed up on a rain barrel and then pulled himself onto the roof. He crawled up and across the roof with the agility of a spider and crept up to the wide outer edge of the enormous nest. The birds were gone beyond the village boundaries, and he had some time to investigate. The nest was saucer-shaped and had an indentation in the middle so that the eggs wouldn't roll out. The nest seemed big enough to hold even Peter, and he smiled at the thought.

Maybe I can get inside and see what it's like to sit in the middle of it! He held on to the edge of the nest and turned to look out over the fields. How beautiful and big the world was from that height! *The farm and fields look so different from here! Like a big map! I could draw one with the shape of the fields and the paths and the …*

"AAAEEEEE!" Peter heard Daria shriek and almost lost his balance. He looked down at her and realized how high off the ground he was. His stomach felt queasy. *How did I get so high?* he wondered. He had never even liked it when Papa carried him on his shoulders when he was smaller.

"Petrush!" she screeched. "Have you lost your mind? Get down or I'll tell Mama!"

From that time on, Peter promised to do all of his observations from the ground. He had watched the storks before the war when he was much younger and had been fascinated by them. Now they were back, and he was old enough to understand more of their habits. He didn't know why they fascinated him so deeply, but he knew he loved them and was drawn to them instinctively.

"Petru," Papa loved to tell him, "remember the time you came out with Mama to bring us lunch when we were cutting hay? You were no more than three. You followed a little way behind me to stay safe from the path of the scythe." Peter remembered the pleasant swishing sound of the scythe and the way it cut so neatly. "You walked after us for a while," Papa went on, "and then I saw you turn very slowly. You must have heard a noise behind you and probably thought it was one of the boys. When you turned, you saw it was a stork! It stood so high!" Papa held out his hand to show the height of about one meter. "I thought your eyes would pop out of your head!" he said, chuckling.

Peter blushed. He needed no reminding. He remembered that meeting when he and the bird were about the same height. He looked straight into its shiny round black eye. The bird was unconcerned with the child and after looking at him briefly, stepped around him and continued to walk behind the workers. Peter was frozen to the spot where he stood and watched the bird walk on with its deliberate, lanky, almost man-like gait.

Papa continued with the story and a brief nature lesson for Peter. "They often follow us like that when we're in the fields. They look for food—mainly snakes or toads that we scare up when we walk along and cut the hay."

Peter listened to his father talk about storks and their habits and never ceased to be mystified by that species of bird. The deliberate walk and the handsome colors of the feathers, beak, and legs made the bird unusual, but it was the steady stare from the deep, intelligent eyes that gave Peter chills as he felt a form of quiet communication with a nonhuman creature. At the age of three the impression was made, and it was never lost.

Peter, now seven, watched as the storks guarded their eggs. He nodded to whichever bird was on the nest anytime he was on his way to or from the barn, and the bird always stared back quietly. They never hissed or made any of the usual warning noises when Peter was near, and it pleased him that he was trusted.

One by one the eggs hatched. There had been a total of five eggs. Peter was sure of the number because he made one more illegal trip up onto the roof one morning when no one was home. In time four little scrawny necks held up fuzzy heads above the edge of the nest. The parents flew back and forth tirelessly all day between the nest and the distant fields and marshes to secure food for their young. Peter waited for the fifth head to appear. Finally, one morning he found a broken egg on the ground with only a partially formed chick inside. He showed it to Daria, and she told him that the parents threw the egg out of the nest when it failed to hatch.

"In nature, if something is imperfect, it's destroyed because it wouldn't be able to live normally. Remember the stork chick you found on the ground once before the war? It didn't fall from the nest, it was cast off. Something must have been wrong with it."

Peter held the egg in his hand and thought of how cruel nature was sometimes. How cruel life could be. He had seen so much cruelty among people in war. *Life, new life,* he thought, *can be so beautiful, but then there are broken eggs too.* He looked up at the stork on the roof. The bird looked back at him calmly.

Spring had come. With it had come rebirth. Rebirth was really the continuation of life that had existed before, life that had been cast into oblivion for a time, but life that perhaps could go on.

Chapter 16

Prowlers in the Sunflowers

For as long as Peter could remember, Mama Cow had been part of the family. She had come to them when Peter was only three years old, had suffered the Muscovite occupation with them, had wandered with them, and then had helped them rebuild their lives once more. She was one of the barn animals, but that did not lessen her role as a real family member. She was a remarkable, intelligent creature who understood the rules of the pasture, was incredibly sure-footed, and had a deep love for all her calves and for the boy with the grey eyes who always came to talk to her in the barn. She seemed especially pleased that he alone had the task of taking her to pasture. Through all that life brought her, she sustained both her calves and her human family with good sweet milk.

A family tradition became established during the war years when food was scarce. When Maria went to milk the cow in the evening, all the children would follow, carrying their tin drinking cups. She would begin to fill the pail with the warm, creamy milk, and then the ritual would begin. Each child stepped up with his or her cup to have it filled. After the children, the farmyard cats lined up in a row, mewing hopefully. Maria often filled a large plate with milk for them, or sometimes if she felt playful, she would squirt the milk across the stall at the cats' open mouths. Pundyk never missed the chance to come for his portion and quickly lapped it up, leaving a foamy moustache around his mouth when he finished. When food was scarce, sometimes that portion of milk in the evening was the only supper any of them had. The milk was good, and even if there was no bread or soup to eat afterward, the warm liquid in their stomachs made it easier to go to sleep.

When they first bought Mama Cow, her name was "Patches" because of her red and white spots. When she was expecting her first calf, they nicknamed her "Little Mama." Later when she became a real "mama" to everyone by giving milk from her body to sustain them all, the name "Mama Cow" was the only name the family used.

Peter took her to the common pasture as often as he could. The common pasture was a large field owned by a local wealthy landowner. Peasants who used it for their livestock paid for the use of the pasture by working a certain number of hours for the landowner in one of his fields or cutting trees in one of his forests. Even if a peasant was fortunate enough to own land, as Peter's parents were, he usually had so little that it was too precious to use as pasture. Instead, the small farms were planted intensively with grain or vegetable crops. The wealthy landowner and the villagers employed wardens to patrol the pastures and fields to make certain that the peasants used only designated areas. Anyone caught trespassing on private fields or woodlands was punished by local authorities. When Peter began his task as cowherd, he was careful to follow all the rules.

Mama Cow made Peter's work easy. She was always obedient and gentle and stayed in the boundaries without the need of a rope or stick to keep her nearby. She ate only the pasture grass and never nibbled at the edges of neighboring crops. When other cows wandered off into forbidden woodlots and had to be retrieved, Mama Cow would be found standing alone and calmly eating grass, right where she was supposed to be. Peter only had to walk over to her, pat her bony back, and praise her obedient nature. She knew the rules and followed them strictly when she was on the commons, but as with so many creatures of superior intellect, both human and nonhuman, mischief was a way to dispel boredom. Peter and his cow appeared to be angels most of the time and supposedly never got into trouble, but given the opportunity, they were really happy partners in crime.

Prowlers in the Sunflowers

The common pasture was set aside for use by all the village livestock, and heavy use made the quality of the grass less than good. Peter felt that the better the grass was, the better the milk would be. Mama Cow seemed to enjoy testing his theory because she indulged in a feast of lush green grass whenever she could find it. Because land was so precious, few farmers used fences to delineate their fields. Instead, narrow grassy paths between the fields served both as borders for the crops and as easy walkways for the workers who went out to tend the crops. The paths separated fields belonging to different farmers or fields bearing different crops owned by one farmer. Whichever the case, the paths were private property. If someone was headed out for a distant tract of land, no one minded if the person used the paths as long as crops were not disturbed in any way. But any other use of the paths was considered trespassing. Peter and Mama Cow were habitual trespassers.

Peter reasoned that the green grassy paths were long skinny pastures, and Mama Cow was happy to take every opportunity to keep the paths nicely mowed. No village wardens agreed with Peter and Mama Cow's point of view. They feared that foraging animals could damage the edges of the fields, and to be caught with a cow or goat on such a path was a serious offense. That made life exciting for the boy and his cow. It was a test of who could outsmart whom. If Peter were caught, it would mean trouble for him, his family, and even the entire village, depending on where the offense was committed. A broken rule could bring loss of pasture rights or a stiff fine. Peter and Mama Cow had some very close calls, but those only helped make life an adventure. For two crafty cohorts in crime, life without adventure would have been unbelievably boring.

Peter and his cow began their life of mischief slowly and in relative safety, but in time they developed strategies. They began their use of the paths on Mr. Kazhanko's land. Ivan introduced them to that particular network of walkways, and the boys made a rather risky habit of pasturing their cows on those secluded paths whenever they could. More than once they were spotted and chased, but they were never caught. Kazhanko would bolt out of his house swinging a long wooden club whenever he heard an unusual noise in his fields, but the boys were confident they could outrun the old man. Kazhanko would never hurt Mama Cow or Ivan's Rusty. It was the boys he was after in his anger. For all that, Mama Cow wasn't a bad runner when she got going. He probably couldn't have caught her either.

One morning, Peter, Ivan, and some other boys had just finished a game of "Piggy, Piggy" on the side of the common pasture when Ivan had to head for home. Peter left with Ivan, but led his cow home by a different route and ended up on the forbidden paths of Kazhanko's fields. He chose to spend the rest of the afternoon tending his cow there.

Mr. Kazhanko was a grouchy old man who owned a large tract of land, and he liked no one. The soil there was especially fertile, and his crops were plentiful. Sometimes Peter heard grown-ups talking about Mr. Kazhanko and his land. "I wonder why his crops don't whither under his mean, glaring eyes," he heard them say. Peter had his own theory. He thought the plants tried harder out of pure fear of the old man. Maybe he threatened the fields with fire if they didn't produce. Whatever the incentive, even his narrow grassy paths bore a soft green grass that was more luxuriant than any other in the village.

It was late summer, and the sunflowers stood tall in the fields. In the warm, still afternoon, Peter picked out a grassy path that was well shielded from the distant house by a field of huge sunflowers. Mama Cow couldn't be seen at all. She enjoyed herself on these little adventures and happily ripped up mouthfuls of grass before swallowing them. Peter watched her for a while, but as he sat there near the sunflowers, his eyes grew heavy.

"I'll lie down for a while and put my hands behind my head. Then I can keep watch and rest at the same time," he told himself. It seemed like a good plan, but he soon fell asleep. Mama Cow finished mowing the path on one side of Peter. She looked at him asleep in the path, carefully stepped over him, and continued the grassy feast on the other side of her little cowherd.

Prowlers in the Sunflowers

Peter was awoken by a horrible burning pain. It felt as if his skin was being ripped off his face! He opened his eyes and saw something huge and red only a few centimeters away. Again he felt the heat and horrible ripping sensation on the side of his face. He yelled out before he realized that he was nose to nose with Mama Cow. She drew back for an instant when he shouted. Her enormous pink tongue came in his direction again and the roughness of it as she licked him practically stood him up. His nap had lasted too long. The sun was starting to sink in the west, and she felt the need to return to the barn for milking. She mooed softly.

"You're right," Peter whispered. "We have to go."

Peter peered through the sunflowers toward Kazhanko's house, and his eyes popped open wide. His shout had been heard! Old Kazhanko was standing on the edge of the field squinting in their direction. Peter felt a cold sweat on his back as he quietly took Mama Cow's rope to lead her back toward the road home. If he could have convinced her to crawl out of there, he would have. They went slowly so that none of the sunflowers would be touched. Any sway in the plants on an afternoon with no breeze would give them away. They got back to the border of the field in time, but Peter's knees felt like jelly.

"We could go home the quickest way," he whispered, "but I have a favor to ask. Could we hurry around the border of Kazhanko's fields and go home by the main road past his house? He'd never suspect that we'd do that if we were the ones he heard."

The cow looked at him and blinked. Her big eyes always looked at him in the same gentle way. She was never angry or impatient with him, but sometimes she embarrassed him because she would nudge him the way she did one of her calves. It was obvious she was eager to go home, but she didn't object when he turned in the opposite direction. They hurried around the huge field, and finally they reached the road.

Peter stopped a moment, took a deep breath, and began a slower, steadier walk home. As they passed Kazhanko's house, they saw him returning from the field.

Chapter 16

"Glory to Jesus Christ," Peter said respectfully and removed his cap.

"Glory forever," the old man grumbled and continued to mumble something as he threw down his wooden club and stomped into his house.

Mama Cow was thirstier than usual when she got back to the barn, and she ate a portion of hay in spite of her banquet of grass. Peter's mother noticed this when she came out to do the milking. She also noticed that one side of Peter's face was very red.

"Is anything wrong, Petrush?"

"No, Mama."

"Petrush, do you know why Mama Cow is so warm and sweaty?"

"We walked home kind of fast. We forgot to watch the sun and were afraid we'd be late for supper."

The cow and the boy looked at each other and volunteered nothing more. Mama, in her wisdom, chose not to ask.

Chapter 17

Ride like the Wind

Peter enjoyed the time he spent tending cows. He knew them to be intelligent beasts that could be both spirited and extremely gentle. For great fun, though, Peter dreamed of the day when he would be able to ride a horse well.

During the war, there were no good horses in the village. The only ones around were like Mr. Janko's old Dusty. She did her best during the wanderings, but in spite of her good, easy-going nature, she was so old that when winter came without the shelter of a real barn, she gave in to the problems of old age and never saw the spring. Peter dearly loved horses, and although Dusty had belonged to someone else, he felt very sad when she died. She had suffered through the rains and misery with the rest of the wanderers, and Peter had grown fond of the saggy old mare.

The horse that stood in front of him now was barely more than a yearling. It was their red-brown filly, the one who had drawn the attention of the Prussians. Her dainty head and frisky nature seemed to demand an extraordinary name, but the family just called her "Brownie." Papa had begun to teach Peter how to groom the young horse. Papa had respect for all the creatures he raised and housed in the barn, but he admitted that horses were always special to him. When he heard the story of how Brownie had come to them, he was pleased not only by the good fortune, but also by the fact that she was a very good horse. She would be good for some work in the fields and yet would never be a dull, bored creature who simply pulled a plow or wagon. She had too much personality and spirit of her own.

Peter was determined to learn to ride that summer. A lot of boys learned at a younger age than he, but because of the war, Peter hadn't had the chance. He tried to ride and wasn't discouraged by the number of times he fell off. The family never owned a saddle. The boys learned to ride bareback with only a bridle and reins, or sometimes they just held onto the mane or the neck.

One evening Peter was fetching water when he overheard his parents talking.

"You should've seen Petrush today. He won't give up till he learns how to ride."

"Yes, Myhailo, but Brownie is so frisky. She might throw him. He could get hurt."

"No. I wouldn't worry. He has a natural sense. I don't know how many times I saw him fall today! He rolls like an apple on the ground and then gets up to jump on again!"

Peter felt as though he had grown a whole head taller when he heard Papa talk about him like that. *It would be wonderful,* he thought, *to chase the wind on horseback like one of the heroes in the stories in school.* He longed for the day when he could sit on the filly's sleek back at full gallop and hear the wind whistle past his ears. He envisioned himself in armor and heard the cheering crowds. *I would be "Peter the Mighty"!*

One hot, humid day, Peter was at home tending the animals. Brownie tugged at her rope and seemed unhappy in the barn. Peter untied her and decided to walk her down to the river for a drink. As they walked along, he looked up at her and patted her neck. *I'm getting better at riding,* he thought. *I wonder if I could take her for a little ride.*

He led the horse to the side of the road and mounted onto her gleaming back. Brownie was used to him and was gentle. She began to walk at a slow, steady pace, and Peter felt very confident. He sat tall and proud and daydreamed about armor and crowds. As they neared the river, they passed by some bushes. Flies and gnats flew out from the foliage and settled on Brownie's hindquarters. It was humid, and the flies were stubborn and vicious. She flicked her tail, but instead of being swished away, the flies bit her with such fury that Brownie kicked her hind legs! Peter was thrown forward and slid up onto her neck. He pressed his knees against her neck and grabbed her ears with his hands. The bites were painful, and she broke into a wild run!

"Brownie—*stop*! Please stop! Stop, girl! Oh, please!" he wailed in her ear.

The horse took no notice and raced past people who were walking along the road. Peter clung to her for dear life and begged her to stop. Some of the villagers turned to watch, but instead of helping, they began to point and laugh. Peter was scared and humiliated. He didn't know how long he could hang on. One man laughed and shouted, "Look here! The boy rides as if he's trying to bring home holy water!" Peter knew what he meant, but it was no time for jokes. The horse raced on as Peter yelled to her to stop, and his tears blurred his vision. Brownie neared the main road to Lubachiv. Once she came to the big road, Peter didn't know what she would do.

Three men were walking to Opaka from Lubachiv. They heard Peter's cries and began to run to help stop the horse. They yelled and waved their arms. The biggest of the men grabbed the lead rope and ran along side them to slow the tiring horse as she sped by. When Brownie finally stopped, Peter slid off her neck.

"Thank you for your help," he gulped. He was grateful but very sore. His bottom felt painfully raw, and it hurt to walk.

The men smiled and patted him on the head. They saw his discomfort and didn't tease him or laugh.

The man who held the horse looked down at Peter. "This is a fine animal, and you're very brave to ride her. You should be more careful though. What happened?"

"I'm not sure. Something frightened her, and she ran. Thank you again for your help," Peter said sheepishly. He knew his face was red from crying. He was glad no one knew that he'd been playing at being an epic hero. That would have made it worse. He wished he could vanish from that spot or at least run somewhere and hide, but he was in so much pain, he could hardly walk.

Peter took the rope and limped to the river to let Brownie have her drink. Each step hurt more than the one before. His knees felt wobbly and weak. After she had her drink, Peter slowly led her home. It would be a whole month before Peter the Mighty would ride her again. Raw skin and hurt pride take quite some time to heal.

Chapter 18

Ivan's News

Peter and his family had just come in from the fields, and his mother was preparing a quick supper for her hungry family. Peter stepped out of the komora with a small bowl of flour and the onions Mama had asked him to get and saw Ivan running into the yard.

"Petru! There you are!"

"Hi, Ivan! What's wrong?"

"Oh! I wanted to come last night, but Mama said it was too late, and today you weren't at school!" He was out of breath. "Where's Daria?"

"Come inside," Peter laughed. "You aren't making much sense. Come on."

Peter and his friend went into the house, and Ivan removed his cap. "Glory to Jesus Christ," he said, remembering his manners.

"Glory forever," Maria answered, smiling. "Ivanchu, your face is all red. Did you run all the way here? Is something wrong?"

"Oh, Mrs. Fedyk, you should have seen! Matchmakers were at our house last night!"

Maria chuckled, and Daria's eyes brightened. The news had traveled through the village the night before, but they let Ivan do the talking.

"That Stephan from Felzendorf sent them—at least his parents did. They came to arrange a marriage between Natalia and him. I wasn't allowed to stay and listen. I had to go out with Bohdan to do chores. But when the matchmakers left, they had linen towels tied to their sleeves, and the wedding is arranged!"

"That's wonderful, Ivan. Your Mama says Stephan comes from a good family. There aren't many young men around since the war." Mama noticed Daria's smile fade briefly but went on. "Tell Natalia we'll all help with the preparations. A wedding is just what this village needs! Something wonderful to celebrate! Laughter, singing, and good food!" She gave Ivan a quick hug.

"A party will be fun," Ivan said happily. "I just want Natalia to hurry up and marry him. Ever since they met at market in Lubachiv, she acts so silly. She primps and fusses just to get ready to go sell eggs! Then when they see each other, Natalia tells me to go find Mama when she is just at the next booth. Then Stephan gives me money to go buy some candy. He does it so I'll go away. Does everyone get so silly when they get older?"

Daria smiled and shook her head at Ivan. "I'm sure you'll think all the eating and dancing isn't silly at all when the day of the wedding comes. Think of all the sausages and cakes there'll be. It will be quite different from last winter, won't it?"

Both boys remembered the winter without good shelter and enough food, and then visions of sausages and breads and cakes filled their heads.

"I guess so," Ivan admitted sheepishly. "Things at our house are changing already. Papa said Mama's like an old hen since the matchmakers left. He says she smiles and clucks and keeps measuring a piece of linen in her trunk. This morning she looked at our geese and murmured something about pillows for the newlyweds. Papa told one of our pigs this morning that there will be extra potatoes in its slop starting tomorrow. Natalia comes home from the fields singing. She keeps hugging me and tickling me for no reason. That's one reason why I came here for a while."

Maria laughed and patted Ivan on the head. "Don't complain, Ivanchu! She's in love! Enjoy the smiles." Ivan rolled his eyes. Maria continued, "Want to have supper with us tonight?"

"No, thank you. Mama told me to come home for supper. She wants to measure me for a new shirt tonight." He made a face.

Daria laughed. "Do you know when the wedding will be?"

"Mama says after harvest. Papa says in November. Natalia and Stephan will go to see Father Ivan in Lubachiv. They'll set the date for the wedding then. It has to be a Saturday when he can come to Opaka."

"Let us know when there is more news."

"Oh yes, I will," Ivan said, feeling very important.

"Come on, Ivan, I'll walk you to the front gate," Peter offered.

After polite good-byes were said, the boys took time to discuss their own "news" on the way out to the gate.

"What days will you be out in the pasture?" Peter asked.

"I'm not sure. I think I'll take Rusty out on Wednesday morning and maybe Friday. I'm going in to school on Thursday. Madame Teacher told me if I don't learn my letters pretty soon, I'll never be able to read in time for the first visit by the school inspector."

"Yeah, he's a mean old fox. He sort of looks like a turtle—but he's quick. He doesn't miss anything. If you forget to say even one 'please,' he makes you kneel in the corner on dry rice for half an hour. And if he's feeling mean, he makes you do it while you hold heavy dictionaries over your head."

"Ow! Really? How many times has he questioned you?"

"None."

"Then how do you know?"

"Oleksa told me. He really does look like a turtle, though. I can say that for sure because I saw him once in Lubachiv on market day."

"Market." Ivan closed his eyes. "The only one I'm ever told to look for is," Ivan made his voice high and fluttered his eyelashes, mimicking Natalia, "Stephan."

Peter burst out laughing.

"He's got nice horses, though. He let me sit in his wagon once and hold the reins."

"Well, then, he can't be so bad."

Ivan grinned. "See you Wednesday. Bye, Petru."

Chapter 18

Ivan's news was followed by a happy time in the village. That year harvest work seemed lighter even though the crops were abundant. Cellars and komoras were being filled with good things to face the coming winter and to contribute to the wedding feast.

Natalia's grandmother gave her several meters of soft, white linen that she had somehow saved through the hard times. Natalia would have the cloth to make Stephan's wedding shirt and luxuries such as a fine tablecloth and towels.

Peter's mother had unearthed her wooden trunk of family treasures months earlier and now decided to give Natalia two embroidered icon towels for the wedding gift. Peter thought back to the look on Mama's face when she opened it and saw that water had leaked in and stained the contents.

"A good washing and time in the sun will make our things fresh and white as snow again," she'd said, only half-believing it.

Then she had unwrapped her treasured fine wool shawl with the beautiful pink and red roses. The white background was stained with pale brown and grey patches. Mama's eyes glistened with tears. There were some tiny holes here and there in the precious shawl. Little worms had invaded the chest and had begun to eat some of the fabric. She sighed and hugged the shawl to her.

"Look, Myhailo," she said sadly. "Your lovely gift has been damaged."

Papa looked at the shawl and then hugged Mama. "Maria," he said softly to comfort her, "we've all been a little damaged by the war. Does it really matter? Your beauty shines through to me in spite of everything the years have brought. The shawl is the same. Its beauty is still there. Here, do this," he said, lifting it up. "Look at it all at once. Hold it out at arm's length. See the beauty of the whole thing. Some things, just like some memories, shouldn't be examined too closely."

She smiled at him and shook her head slowly. "You're right. I remember praying that I'd give up everything I owned if only all of us could be together again. My prayers were answered." Mama never mentioned her sadness over the damaged things again.

Peter finished his daydreaming and watched his mother test the iron before she pressed the embroidered towels.

"Do you think Natalia will like the towels, Petrush?"

"Oh yes, Mama! She's always admired them when you put them over our icons during holidays. She'll be very pleased!" His mother smiled.

"Mama?"

"Hm?"

"Mama, next time you open the chest, can I see your shawl?"

"My shawl?"

"Yes, Mama. I like all the colors, and I like to see it wrapped around your shoulders. You look so pretty with it on."

Her brown eyes sparkled. When she finished ironing, she opened the chest and tenderly lifted up the shawl to let Peter look at it.

"Put it on, please, Mama." When she did, he looked up at her. "You look beautiful."

Mama became very still and looked at Peter. "You are so like your papa, Petru. So like him. Someday when you marry, this will be my gift to the wife you choose."

"But Mama, there's Daria or Kashia. They're girls. They'd love it too."

"No Petrush. It will belong to your wife. I'm your father's wife, and he's made me happy because he is a good man. You're like your Papa. Someday your wife will have it."

"Thank you, Mama," Peter said and felt a little embarrassed and very honored all at the same time.

Daria came into the house. "Oh, Mama," she said, "the towels are beautiful! When will you give them to her?"

"Stephan and Natalia should be coming here today or tomorrow," Maria answered while she folded the towels. "Aunt Pashia is coming this afternoon to help make poppy seed cakes for the wedding. Would you like to grind the seeds for me?"

Peter's ears perked up at the mention of good things to eat. All week long, most of the gossip in Opaka had had to do with food. The intoxicating smell of smoking sausages and meats was in the air. Natalia's mother was down at the river that morning with some of her neighbors. They had taken veal and pork that had been boiled for hours and hours, seasoned it, and put it into pots with the natural broth from boiling and were setting the pots into the cold river. The cold water would chill the broth and meat and turn it into delicious jellied meat called "studenetz." The thought of all that studenetz served with a touch of vinegar and thick slices of fresh rye bread—it was almost more than Peter could stand! Weddings were wonderful.

Ladies in the village were baking breads, honey cakes, little nut and prune-filled cakes called "perishkeh," and all sorts of other marvelous creations. Children sat in awe while they watched their mothers use real store-bought white sugar in their recipes.

Mrs. Gont was preparing a compote of apples, pears, and prunes. Every now and then, she added some brandy and let the compote age some more. Brandy and strong drinks weren't just for compotes. As soon as hints of a coming celebration were spread through the village, special brews and concoctions were begun and tended. Now that the wedding was only days away, there was a considerable amount of tasting going on.

Ivan spent most of his time running errands for his mother and had little time to visit with Peter. Two days before the wedding, he walked very slowly through the front gate of Peter's farmyard and saw Peter sitting on a bench near the door. He came over to Peter and sat down slowly and stiffly.

Peter watched him and smiled. "Well, Grampa, have a hard day?"

Ivan sighed. "Don't make fun of me. My legs are sore! I think I ran all over the village and countryside at least five times in the past two days. If Mama says 'Ivan, run over to …' one more time, I'll run and hide in your loft till Natalia is a grandmother! I can't wait for the wedding to be over. If it wasn't for the promise of all those sausages and cakes, I'd tell Stephan to kidnap Natalia and get Father Ivan to marry them in secret." He paused just a moment. "And the giggling! Your sister is one of them too!"

"Daria?" Peter pretended to be shocked.

"Yes, Daria! We've had so much giggling and cackling at our house lately, it sounds like a chicken coop. And *then*, I always miss the good stuff that happens!"

"Like what?"

"You remember when Daria was coming over with all the girls—even your mother came a few times—to help strip goose feathers to make pillows and quilts for Natalia's dowry?" Peter nodded. "One evening, the one when I went to my grandpa's to help with chores, some of the girls and women were stripping feathers. Mama always insists that everyone sit quietly and work. You can hardly breathe around those feathers, or it starts to look like a blizzard in the house. Well, Stephan and some of his friends came over to visit. That was really silly to begin with because Natalia gets all giggly when she sees him. Anyway, he came over for mischief. At first he and his friends were very polite and serious and talked about harvest work and somebody who died. Then before you knew it, he and his friends started telling jokes. They saved the best one for last, and soon all the women were laughing and sneezing so hard you couldn't see across the room. Bits of feathers were flying everywhere. I came home and couldn't believe what I saw. Everyone was gone by then, Natalia was still giggling, Bohdan and Papa were wiping off the beams, and Mama was angry and sputtering like a wet hen, saying that Stephan was a young devil and should've been made to clean the house himself."

Peter laughed. "I didn't hear about that! Mama and Daria must have stayed home that night. Mama has been tired. Papa told me she will have a baby in the spring."

"Oh, good, Petru. Maybe you'll get another brother. I'm getting a brother-in-law. I think he'll be a good one. My brother Bohdan is all right, but he is so serious. Stephan is serious too, but he knows a good joke. He likes to tease Mama, and even though she gets angry and yells at him, it isn't long before he gets her to laugh too."

"Two more days, and he'll be your real brother-in-law."

"And my sister will be a married woman."

"That's hard to imagine, isn't it?"

"Tonight the girls are at our house again. Your mama and Daria are there too. They're making Natalia's wreath. You should've seen the ribbons and things piled on the table." Ivan sighed and stood up. "I'm going home now. Stephan is coming over. Natalia finished his shirt for the wedding. You should see it! She embroidered the collar and the cuffs and even put designs on the front panel over the chest. He's coming over tonight to 'buy' it. I asked Mama why he has to haggle over a price and try to buy it when Natalia made it for him. Mama says, 'It's tradition!' I want to be there to make sure he pays a lot!"

"What?" Peter chuckled.

"I want him to pay a lot. Stephan always gave me a little money at market so I'd leave them alone. Once they're married, I won't get any more. If I help Papa with the bargaining, maybe I'll get a little yet tonight." Ivan smiled shyly.

Peter burst out laughing, and Ivan's face broke into a wide grin.

"Good night, Petru. I don't think I can come over tomorrow. Can you come over the morning of the wedding and help decorate the wagon?"

"I'd really like that! See you then!"

Peter watched his friend start off down the road. As sore as Ivan may have been, he broke into a run. He'd been running so much lately, he had forgotten how to walk.

That night, after Peter was already in bed, Mama and Daria came home. They told him how Ivan was quite a little businessman and had whispered to his papa to keep the price of Stephan's shirt high. Stephan finally got his shirt, and Natalia tied a beautiful flowered scarf around his arm. Stephan would wear that scarf at the wedding too. Peter listened to all they said and fell asleep thinking about what hard work it was to get married.

Chapter 19

Natalia's Wedding Day

After chores, Peter washed up at the well and then put on his best clothes. Mama had embroidered little bands of designs on the collar and cuffs of his Sunday shirt, and he felt very elegant. His dark wool pants looked like new after Mama had brushed and pressed them. After he tied his shoes, his mother insisted on combing his hair herself.

"If you don't run around too much or hang by your knees from the apple tree, your hair should stay nice until the wedding. Behave yourself, Petru."

"Yes, Mama."

With that advice, Peter left for Ivan's house. The entire village was buzzing. People carried flowers and food and headed in the direction of either the church or Ivan's house. When Peter arrived, he saw Ivan in his new clothes. Ivan's hair was wet and combed, and it looked like he had orders from his mother to stay neat too.

Women and young girls were busy helping in the house. Daria was already among them and was dressed in her best clothes. One woman carried long pieces of myrtle vine. It was to be used to decorate the bride's wreath and the wedding bread. Some of the other bridesmaids were in front of the house and already had ribbon wreaths in their hair.

Peter and Ivan tied ribbons and flowers and greenery to the wagon. Usually a bride walked to church in the village, but Stephan insisted that his bride would ride in a decorated cart behind one of his best horses.

After a while Stephan arrived with his family and some of his friends. Natalia, her parents, and all the bridesmaids came out of the house. Natalia looked beautiful. Her long braided hair was arranged on top of her head like a crown. On top of the thick braids, she wore the ribbon wreath that her bridesmaids had made. Fresh myrtle vine and autumn field flowers had been added that morning. She wore an embroidered blouse and a royal blue woolen skirt. On her feet she wore red boots. Her face was beaming, and Stephan couldn't keep from looking at her. He stood there tall and proud with a little smile on his face. He wore polished black boots, dark pants, his wedding shirt, and the beautiful red-flowered scarf that Natalia had given him. It was tied around his left arm above the elbow. He looked very handsome.

All the bridesmaids gathered around Stephan and began to walk with him to church. One of Stephan's groomsmen helped Natalia into the decorated wagon and sat next to her while he held the reins. The other groomsmen walked alongside the wagon, and they started to ride to the church. The families and friends followed behind.

When the procession reached the church, the bridesmaids led Stephan through the bell tower archway near the road and into the churchyard. The groomsmen led Natalia into the churchyard soon afterward, and Ivan and Peter followed along. Peter saw Daria near Stephan and smiled back at her when she saw him.

Father Ivan came to the door of the church and greeted the bridal couple. Because they were to be married according to the Byzantine or Ukrainian Rite of the Catholic Church, there were no vows as there are in a Roman Catholic ceremony. The couple was asked two questions that seemed simple but had profound meaning. The priest asked them if they were there to be married and if they came of their own free wills. The bride and groom answered "yes" to each question. He blessed the rings and placed them on their fingers. The commitment was made, and as the bridal couple entered the church holding lighted candles, they entered as married people who were bringing their union into the church to be blessed and sanctified through a series of ceremonies.

Intertwined in the liturgy was the ceremony of crowning. In wealthy churches in cities, real crowns were placed on the heads of the couple to signify that their marriage was part of the Kingdom of God. In this little village church, the crowns were circlets made of myrtle vine. The couple received communion, the Eucharist, as the seal of their marriage, and near the end of the ceremony, they joined hands and walked with the priest around the tetrapod. The tetrapod was the table in front of the iconostas. This little procession showed that now Natalia and Stephan were in the stream of life not as single people, but as two souls united by God. When they were baptized as infants, they had been carried around the tetrapod to show that they entered into the stream of life of the Church as new individual little members. Now they continued in it together.

All during the ceremonies, the people chanted the responses to the prayers of the priest. The fragrance of incense and the gold of the sunbeams gave light and mystery to the things taking place in the little church. Peter watched and listened to it all and thought how beautiful the sunlight looked as it was reflected by the gold of the priest's vestments and the chalice and the gilt paint of the icons. He gazed at the billowing smoke from the incense and at how the sunbeams played with the haze and shadows. Through the haze, Peter saw Daria standing with the girls and thought, "I hope Daria has a day like this too."

The hours in church slipped by, and the wedding ceremony was finished. The priest congratulated the bridal couple, and the entire congregation sang a song wishing them many long and happy years together.

Natalia and Stephan rode back to her parents' home in the decorated wagon for the first wedding feast, which would last all afternoon. After the villagers left to take care of evening chores, all the guests and the bridal party planned to go to Felzendorf to continue the celebration with more food and music played on violins and "tsimbaly" (dulcimers) by Stephan's uncle and some of his friends. The eating and drinking and visiting would last all of the next day and each evening after chores for the rest of the week.

Chapter 20

Christmas

Christmas came each year to Opaka. It had come for as long as Christians had lived there. It had come during the long past years of serfdom. It had come in kinder years when straw roofs held in the warmth of wood stoves and the men of the village were present at the festive meals. It had come during the Muscovite occupation. And it had come in silence under icy stars when survivors huddled together in shanties after the war and knew what it was to be warmed by the breath of an ox or horse. Christmas came. Nothing could change its coming. Only the hearts of the people made the difference as to whether it was welcome or not. Peter's family rejoiced in the holiday and all its ritual. Christmas held all its usual wonder as well as the deeper understanding that comes with time.

"Remember, Kashia?" Papa asked. "We told you about the hay and straw we place on and under the table. It reminds us that Jesus was born in a stable and slept on straw."

Kashia looked up at Papa with her shining face and smiled. "Yes, Papa, I remember. Last year we didn't have to set the table over straw and hay because we were already in the little shanty with Mama Cow and Bura and Brownie."

"You have a good memory, little one," he said softly.

Christmas Day was special, as it always had been, but this year it was the second day of Christmas that Peter anticipated. That evening he and the other young boys were going caroling. They had practiced all during Advent and had carefully memorized the words and melodies. Peter had even composed short speeches of greeting and good wishes to deliver at various homes in the village.

After supper, while the boys bundled up for their evening out in the snow, the door opened, and Papa came in with the large, wooden, eight-pointed star that he had made. It was mounted on a long pole like a broom handle. The star had two faces, mounted back to back with the pole attached in between. In the center of each side Papa had glued a picture of the nativity scene. Such a star was traditionally carried by carolers as they made their rounds. Papa had spent a lot of time carving designs around the edges of each point. Mama had made colorful tassels out of thread, and Papa had decorated each point of the star with a short tassel. Peter had watched him work on it during Advent, but Papa had let no one see it finished until now. It was beautiful!

"Here's the Christmas star for my carolers! Sing beautifully, and everyone will think you're angels," Papa said with a happy grin. "Only we will know for sure," he whispered.

Peter and Oleksa proudly took the star and thanked their parents. They went to meet the other boys at the crossroads near the village roadside crucifix. Ivan was already there and was helping little Roman with his sack. Roman was only four years old but had begged so many times to go caroling with the older boys that they had finally agreed to let him come on the condition that he would carry the sack. The sack, almost as big as Roman, was for all the treats and coins the boys hoped to receive for their efforts. They had high hopes for the generosity of their neighbors. Oleksa's friends Ihor, Maxim, and Bohdan came up to meet them.

"Oh, look at the star! It's really nice!" the boys said, admiring it. "Is everyone here?"

"My older brother will join us when we go to my house," Roman said. "He had to help my papa with chores."

"Let's start then," Oleksa decided, and the boys walked up to the first house where he called out in a loud voice. "Will the master of this house allow us to carol?"

A voice answered from the house, "Carol! Carol!"

Chapter 20

The boys chose to sing Peter's favorite, "God eternal is born this day ..."

The family came out of the house and listened to the boys sing. After they finished, the boys shouted, "Christ is born!" The family answered, "Glorify Him!" Peter stepped forward, cleared his throat, and began his speech.

"We greet you on this joyous day and wish your entire family good health! May your rye and wheat and all your crops grow well. May the coming year be better than the one passing." Peter knew the man was one of the village beekeepers, so he added, "And may your beehives be filled with light honey in the coming season!"

When the mother of the family offered them a small loaf of Christmas bread, Roman stepped forward. Oleksa said proudly, "Here, Romko, put this in your bag." In a half whisper he added, "And no nibbling!"

Everyone laughed while Roman carefully put the Knesh into the sack. The boys thanked the family for their generosity and bid them a good evening before going on.

They came to the next house and asked, "Will you allow us to carol here?" A gruff voice shouted from the house, "I don't need carolers like you! I'll carol for myself!" The boys looked at each other. Oleksa lifted his eyebrows and then whispered to Peter, "Not everyone welcomes Christmas in the same way." The family there was Polish and celebrated Christmas according to the Gregorian calendar in December. Peter's rite followed the Julian calendar for church holidays, and Christmas came on January 6.

The next house was Roman's. They sang two carols and let Roman give the greeting. His parents beamed proudly as their littlest son gave the holiday speech. His mother gave the boys coins and pampushky for their efforts. Each boy ate his pampushok then and there and gave the coins to Roman to put in the sack. Roman's brother joined the group, and the boys went to visit so many houses that evening that they lost count. They returned to Roman's house to divide the treats and money among themselves and planned to meet again the next evening and for as many evenings as they would need to finish their rounds of the entire village.

Christmas

On the third day of Christmas, Papa asked Peter to stay home with him to complete still another ritual. The rest of the family went to church while the two of them did morning chores. After all the animals except Brownie were fed, the cows were milked, and the other tasks in the barn were finished, Papa told Peter it was time to get ready to share Christmas with God's creatures. They went into the house with a pail of oats and set it on one of the side benches. They moved chairs out of the way and bundled up all the straw and hay that had covered the table and floor since Holy Supper. Peter then helped Papa to put all the bundles outside the door.

Papa returned inside and looked around. "Now we're ready." Peter followed him out to the barn and stood near Pundyk while Papa led Brownie out of the stall. He spoke to her in soothing tones and patted her neck. Then he led her slowly to the house.

"Go open the door for our guest, Petru."

Peter and Pundyk ran to do what he asked, and Papa led the horse inside. She was a spirited creature, but his steady hand and soft words calmed her. The house scared her because she had never been inside. Each year that there had been a house, the family had carried out this ritual. Each time the gentlest, calmest horse was chosen for it. The first Christmas Brownie was with them, there was no house. That year all of them had truly shared one roof, and there had been no need for this traditional show of hospitality and love. Now, in a more prosperous year, the horse was invited into her master's house to be fed the best oats. It was a symbol of how much the master held all his beasts in high esteem.

Brownie ate her oats. She was nervous but didn't panic. After she finished, Papa carefully led her back to the stable while Peter carried the bundles of hay and straw over to the oak tree. Papa came out and helped him tie the bundles to the trunk of the tree.

"Now the wild birds can share our Christmas too!" Papa said, smiling at Peter.

Peter looked up at his father and felt proud. His father loved animals and respected them. Some men Peter knew in the village believed in using a whip and a curse when it came time to deal with the beasts of the farm. Papa taught animals to obey him through respect and the spoken word. Peter was happy that a strong man like Papa was not ashamed to show affection and concern for fragile little birds that knew hunger in winter.

Christmas was a time of happy mystery when the whole world seemed to come together. Even Father Ivan at church had said something about Jesus's birth changing everything to make all nature different and special. Papa and Peter stood together and watched the birds come to pick at the seeds still attached to the straw and hay.

"Little birds," Peter said softly, "Christ is born!"

Papa looked down at him and smiled. The feathered visitors chattered and whistled while they looked for seeds. "Listen!" Papa said gently and rested his hand on Peter's shoulder. "They're answering you. 'Glorify Him! Glorify Him!'"

Other traditions followed in the cycle of the Christmas holiday. On the eighth day of Christmas, it was considered good luck to have a young boy visit each home. Ivan arrived at Peter's house early in the morning after chores. He greeted everyone and came into the house with handfuls of grain. Ivan walked around the room, scattering the grain, and recited the familiar verse:

Sow and germinate, rye and wheat,
For good luck and good health in this New Year,
So that it may be better than the year just past!

Peter's parents thanked Ivan for the good omen of his visit. Peter took his own supply of grain and left with Ivan to repeat the ritual for Aunt Pashia and Ivan's family.

With the traditions of Christmas fulfilled, everyone waited for the holiday, two weeks later, called "Jordan." Some people called it "Little Christmas" or Theophany. Roman Catholics called it Epiphany. It was the day that recalled the Baptism of Jesus, and it was the day the village river was blessed.

The eve of Jordan is called "Shchedreh Vechir," which means "generous eve." It was a day of Black Fast, but a day of joy as well. It was so special that certain carols were sung only that night. It was also the time Christmas caroling officially ended for the year. In the late afternoon there was a special ceremony at church. Villagers brought pitchers of water to have them blessed. As soon as the ceremony was over, young boys raced home with the pitchers, taking care not to spill any of the water. Then, in Peter's family, Mama took the water and blessed the house, the barn, the farmyard, and everything in them.

Mama also baked special bread that day called "pidpalkeh." It was large and flat, and when it was ready, she gave it to Papa and the boys. They each broke off a piece and ate as they went to the barn. Between Christmas and Shchedreh Vechir, it had been forbidden for anyone in the family to eat outside the house, in the farmyard or the barn. Mama said if they did, mice would ruin their stores of grain. Now, when they reached the stable, some of the bread was given to each of the large animals.

After church at dawn, the people went down to the river in the frigid morning air for the blessing of the water. Father Ivan refused to wear a hat in any weather, so Peter had his own little tradition on Jordan. For as long as he had gone to the river for the blessing ceremony, Peter had watched Father Ivan's bald head turn different colors from the cold. First it turned red, then blue, and finally white near the time the ceremony was finished.

The day before, a cross had been formed from ice blocks cut from the river ice. It stood tall on the ice near the open hole where water could be dipped and was decorated with paper ribbons and evergreen boughs by the older boys and girls of the village.

When the ritual of blessing was finished, Peter smiled secretly because he noticed that Father Ivan's head was white right on schedule. The villagers began to dip pitchers and bottles into the blessed river. Once again young boys ran home with the vessels of water, and the farms were blessed a second time. The tradition of running home so quickly probably was wrapped in some superstition that the strength of the blessing was greater if it was done as soon as possible after the water was blessed. It was so important to rush home that there was even a saying that could be heard whenever anyone was in a big rush to get somewhere at any time of year: "Look, he runs as if he had holy water!"

Chapter 21

The Demonstration

"Petrush, would you like to go to town with me in a few days?"

"Sure, Papa! Do we have to buy supplies?"

"No, we're going to see a political demonstration."

"Demonstration?"

Papa set down the grooming brushes on a bale of straw. He and Peter had cleaned out the barn and were grooming Brownie on a clear, late winter morning. Papa seemed preoccupied with his thoughts, but whatever was on his mind put a quiet smile on his face.

"Yes, Petrush. You know people have been talking about independence ever since the Muscovites left?" Peter nodded. "Do you know what independence means?"

"Freedom."

"Yes, that's one way of saying it. You see, there are many kinds of people in the world. You saw Prussians and Muscovites and Austrians during the war. You know there are some Germans who settled in Felzendorf and Poles in our own village, as well as people who speak as we do. We're Ukrainians. You know that, don't you?"

"Yes, but Poles in our village speak Ukrainian too."

"Yes, most of them do. That's because Opaka is considered a Ukrainian village."

Peter thought he understood but wasn't sure.

"Remember when we were in Lubachiv once and saw a map of Halychyna?"

Peter nodded again.

"Well, Halychyna is the region where we live. For many years before the war, before you were born, and long before Mama and I were married, there was talk of letting Halychyna be divided so that the areas that were mainly Polish and the areas that were mainly Ukrainian could be separate and govern themselves. Well, the time has come for that to happen and for Ukrainians to be an independent people. Before the war a special political group of our people in Halychyna secretly promised the Austrians that if war ever came between Austria and Russia, the Ukrainians would be loyal to Austria. In return, if all went well, Austria said that when the issue of this crown colony was settled, our people would get special favors. It's all very complicated, but that's what happened."

Peter sat down next to his father and was fascinated by what he heard. He had heard portions of that history all his life. Now it all seemed to fall into place.

"Then Emperor Franz Josef died. Do you remember when that happened?"

"It was in the winter after our village burned."

"That's right. In November of 1916. The new emperor, Charles the First, assured the Ukrainian representatives in the Austrian parliament that after the war, the question of the separate Ukrainian "Galician" province would be settled in such a way that it would please our people. Now the Austro-Hungarian Empire is ending, and Halychyna has been declared split. We will now be part of the Western Ukrainian Republic! Someday soon, maybe we and the Ukrainian National Republic—some call it "Greater Ukraine"—will be one nation!" Papa's face glowed. "It won't be long now. We'll govern ourselves and won't be taking orders from Poles or Austrians or Russians! We'll be independent!"

"That sounds wonderful, Papa! Does that mean there won't be wars anymore?"

"No, Petrush. No one can say that." He sighed. "It may mean more fighting, but then we'd have something to fight for. We'd have our own country!"

The day of the demonstration came. Myhal and Oleksa stayed

home to do chores, and the girls stayed home with Mama. The baby was due soon, and Mama didn't go far from home.

Peter and his father went to Lubachiv and saw the banners and parades. They stood and listened to the exciting speeches. Papa and the rest of the crowd cheered at the parts of the speeches they especially liked and then began to sing inspiring words:

Ukraine is risen! The glory! The freedom!
For us of the young brotherhood, there is a happier fate …

Papa looked so happy that Peter grinned and cheered with him, even when he didn't quite understand all the words. It was a magnificent time and a wonderful feeling. All the way home, they talked about what had happened that day in Lubachiv and what it meant.

"Petrush, all your grandparents were gone before you were born. You never knew them. You never had the chance to feel that tie to your past, to your history. They were all Ukrainians who loved their land and traditions, even though they were controlled and ruled by others. Someday I want you to know your history better so that you can really know who you are, the people you're descended from, and who you must always be."

Peter's head was swimming with all the excitement of the day and the powerful words and ideas he had heard. He felt very close to Papa and was honored that Papa wanted to share something so important with him. He wanted to say something wonderful back to his father, but he couldn't find special words. After a moment, he said quietly, "Yes, Papa. I will never forget."

Chapter 22

Easter

Spring always meant new beginnings. There was hope of a new independent government. Fields held new crops. Peter's new little sister, Maryna, was born and already baptized and confirmed according to the Ukrainian Rite tradition. And Mama, now that life could settle into a routine again, was beginning preparations for the celebration of the holiday that was the greatest of new beginnings—Easter.

She spent most winter evenings spinning or weaving cloth, but Mama tried to take as many evenings during Lent as she could spare to work on special Easter eggs called "pysanky." Sometimes Aunt Pashia and her three daughters, Olesha, Evcha, and Hanushia, would come and sit near the big table with Mama, Daria, and Kashia, while they all drew beautiful designs on the smooth shells. Most of the time it was just Mama and her girls, but now and then Peter and Oleksa tried to draw designs too.

Dozens of eggs were decorated during Lent because they were given as gifts to special people at Easter. Some were saved to use as talismans around the farm. The raw eggs were decorated in an ancient way using dyes and beeswax. Mama made the dyes from things like bark, plant roots, seeds and onion skins. The dyes created yellows, reds, oranges, and purple-black that looked beautiful together. Mama traded fresh eggs to the beekeeper for the beeswax she needed.

The instrument used to decorate the eggs was called a "kistka" or stylus, which was a little stick with a tiny funnel wired to one end. Papa usually made the funnel from bent tin. Mama put a little chip of beeswax into the funnel and then held the funnel over a candle flame. The heat melted the wax so that it could flow through the tiny hole in the bottom of the funnel. When Mama touched the funnel tip to the egg and pulled the tip over the surface, a thin line of wax was left behind.

Mama used clean, raw eggs with smooth, even shells. She chose white or very light brown eggs so that the dyes could tint them clear, bright colors. First she drew designs in wax on the white egg. Peter loved to watch how she heated the funnel, scraped bits of wax into the funnel, heated it again and then drew lines and symbols on the egg. Anything covered with the wax would stay white because the dyes could not penetrate the wax. After her designs were drawn, she dipped the egg in yellow dye.

After the yellow dye had taken, she carefully dried the egg and began to draw again. The designs she drew would stay yellow under the protection of the wax she now applied. She drew baby chicks and outlines of leaves and sunbursts. She added little dots and crosses where she wanted more complicated designs. When all parts of the yellow designs were finished, she dipped the egg in orange. After the orange color was vivid enough, she filled in the designs she wanted in that shade. She then dipped the egg in red and repeated the process. Finally when all the designs that she wanted to be red were protected by wax, she gently put the egg in the deep purple-black color.

When she lifted the egg out of the black dye, it looked ugly. The wax, once a pretty honey color, had been blackened by the soot of the candle each time Mama held the funnel in the flame, so the designs had been drawn in black wax. The egg looked all black and lumpy with wax. But after the egg dried, Mama did what almost seemed to be magic! She carefully held the egg close enough to the candle flame to slowly melt a patch of wax, but not close enough to get soot on the egg. When a patch of wax melted, she took a soft cloth and wiped away the wax. Suddenly the colors and designs that had been protected by the wax appeared! The little yellow chicks, the white lines, the orange horses, and the pretty red poppies all came into view! When all the wax was wiped away, Mama set the egg aside in a little wooden bowl.

It took hours to complete one egg. Mama and the girls made dozens in the weeks before Easter. They displayed them on a wooden tray and Peter loved to look at them. He had to be very careful just to look and not touch them. As pretty as they were, he had to remember that they were real raw eggs.

All the symbols had meanings. The ram was a wish for good health. Evergreen boughs and deer stood for a long life and wealth. Flowers symbolized happiness, and a sunburst was for God's blessings. Triangles reminded people of the Holy Trinity, and lines that ran all the way around the egg to meet in a continuous circle stood for eternity and the eternal life that Easter made possible. The egg itself was a symbol for the tomb of Christ. Just as the tomb held the promise of life through resurrection, so too a raw egg held the possibility of new life inside. Pysankas were a tangible sign of people's faith in the intangible mysteries and wonder of Easter.

Some symbols also had amusing and superstitious meanings. Daria chuckled to herself when she showed Peter the egg she had decorated for Natalia. In a double band, like a ribbon that encircled the egg, Daria had drawn a lot of little chickens and roosters.

"You know what the chickens stand for?" she asked. Peter shook his head. "It's a wish for lots of babies. Natalia and Stephan would make nice parents, wouldn't they?"

Peter smiled shyly. "Girls always talk about babies and weddings and things like that. I'm glad I'm a boy." He turned his attention to the egg he was decorating. He chose to draw simple deer using straight lines for their box-like bodies and heads, and Peter was proud of how well they were turning out.

Happy conversation, the friendly glow of the lighted candles, and the sweet honey-smell of the beeswax made evenings spent decorating eggs warm and cozy for Peter and his whole family.

On the day before Easter, Peter and Kashia watched their mother check to see if the big outdoor oven was ready for baking. The special bread, the Easter Paska, was so big it didn't fit in the baking oven in the house, and just before the holiday, Papa had to build an outdoor oven made of bricks.

The children watched as Mama took a clean goose feather and dipped it in beaten egg yolk. She painted the top of the bread with a thin layer of yolk so that when it baked, the crust would brown nicely and be shiny. The feather smoothed the yolk over the decorations that she had put on the top of the bread. Out of the same dough, she had fashioned a braided strip that ran around the top edges of the bread, and inside the circle she had formed a flat cross with curled ends. In each of the four sections divided by the cross, she put a little flower made from dough too.

For a whole year now, Peter had been old enough to take part in the strict fasting laws of the Church. All during Lent the faithful were to abstain from meat and dairy products. They could eat vegetables and grains and use vegetable oil in their cooking. The people who were exempt from the laws were children under the age of seven, old people, the sick, and pregnant or nursing mothers. Children still in their growing years, like Peter, abstained from meat but still had some milk, eggs, and cheese.

Great care had to be taken when Easter finally came. People who had abstained from all meat and dairy products during the weeks of Lent had to begin to eat cheeses, eggs, and meat again slowly. They had to let their bodies gradually get used to small amounts of animal protein over a matter of several days. If they began Easter with big meals of sausage and eggs, they were known to become very sick and even temporarily blind!

Peter thought about these things while he watched his mother brush the bread with the goose feather. Easter was the great and wonderful day when people celebrated the incredible. They celebrated victory over death—and Peter had seen so much death in the war. The fasting and time in church helped to prepare the people to understand the great day of celebration. As Peter grew older, he was proud that he began to understand.

He remembered Palm Sunday when he and his family had gone to church to receive the traditional pussy willows instead of palms.

Easter

After the liturgy was over, people came out of church and tapped each other on the shoulders with the willow branches and recited a verse:

> It is the willow, not I, that strikes you.
> Though it strikes you, it will not harm you.
> Rejoice, for in one week is Easter!

The week that followed had been devoted to Mama's pre-holiday ritual of cleaning house. Papa had whitewashed the inside walls, and everything in sight had been cleaned and polished.

At Easter, a time of rebirth and celebration, everyone had to have something new to wear. Sometimes it was only a new handkerchief or a new pair of shoelaces. This year Peter was lucky enough to have a new shirt. He was growing so quickly that Mama made him a one from linen she had woven from her own spun thread.

Holy Thursday had come with the solemn ceremony at church in the evening. Twelve gospels were read to retell the story of the sufferings of Jesus. Great Friday had followed with the sad, solemn burial service at sundown. Bell ringing stopped on Great Friday, and only wooden clappers were used until Sunday.

Finally Holy Saturday had arrived, and the last baking was being done. Mama was finishing all the foods that would be taken to church to be blessed. Papa had taken sausages to Aunt Pashia's for smoking earlier in the week, and Mama made pressed cheese and churned fresh butter for the food basket.

Papa spent a tearful, choking hour grating the white horseradish roots he had dug up that morning. He gasped and with a thin laugh told his wife, "This job should always be saved for whoever has the worst head cold in the family. These fumes bring their own Easter miracle. They'll clear your head, nose, ears, lungs, everything!"

Mama cooked red beets and grated them before she mixed them with salt, sugar, vinegar, and the horseradish Papa had prepared. The mixture made a pungent condiment for the eggs, cheese, and meats.

Fresh eggs were hard-boiled and dyed a reddish color in a

solution made from onion skins. The solid red eggs, called Krashankas, were the ones the family peeled and ate on Easter.

That evening Mama took two large wicker baskets and prepared them for church. She lined the inside bottom and sides of each with linen towels. Into the round one she put her beautiful shiny Paska that was so large it filled the basket. Into the rectangular one, she put a large link of smoked sausage, some roasted sausage, a plate of pressed cheese, and a little container of salt. She took a knife and carefully carved the shape of a cross into the top of a block of butter. She placed the butter on top of the cheese and decorated the plate with a piece of myrtle vine. The dark red horseradish mixture was put into a small crockery jar with a little cover to keep in the powerful vapors. Finally some peeled hard-boiled eggs were arranged on the cheese and butter plate. Unpeeled Krashankas were put in the basket for colorful decoration.

Another touch of color came from the pysankas Mama tucked into the basket. She put in the ones she intended to give to Father Ivan and friends she would see at church. There was a special one there for old Mr. Janko, one for Mykola Bula, two for Mr. and Mrs. Chorney so that they would have one to display and one to use as a talisman in the barn, and several others for the Soroka family, Aunt Pashia, and dear Mrs. Gont.

Mama covered the baskets with pretty embroidered towels. With that task complete, it was time for everyone to go to bed. Father Ivan was expected to be in the village at around one o'clock in the morning for Easter Liturgy so that he could be back in Lubachiv for sunrise liturgy at his city parish.

When the time came, the villagers carried their baskets of food to church. The contents of each were carefully covered, and the baskets were left outside the church in the cemetery. Everyone entered the church to visit the "tomb" one last time. Each person knelt and kissed the Plashchenetsia, which was a tapestry showing Christ in the tomb. After that was finished, the church services for Easter began.

People left the church for a procession outside around the building. People carried lighted candles and followed the priest and several parishioners who carried banners. The effect of the candles was eerie and mystical. The shadows cast by the flickering lights in the cemetery and against the old wooden walls of the church, seemed to dance and flutter like dark wings of spirits from ages past. Peter looked around him and was both fascinated and a little frightened. The darkness made him think of death, and the candlelight was a small, cherished comfort. After the procession circled the church three times, the chanting ended, and the diak ceased the clacking noise of the wooden clappers.

The doors of the church had been locked when the procession began. Now as the people waited, the priest unlocked them and went inside alone. He reappeared a moment later and joyfully exclaimed, "Christ is risen!" The people shouted the response, "Indeed He is risen!" The church bells rang, and everyone began to sing:

> Christ is risen from the dead, conquering death by death,
> And to those in the graves, He granted life.

The people happily went back into church. The Plashchenetsia was on the altar, and in its place on the tetrapod was an icon of the Risen Christ. Easter Liturgy was joyful and beautiful, and the people sang with smiles and hopeful faces. At the end of the long service, when the church was filled with billowing incense and happy repetitions of the Easter hymn, Father Ivan paused a moment and spoke to the congregation.

"Today all nature, all things, are changed. Today the world is new! Man isn't lost; now his life is eternal. Just as we are nourished by the Eucharist for our spiritual lives, we feed our bodies with the food God grants us. Now let us go out to bless the food you will eat on this holiest of days."

People filed outside to stand near their baskets. Candles were lit again and placed into the baskets. They provided light along the paths where the priest walked while he blessed the food and sprinkled it with holy water. The candles also reminded everyone of the Light that was given to the world by Easter. After the blessing was ended, Mama and others in the crowd went to greet friends and relatives and give out pysankas from their baskets. Candles were blown out, and everyone walked home with their food in the very dim light of a still distant dawn.

After morning chores, the family gathered around the table and said prayers. Papa took some blessed eggs, cut them into wedges, and offered the plate of eggs to each member of the family, while he exclaimed, "Christ is risen!" "Indeed He is risen!" everyone answered, and each took a wedge and ate it first before beginning the rest of the meal. Easter Sunday had finally come, and the time of fasting and abstinence was over.

It had been a long night, and after breakfast, Papa, Mama, Kashia, and, of course, little Maryna took time to rest and nap. The older children were too excited to sleep. They walked back to the churchyard to watch the celebrations that were going on. The brothers watched other boys set off homemade firecrackers, and then Myhal went off to join some friends his own age. Peter and Oleksa joined in organized games with some boys in a nearby field, and Daria went to watch the spring dances. The village girls, dressed in their best clothes, had gone into the fields earlier and picked flowers that they made into wreaths to wear in their hair. The girls stayed in the churchyard and sang while they did pretty spring circle dances. The dancers held willow branches in their hands and gracefully went through many intricate steps to celebrate the new season. It was a happy time, and the weather was beautiful. For the rest of the day, villagers relaxed, visited friends and relatives, exchanged pysankas, and enjoyed the delicious Easter food.

On the way home from the games, Oleksa was already making plans with Peter for Easter Monday. "Tomorrow is Dousing Monday," he said with a wicked grin. "I already know where I want to hide with my bucket of water after liturgy is through."

"I don't think Mama wants you to do that."

"Oh, Petru, it's all in good fun! I want to douse Anna Janczura from school."

"Why do they do that to the girls?"

"Remember Father Ivan says everything is new in the world?

Everything is growing—it's springtime! Myhal told me that because girls adorn themselves with flowers, dousing them with a bucket of water helps keep the flowers from wilting." Oleksa smiled smugly at his own logic.

Peter frowned. "I wonder if Papa ever did that."

"Sure he did, but he won't admit it. He just smiles when you ask him."

"But the girls are all dressed up after church, and they'll get angry if they get wet."

"Which side are you on, the girls' or the boys'?"

"On the boys', of course. It's just that Mama was saying the other day that she didn't think it was nice to be soaking wet in your best clothes."

"Oh, stop it, Petru. You're too good. Myhal is planning to douse that dark-haired Anna from the other side of the village. I think he likes her."

Peter thought about it all. He didn't want to make Mama angry, but he secretly admitted he liked mischief. He wouldn't admit it to Oleksa, though.

"With all the different Annas you and Myhal plan to douse in the village, how can you keep from being confused and dousing the wrong one?"

"What does it matter?" Oleksa chuckled, and his wicked smile returned.

Peter smiled. They were home and couldn't speak of such things in front of Mama.

Chapter 23

The Hoopoe

Spring haying time was fun for Peter and the other boys in the village. After the men cut the hay, the younger boys helped to gather it into bundles for drying. It was great fun to be in the fields, especially during lunch when the boys could rest.

One lazy noon after they had eaten, Peter, Ivan, and a boy named Janush were lying on their backs looking at the shapes of the fluffy clouds in the sky. They rested in the shade of a huge oak tree in one of the fields. Peter looked up at the branches and studied how they spread so broadly into space. Suddenly something caught his eye. He saw a flash of something honey-colored with black and white stripes.

"What was that?" he said, sitting up and pointing to a branch above his head. The tree was leafing out already, but there were a few dead branches with last year's brittle, brown leaves still attached. "There!" he said softly, pointing to a cluster of dead leaves.

There was a rustling sound, and a bird hopped into view on the branch.

"That's a hoopoe!" Ivan whispered.

"Yeah, it is," Peter agreed quietly. "Do you think it's got a nest in this tree someplace? Look for an old knothole. See anything?"

All three boys quietly watched the bird that sat above their heads watching them. After a time, in the still air, they heard soft cheeping noises.

The Hoopoe

"Hear that? There must be a nest around here," Ivan said softly.

The boys saw the bird flutter to another branch and hop over to a hole in the side of the tree. The cheeping became louder while the bird gave its offering to its young. It was an impressive sight. The bird had a honey-colored body with bold black and white stripes on its wings and tail. The head was usually smooth and round, but if the bird became upset, feathers stood up on the crown of the head, making a very elegant crest. The bird fed its young, took a long look at the boys below, and left again to search for food.

Peter felt his insatiable curiosity get the better of him. Mama didn't like him to climb trees. He remembered that he had even had to promise not to climb the barn to get a better look at the storks, but out here, well, no one would tell on him. The old sturdy oak would be easy to climb and would easily hold his weight. "I want to get up there to see the babies," he whispered.

"Are you crazy?" Ivan squeaked. "The old bird'll be back soon, and if you touch its babies, it may abandon them! Besides it's too high up. You'll fall and crack your head."

"You sound like my mother," Peter muttered, eyeing the nesting hole. "My papa told me about hoopoes. I don't think they'll abandon their babies."

The old bird returned with more food and soon left again. Peter climbed up as quickly as he could. The nesting hole wasn't very far up, and he was at the main branch near it in a few moments. He straddled the broad limb and edged closer to the hole where he already could see tiny beaks in the opening.

When he reached the hole, he was so fascinated with the little birds he didn't notice the stench coming from the nest. He reached in and lifted out one of the birds. It had the long curved bill of the species, but the tiny thing was still covered with down and had prickly pin feathers on the wings. The bird jabbed Peter's finger and tried to bite it. Peter could feel its tiny heart pounding under his fingers, and the little thing squirmed and wriggled in a brave attempt to get free. He put the bird back gently and reached for another. He noticed the second one was probably a little older because the pin feathers were more developed.

Chapter 23

"Hey, Petru," Ivan said in a raspy whisper. "The old one is coming back!"

Peter put the chick back and began to pick his way down as fast as he could until he finally jumped to the ground. The adult bird sat high in the tree and chattered an alarm. Its crest was standing high and full. The bird was definitely upset.

"Uh oh! It's angry!" Janush said softly. "Oh, you shouldn't have bothered them!"

"Just watch," Peter said, smiling.

The old bird chattered a few more times and glared at the boys.

"Think it'll come after us?" Ivan asked, nervously eyeing the falcon-sized bird.

"No. Shh," Peter said, although he wasn't sure if it would or not.

The bird sat and chattered once and then hopped down to the hole to feed its young.

"See, it didn't abandon them. It didn't sense my smell on them at all."

"Since you said something about smell …" Ivan began.

"Something really stinks!" Janush said loudly. "Phew!"

"The wind didn't change. What is that?" Ivan said, holding his nose.

"It's you!" Janush said and pointed at Peter. "You stink like manure!"

Peter had noticed the smell but was so interested in birds, he hadn't thought about it. He lifted his hands to his nose and sniffed. He smelled like a dirty barn. He rubbed his hands on his pants, but it didn't help. It just made his clothes stink.

"The old bird didn't abandon its babies because it couldn't smell anything over that stench!"

Janush grinned. "The old bird didn't abandon its young, but if you go home like that, your mama might abandon you!" Janush laughed and sat on the grass holding his stomach and his nose at the same time. "How come you're never happy just reading about some things, Petru? You always have to get right in there and …"

Ivan was laughing so hard there were tears on his cheeks. "You know," he choked, "My papa told Bohdan once when he was really dirty that he smelled like a hoopoe. Now I know what he meant!"

Peter felt his face flush. He was embarrassed but proud of himself at the same time. "I guess I better go home to wash," he said sheepishly. He was sure Mama wouldn't abandon him, but she wouldn't be very happy with him either. Papa would probably laugh.

As he walked across the field toward home, he saw the old hoopoe lazily fly by and heard the soft, low, far-carrying call, "Poo-poo-poo."

Chapter 24

Night Pasture

The hot, humid air made even taking a breath hard work, and yet each chore was accomplished too quickly. Time seemed to crawl by, but finally suppertime came. Peter downed a large cup of milk, and in a very serious, grown-up manner, he announced that he was going to leave soon. He took his rolled blanket and kissed Mama good-bye. She gave him two thick slices of bread that she had buttered generously and then carefully wrapped in a clean cloth. He put it in his jacket. The time had come.

He went into the barn, patted Pundyk on the head, and jumped on Brownie's bare back. "I'll play with you when I get back tomorrow," he promised the dog.

He waved good-bye to his mother, wrapped his arms around the horse's neck, and road out of the village for night pasture. Night pasture! Peter's first time! Mama told him he was becoming a very responsible young man, so he could begin to go to night pasture. Papa had given his permission. After all, Peter was eight years old. He was filled with anticipation. He would sleep on the ground and share in the camaraderie of the bigger boys.

When the weather was good, the villagers pastured their horses at night out on the commons. The horses were used for work during the day and yet needed some time out on the open pasture in addition to their feed. It was a common practice for the farmers to send their horses out with teenage sons or neighbor boys, who would watch the animals. There were always some younger boys, Peter's age, who went along to learn how to tend the animals so that they could be the leaders of the group when they were older.

The camp had a military feel to it. The leader of this outing was young Voytko Krupka, the son of one of the local wardens. He shouted out orders as boys arrived at the commons. First, each boy was to tether his horse to keep it from wandering into forbidden fields and forests. Then the boys were free to play games, eat a snack, or just talk. Peter carefully tied Brownie to a stake and affectionately patted her nose and neck. He watched as she eagerly began to graze before he ran off to join the other boys.

When it began to get dark, the boys were commanded to go into the nearby forest to gather dry wood for the campfire. After starting the fire, the boys began to pick out places to sleep. Peter unrolled his blanket and decided to bed down near the edge of the forest. He liked the sound of the wind in the pines and could sit there to watch what all the other boys did. Off in the distance, Brownie was grazing contentedly, and Peter congratulated himself on his choice of location.

I picked a good spot, he thought. *I can enjoy the pretty dancing flames from a distance, but I don't have to worry that the light or hot fire will keep me awake. I don't think it'll cool off much tonight.* He sat by himself and felt a little lonely. *I wish Ivan could've come. He went to visit his grandpa. Wish I had a grandpa who could sit down with me and tell me about the world.* His bread-and-butter snack tasted especially delicious. The freshness of the wind sighing in the trees and the good snack made him sleepy.

Suddenly Krupka shouted, "Everyone get up!" Peter and the other boys stood. Peter noticed that two little boys his age were already asleep and didn't hear the order. "Kneel!" Krupka shouted. "Pray that we and the horses will be safe from night devils!"

Night devils? Peter thought. He felt a prickly sensation along his spine, but shrugged it off. *Nothing will harm us,* he told himself. *I'd say my prayers even without Voytko's commands. Mama taught all of us to do that when we were babies!*

When the "Our Father" was finished, Peter crossed himself three times and then heard, "All sleep now!" That order was followed happily by everyone. Peter fell asleep, and the last thing he remembered was seeing two of the older boys head off to the far end of the field for one more check on the horses.

In spite of the prayers to keep them away, "devils" did come out that night. It was common knowledge that those mischievous spirits roamed after midnight and led a smoke-grey horse. What Peter did not know was that the devils who would visit the camp that night were not the little black creatures of the legends, but rather some older boys who enjoyed playing pranks on the unsuspecting younger boys. These "imitation devils" were just as mischievous as the legendary ones, and for the right effect, they too led a smoke-grey horse. For victims, they usually chose the little boys who fell asleep before prayers. These same devils *always* chose newcomers to night pasture whether those boys said their prayers or not. So it was that Peter was chosen that night for their favorite prank.

As he slept peacefully and soundly, he was gently lifted onto the grey horse. The horse was led far enough into the forest to confuse the child if he awoke and have him lose his bearings. He was gently laid down in a fern bed, and the "devils" took soot and smeared Peter's face so that if anyone saw him, they would think he was a real night devil. As the big boys left Peter alone and asleep, they began to make hooting and chattering noises. Peter awoke and saw nothing but blackness.

Where am I? he thought. *It's so cold and damp. Where is the fire? Where are the other boys? Maybe I'm dreaming.* He reached out and touched the ferns. He didn't know what they were. *What is that?* he shuddered. *Feels like spider webs in the hayloft. But they don't crumple up like webs do.* What he felt seemed unreal, feathery, and somehow unattached to the world. He looked up and saw patches of tiny lights above him. *Stars? Must be stars. But why are they in little bunches?* He stopped a moment and recalled, *I saw stars like that when we were wandering and slept in forests.* The air smelled sweet and moist. *Maybe I'm in the forest. How did I get here? I must be dreaming. Dear Mother of God, I hope I'm asleep!* He began to sweat from fear. *I want to wake up.*

He remembered how frightened he had been in the dark forests during the war. The hooting began again. Peter leaned through the feathery webs and pressed his face to the cool, moist earth. He clamped his hands over his ears to block out the sounds and wanted to wake up and find himself either at home or on his blanket in the field. Hot tears ran down his cheeks, but he didn't whimper. Mama said he was getting to be a big boy. After a long, frightening time, he fell asleep thinking of Mama and good bread and butter.

Shimmering sunlight filtered through the leaves and created dancing patches of many shades of green on the forest floor. Glistening dew and the sparkling morning light transformed the woodland into a fantasy world for Peter. He sat up and saw blue sky where the stars had been in the night. *I am in the forest!* he said to himself. Peter reached out his hand and brushed it against the ferns. The swaying, feathery feel came not from webs, but from filmy leaves on thin stalks that really grew from the earth. He looked around him. *I know this place!* he thought. *Papa brought me here last fall when he looked for honey mushrooms. We filled two baskets near that stump over there!*

He heard voices, and when he turned, he could see some boys and horses through the trees. He ran as fast as he could to get Brownie. Some older boys saw him and laughed. Somehow he had ended up in the woods, even after he properly said his prayers too! The boys must have laughed because they saw him run out of the woods. He found his blanket where he had left it and folded it as he ran to Brownie. He jumped on the horse's back just as Krupka shouted, "Back to the village! The horses are needed for work!"

After the confusion of awaking by himself and running to get Brownie, Peter nestled against her neck and relaxed during the ride home. He noticed three other little boys his age had very dirty, black faces. He laughed to himself and thought, *They must've rolled into some mud.* As the riders neared the village, they met some children taking cows out to the pasture.

"Hello! Where've you been?" the cowherds asked.

"To night pasture."

One girl laughed and shouted, "You look like devils or black ghosts, you're so dirty! Didn't your mamas ever teach you how to wash?"

One of the little sooty-faced riders called back, "There wasn't any water for washing. We camped out near the mud flats." He didn't seem to understand why everyone was laughing.

The cowherds burst into even heartier laughter and went on their way. The horses reached the village and carried their riders home.

Pundyk came running out of the barn when Peter rode into the farmyard and slipped off the young mare. The dog yipped his usual greeting and then whimpered when he saw Peter's face. Peter thought that was odd, but only said, "What's the matter, boy?" as he led Brownie to the barn. Mama was milking Mama Cow and looked up when Peter came near the stall. When she saw two light grey eyes staring at her from a sooty face, she jumped from the shock. The cow also jolted, not only because of the sight of her favorite little Petrush who had turned black, but also from the unintentional pinch she got from Mama. The cow almost kicked over the bucket. Mama laughed and patted the cow to calm her.

"Easy there. It's only our little Petrush, home from night pasture. It looks as though he's had quite a night. Did you have fun, Petrushu?"

"Oh yes, Mama! I want to go again! Soon!"

Mama smiled. "Yes, you'll go, but maybe next time, you'll pick a spot closer to the fire where the night devils won't find you."

Peter looked at her and blinked. How did she know?

"Go wash at the well. Your hands and face are dirty. Then go eat the porridge I left for you."

Mama tried to talk with a straight face, but a smile tugged at the corners of her lips. He didn't see her lean her forehead against the side of the cow and begin to shake, but he did hear her laugh softly as he ran off. Peter drew a bucket of water at the well. He began to wash his face and hands, but it seemed the more he washed, the blacker his hands became. He finally realized that he too was one of the "devils." Only Pundyk was there to witness Peter's dawning realization, but he was embarrassed anyway. After he used the soap to really scrub his skin, he went into the house with a red face instead of a black one. The joke had been on him too.

Chapter 25

Partners in Crime

One cool, clear morning later in the summer, Peter was finishing his breakfast when his mother came in from the barn with a pail of milk.

"Petrush, Bura's hoof is sore today, and I don't think she should aggravate it with too much walking. Leave her here and just take Mama Cow out to pasture."

"That'll be fine, Mama."

"It looks like the weather will be good today. Remember to watch where the sun is. No napping. Be home in time for supper."

"Yes, Mama." Peter kissed her on the cheek. "We'll be home in plenty of time."

Peter took his lunch and went out into the chilly morning air. The sun had been up about an hour, and the dew sparkled on everything Peter could see. The dew was so thick on the fence that the boards looked as if they were covered by a fuzzy, pale grey moss instead of water droplets. It was a magnificent scene to see, and Peter paused to admire it before he went into the barn. While he looked at the beautiful morning, he planned his day. *Hmm,* he thought. *Where shall I take Mama Cow for pasture? Ivan won't be at the commons today, so I'll take her out on the field paths. But which ones?*

He stood there camouflaged near the dew-covered fence, in his grey jacket and pants. His hair was covered with his cap, and he stood very still. He heard a tapping noise and looked in the direction from which it came.

Chapter 25

Mr. Tenuch lived two farmyards away from Peter, and he was outside tapping his walking stick against a fence post. Each time it hit the fence, sparkling drops of dew flew off in all directions like shattered stars. Tenuch was one of the village wardens, and the walking stick was a symbol of his position as warden. It aided in the long walks he had to take and could also be used as a weapon against any offender he might chase. Poachers could be a mean lot to deal with in the private forests, but Tenuch rarely went looking for them. He preferred to catch less dangerous cowherds who did not tend their animals carefully enough. He liked to make his job sound terribly dangerous and important. "Only someone of great cunning can be a warden," he'd say. He and Mr. Brama, another warden, were hired by wealthy landowners outside Opaka to make systematic patrols of the fields and woodlots to make certain no villagers or livestock trespassed.

Tenuch tapped his stick and talked to Brama. In the early morning stillness Peter could hear every word they said.

"This morning we'll go out to where they mowed hay yesterday."

Peter knew that the mowing had taken place south of town for the last few days. He stood quietly and watched the two men head southward.

"If they go south, I'll go west or north. The farther away from them we can be, the better."

Peter greeted Pundyk at the door of the barn, and the dog went inside with him to get Mama Cow out of her stall. "Be good, Pundyk, and watch Bura for me today." The dog barked and looked as if he'd rather go to the fields with Peter, but obediently he stayed behind at his post.

The boy and his cow left the farmyard and headed westward. Once they were beyond the village, Peter began to make his selection of which path to the north would give the cow good grass. They stopped at one that looked lush in the dew, and he stood guard behind her to watch in case someone should come. Mama Cow began to chomp away happily, and Peter removed his cap. His honey-colored hair was the same color as the rye, and with his cap off he was less conspicuous. The rye was so high, it hid both of them.

The cow ate as if she had been starving. "Must taste good, eh? You make me feel like no one ever feeds you. You know that isn't so," Peter teased. The cow mooed softly. Peter directed her toward the crest of the hill that they were approaching. The end of that particular path was just on the other side of the rise, and Peter had already planned where they would go from there. Peter glanced back at the village and saw two men walking in his direction.

Who is that? he wondered. He peered through the rye until he recognized the stiff, almost military walk of the men. When he saw them swinging their walking sticks, he almost choked. "Oh no!" Peter whispered to himself. Brama and Tenuch had changed their strategy and ruined his. "If they catch us, there'll be trouble for the whole village."

He bit his lip and started to plot his next move. It was just habit that made him glance at the ground while he thought, but what he saw scared him. The dew! That lovely, silvery dew he had admired that morning suddenly became a threat. He looked back along the path. Each step that he and Mama Cow had taken was neatly recorded. Each mouthful she had lovingly ripped up was outlined so clearly! Peter gritted his teeth.

"They'll see the dew has been disturbed on this path, and they'll come after us!"

He turned and chased Mama Cow toward the crest of the hill. The rye was tall all over the fields, but to make certain they wouldn't be seen, Peter slowed the cow and then stopped her before they reached the crest. He waited until the wardens passed by, about twenty-five meters away, on a parallel path at the other edge of the narrow field. If he let them pass by so closely, the rye would hide Peter and his cow better than if they kept running. At a distance, the rye appeared to flatten out, and the slope of the hill was such that they would have been easier to see. By standing still and waiting, they were better hidden, but their timing had to be perfect. When Brama and Tenuch passed them, Peter whispered to his cow to run. They had to get over the crest of the hill and down the other side before the men came around to the entrance of the path and saw the dew. Mama Cow was feeling frisky that morning, and the excitement of being on an adventure again made her light-footed. Peter had a healthy amount of fear to move him, and they soon found themselves on the other side of the hill in a shallow ditch. They followed the ditch at a full run until Peter saw the beginning of the paths of his family's rye fields. They ran past the last neighboring field and then quickly up out of the ditch onto a path his family owned. The neighboring crop was also rye, and it shielded them from view. Peter stroked his cow's neck to calm her and then took the rope he carried, looped it, and put it around her neck. That was her signal to stay put and graze while Peter went off somewhere.

He carefully made his way to higher ground. He raised his head just high enough to be able to peek through the waving rye to see where the wardens were. They stood at the crest of the first hill. Both of them were waving their walking sticks in a menacing way and shouted for someone to stop. There was no one else around. Peter was certain of that. The men were only trying to intimidate the offender.

Peter returned to Mama Cow and smiled when he noticed that the side of the ditch where they had crawled up to reach their path was bathed in sunlight. The dew was gone there! The sun had gently dried it. Aside from some lightly trampled grass, there was no sign that they had come out that way. They ran down to the end of their path and came out on the road near the common pasture. They joined the others in the pasture and then slowly moved up into the meadow.

Tenuch and Brama appeared later and made their way systematically across the commons. They stopped to speak to each young cowherd they met. They asked each one if he had been up in the area called the Opshar. All of the young people looked at them in surprise and said they had no information to give them. Peter carefully watched the real surprise and responses of the others, and when he was questioned, his innocent face betrayed nothing.

The two wardens cursed and spat on the ground. Then they started to shout so that everyone could hear them. "No one has ever gotten away from us!" Tenuch yelled.

"No escape!" Brama added.

"We're experts! No one can outsmart us!"

"We always catch trespassers!"

"I'll bet they headed toward the river! We'll find good clues on the soft banks, and then we'll get them!"

Peter watched them go off. "Good luck, you two experts," he whispered and smiled. He spent the rest of the day in the pasture with Mama Cow. On the way home, Peter and his cow used the village road. As they neared their farmyard, they passed Tenuch's place, and the two wardens were involved in a very animated discussion. Their arms were waving, and when Peter passed by, he heard parts of what they were saying.

"The whole day … nothing … we'll get 'em!!"

Mama Cow walked calmly by and mooed softly to Peter. Peter patted her on the neck. He couldn't help laughing while he filled her trough in the barn. She in turn gave him a friendly nudge.

Chapter 26

The Two Soldiers

Winter was just beginning. Peter and Papa were in the barn early one morning to repair one of the walls that had come loose between the stalls when Peter realized he was late for school. Oleksa hadn't come to get him because he had left early to meet friends, so Peter grabbed his notebook and pencil and ran as fast as he could down the road.

He ran to the end of the lane that went past his farm and turned onto the main road that cut through Opaka on its way south. Peter slowed as he neared the roadside crucifix, crossed himself as he passed, and had started to run again when he saw a patrol of two young soldiers from the Ukrainian Army. He slowed to a walk so that he could watch them. Their horses stood in the ditch and were partially hidden. The soldiers saw Peter but paid no attention to him. They were looking to the west, in the direction of the distant city of Jaroslava, and seemed to be searching for something on the horizon. Everything was very still and quiet.

What Peter and the soldiers did not know was that some Polish troops had come to Opaka by the back roads past the fields. They had approached the village from the west and were nearing the main road. Moments before they reached the church, the two Ukrainian soldiers spotted them, though Peter saw nothing. The Ukrainian soldiers quickly pulled their horses up to the road, mounted them, and galloped off as fast as they could toward Lubachiv.

Peter was frightened by the urgency of their moves and wondered what had made them jump into action. As if by instinct, he knew enough not to stand out in the open to watch, but ducked behind one of the tall poplars along the edge of the road. From his vantage point he watched them ride and then heard shouts coming from the direction of the church. He saw Polish soldiers there, and suddenly they opened fire on the fleeing horsemen. With bullets flying so near, Peter was afraid that the Ukrainian patrol would be hit, but they turned their horses toward the little bridge that led toward Felzendorf. They crossed it and turned again to a narrow lane that cut across the fields. They escaped by that route and finally, by making a wide circle, reached Lubachiv.

That was the first encounter between the Ukrainian Army and the Poles in the area surrounding Opaka. Ukrainian newborn independence was short-lived. Poland wanted all of Galicia and had decided to take it by force. Uprisings had begun with small pockets of the Polish Underground, but now war was unleashed. The Polish government had sent in its army.

Peter was afraid to move at first, but he wasn't far from school. The soldiers stopped shooting and gave their attention to their officers, who were shouting orders. Peter took his chance and ran to the school. His heart was pounding in his ears, but he didn't stop running until he had slammed the school door behind him. His teacher was waiting for him inside.

"Are you all right, Petro?" His teacher's voice was high and shrill even though she was trying to keep calm in front of the students. "I saw you out there when I came to the window after the first shots!"

"Two soldiers … from the Ukrainian patrol … the others shot at them … I think they made it … they went toward Felzendorf … then turned over the fields …" Peter gasped.

His teacher looked at him sympathetically and stooped to pick up his hat when he dropped it, while he nervously tried to take off his coat and hang up his things. She looked worried and peered out the window in the direction of the church. She could just barely see the Polish soldiers still waiting there.

Chapter 26

"Sit down, Petru," she said softly. "Children! I want all of you to open your notebooks and copy the words I wrote on the blackboard. Those of you working on mathematics, show all the steps you go through to find your answers. All of you get to work and stay quiet."

She stayed near the window and continued to watch what she could see of the soldiers. No one did any work. They sat quietly with their pencils in their hands and their notebooks open, but everyone looked at the teacher. The only sound in the room was some hissing from a damp log in the stove.

After what seemed like a very long time, muffled shouts were heard from outside, and everyone heard the sound of wagons, horses, and troops on the move again. The Polish troops continued through Opaka, took the back roads, and headed out to the distant fields beyond. As soon as they were out of sight, the teacher came to the front of the class.

"We all know what kind of danger we have here. I don't know if they'll be back. I'm going to dismiss you now. I want you to go straight home. No playing along the way. Go home and wait inside for your parents. Understand?"

Heads nodded, and the room emptied quickly. Everyone headed for home, and no one spoke along the way. Most of the children kept glancing over their shoulders to see if the roads were still clear. War was coming again to Opaka, and this time even the little children knew what it could bring. They were afraid.

Fighting began all over Galicia, and Opaka was included in it. The villagers were not warned to leave as they had been by the Muscovites, but rather the two armies clashed right outside the village boundaries. For a time, Lubachiv was held by Ukrainian troops, and the Poles positioned themselves on the outskirts of the city.

A man from Felzendorf named Derzhak worked with the Poles, and because of his knowledge of the area, the Polish army was able to make some cunningly strategic moves in the battle to win Lubachiv. He knew the terrain and all the back roads near the fields. Felzendorf was situated between Opaka and Lubachiv, and the

Poles, who decided to base themselves in Felzendorf, needed to come no farther than the river bank for a good fighting position. They set up their big guns and shelled Lubachiv. The major battle continued for three days and nights. The shooting and loud thunder of heavy artillery were a living nightmare. When the shelling died down for a time, Peter went with Papa to the barn to tend to the animals. He saw the wild look in the eyes of the frightened beasts. Every living creature was nervous and afraid. Even brave and loyal Pundyk, who never left his post, whimpered and even howled when the shooting was especially heavy.

The Poles cut the supply routes to the Ukrainian soldiers in Lubachiv, and the Ukrainians' ammunition began to run out. The army did all they could to hold the city but finally had to retreat to the big city of Lviv far to the southeast.

The villagers stayed huddled in their homes during the fighting. Some of those on the edge of town close to the guns even went into their root cellars or ran to stay with neighbors in safer areas. None of the villagers were hurt or killed, but many soldiers died. Both sides lost a great many men. When the Polish troops moved in to take over Lubachiv, two mass graves were dug. One was for the Ukrainian soldiers who had fought to defend a part of their new country. The other was for the Polish troops who had set out to take the city from them and succeeded.

The war with Poland did not end with the Battle of Lubachiv. In fact that encounter was one of the first clashes between the two armies. The Poles moved into the area early in the war and held that section of Galicia throughout the fighting. There weren't many battles near Opaka after the one in Lubachiv, but the occupation of the area and the resentment of the Ukrainians began a time of conflict on a different level.

Some buildings that housed Polish officials in Lubachiv were bombed by nationalists from the Ukrainian Underground. Most of the harassment took place in the city, but Polish dominance was soon felt even in Opaka. Polish families were not bothered, but Ukrainians were under surveillance. Across the road from the blacksmith's shop, the building that served as a town hall and library was closed. Young people were forbidden to meet there anymore. The Poles said that the ones who came there plotted against the government. Sometimes local people were arrested because they were suspected of being subversive. Most of the time, however, arrests were made for such so-called offenses as using the Ukrainian language at public meetings. A display of nationalism of any kind, even something as simple as wearing an article of clothing embroidered in a traditional Ukrainian design, was considered an insult to the occupying government.

Mama and Papa tried to keep the family routine as normal as possible, but no one could ignore how the world was changing. Peter often saw Papa talking to other Ukrainian men in the village. The discussions were always brief, and hand gestures made it look as if they spoke of the weather or work in the fields. Peter wondered if Papa knew about the sabotage in the city. One time he even asked Mama about it. She quickly silenced him with a stern look and a whispered command to be quiet.

"Papa was away so long in the war, he wouldn't do anything that would take him from us again!" she said softly but firmly.

That really didn't answer his question, but because Mama seemed so frightened when she said that, Peter didn't ask anymore. Papa never left to go anywhere except for work in the fields or to buy supplies in the city. He was careful not to do anything that might bring trouble to his family, but still certain men would stop by to talk with him. They always spoke in low muffled tones.

Once Peter was in the barn with Papa, and he asked, "Who was it Mr. Baran was talking about last night, Papa?"

"Don't concern yourself, Petru. He just brought news from Lubachiv. I like to know what's happening near our village. That's all." Papa said no more about it and began to talk about weather and how the barn needed repairs.

Peter became skillful at slipping quietly and unnoticed into shadows. Whenever he happened to see Papa talking with old Mr. Baran or one of the other men who came to see him, Peter tried to hide nearby and listen. They always came and asked to use some of Papa's tools to sharpen a scythe or repair a board on the side of a wagon. They never stayed long, and Peter saw very little sharpening or repairing being done.

Over the winter and spring months, Peter learned as much as he could from his shadowy eavesdropping. He learned that in February the Poles wanted to negotiate a peace. They wanted one-third of Galicia and Lviv as part of the settlement, and the Western Ukrainian Republic refused the proposal. Peter was happy when he heard that.

One evening in late spring, Peter was up in the hayloft. He went up to look for a book he had borrowed from his teacher so that he could finish reading it before he had to return it the next day. He liked to read in the loft where it was quiet because he didn't like interruptions. He was reading the last few pages in the fading light when he heard Papa come into the barn. Before Peter shouted out a greeting, he heard Mr. Baran come in too. Peter, hidden by a large mound of hay, watched the two men over the edge of the loft and listened to their conversation.

"Myhailo," Baran's deep voice wavered, "word came that all is lost."

Papa put up his hand, gesturing to the old man to speak more softly. "No! What do you mean?" Papa said in a half whisper.

"A few weeks ago the Poles made another proposal to the Ukrainian delegation." Papa nodded, and Baran went on. "It was more favorable, and the delegation accepted it. That was on the 13th of May. Negotiations for peace were to begin right away."

"I heard that." Papa's eyes searched the old man's face.

"Myhailo. Then you have to know too that two days later they launched their all-out offensive against our side." Papa angrily muttered something under his breath, and Baran continued to talk. "Their main strategy, it now appears, was to cut off our supply lines and all communications with the Czechs."

"Can't our allies find another route?"

"It's too late," the old man said, shuddering. "The lines have been cut. It's only a matter of time. Already there are rumors that the Galician Army is planning to cross into the east to help the National Republic against the Bolsheviks." Baran sounded weak and tired.

Papa placed his hand on the old man's shoulder. He looked at him intently, and even from a distance Peter saw the sorrow in his father's eyes. He knew his father's silence said a great deal. The silence spoke of Papa's understanding of war. War involved such enormous losses that words were often useless. The two men stood and said nothing for a long while.

"Well, old man," Papa finally said softly and with affection, "it's time for supper."

Old Baran stood rooted to the floor. Papa's hand still rested on his shoulder.

Myhailo spoke in a raspy whisper, "The hymn said that we resurrected. Resurrected! We can't die anymore. The spirit lives on no matter what happens, and our spirit is so strong. Someday, Baran. Someday." He patted the old man's shoulder.

Baran turned to go. At first he seemed stooped and defeated, but he turned again to look at Myhailo and straightened his back. He nodded his head in a silent gesture of farewell and left.

Peter had begun to cry without realizing it, and before he could stop himself, he sobbed loudly. Papa heard him and looked up. Peter was afraid that his father would be angry to see him there.

"Petrush," Papa said gently. "It's time for us to go in for supper. Come down from there."

Peter crawled down. He walked over to his father and stood in front of him. He wiped his streaked face in his sleeve and then reached out to take Papa's hand and walk with him to the house. He hadn't done that for a long time because he thought it was something only little children did. At that moment, it didn't mean anything like that. Peter and Papa held each other's hand and walked slowly to the house.

Chapter 27

Polish Harvest

Hatred and oppression did not end with the defeat of the Western Ukrainian Republic. Although the Poles were in the minority in that part of Galicia, they made certain that their culture would dominate along with their government. By autumn there were mass arrests and deportation of Ukrainians throughout the area. Land held by some Ukrainians was seized and turned over to Polish settlers. Somehow, Peter's family was not torn apart during this persecution. The family farm had come to Mama from her first marriage. Her first husband had been Polish, and most of it would be inherited by his two children. Perhaps that was why no one bothered them. Other Ukrainian families in Opaka were left alone too. There were individual reasons as well as the fact that some Polish families had already lived in Opaka before the war. Because the area was somewhat "infiltrated" in that way, the attention of the governmental authorities was focused more on Lubachiv and other areas with heavier Ukrainian populations.

Papa continued to have quiet talks with other villagers, but took care not to arouse suspicion. In his eavesdropping, Peter heard that over 20,000 Ukrainians were in Polish prisons and internment camps, and the numbers were growing. Peter pieced together what information he could get. He wasn't certain what an internment camp was like, but the mere mention of it struck horror in people. The number of prisoners seemed so huge. Peter found it hard to picture 20,000 of anything, let alone 20,000 human beings.

Papa was brushing Brownie one day when Peter wandered into the barn. Peter watched his father's coarse hands while he groomed the horse with almost graceful strokes. Papa was usually in a good mood while he did this task that he enjoyed so much.

"Hello, Petru. You look troubled. What is it now?"

"Nothing, really, Papa. I'm just trying to imagine something. In mathematics, the teacher talks of thousands. I'd like to see how large a certain number really is."

"What's the number you had in mind?"

"Twenty thousand."

Myhailo stopped brushing for a second. He knew why that number was significant to Peter. The boy must have overheard one of the discussions with old Ihor from Lubachiv.

"Think of a field of wheat or rye. Think of a hundred bundles lying in a long row. How many rows would it take to make twenty thousand?"

"Two hundred rows," Peter whispered in awe. That would require an enormous field.

"Twenty thousand bundles of grain would make quite a harvest."

Papa said "harvest." Peter thought of wheat cut and lying on the ground before it was gathered and taken away. "People are cut down like that too," he murmured.

Myhailo watched Peter's face. "Remember this, Petrush. Even after the crop is gathered and taken away, some seeds are scattered or overlooked. No matter how careful the farmer is, some of the ones left behind will grow into wheat again."

Peter stared at his father. Although they talked in symbols and numbers, they both meant and understood the same thing. Ukraine, the great breadbasket of Europe, was often symbolized by stalks of wheat. Peter saw the stalks to be the people.

The mass arrests missed the family, but there were other torments that came. An aftermath of the war and the terrible conditions of the prison camps was the spread of disease. Large areas of Galicia were stricken with outbreaks of typhus and dysentery. It was typhus that came to Opaka, and the disease hit with no regard for ethnic background. Many people Peter knew died. Old Mr. Janko and the Chorneys were too old and frail to fight it off. Some little babies were too weak. Even Mrs. Kucharski's little grandson died of typhus.

Peter couldn't recall much about the illness. His fever and delirium wiped out most of his memory of it. Everyone in the family came down with it at the same time, even little Maryna. Everyone except Mama. She took care of her husband and children through the fever and its wretched symptoms. They were all so weak she had to do everything for them. She also had to do the barn chores herself until some of them recovered enough to help. Finally, when Papa and Daria began to recover, Mama fell sick.

They celebrated Christmas very simply and quietly that year. It had never been part of the family custom to exchange gifts at Christmas, but that year Mama said that they all received a great gift. They were together and had all regained their health. It was true—all of them had lived through the fever—but Peter noticed Papa seemed very tired most of the time. The typhus had weakened him more than anyone else, and Papa looked old to Peter.

There were changes at school that winter. Peter's teacher was replaced by a Polish woman. Classes were conducted in Polish, and Peter no longer practiced penmanship with the Cyrillic letters of the Ukrainian alphabet. Only the Roman letters of the Polish alphabet were allowed. No one greeted the teacher anymore with the exclamations of "Glory be to Jesus Christ!" or "Christ is born!" Ukrainian customs and traditions were eliminated. Ukrainians weren't even to be called Ukrainians any more. They were no longer to be thought of as a separate people. They were to be called "Rusyns" as if they were just a little segment of the people called Russians. The Ukrainian language was not to be used in school or in any business transaction. The Poles said that Rusyns didn't really have a language. The Rusyns spoke gibberish. In fact, the Poles said, it was really the babbling of fools. Peter heard all these things and was so angry his head pounded.

Chapter 27

"Babbling, is it? They never read the poems of Taras Shevchenko. No one who writes like that can be called a fool. He would never use Polish to say what he did!" Peter mumbled these thoughts only to himself. The anger he felt ran very, very deep.

The biggest visual jolt Peter received was on the day he walked into school and saw that the big map of the Austro-Hungarian Empire was gone. Ukrainian independence was so short-lived that there had been no time to get a map of the infant republic. Now the huge map that hung in front of the classroom was one of Poland. The Poland it showed included Galicia. When Peter saw it, he felt as if he had been slapped. He knew the teacher was looking at him and had seen the expression on his face. He nodded respectfully and took his seat. He tried to act normally and hoped his feelings would not show too much. He couldn't explain the feeling yet. He hated having to learn and use only Polish in school. He didn't like the changes in class routine. It was all happening so quickly that there wasn't time to think it through. The new map symbolized the finality of it. He still had his family, but something else very precious was lost. It was how he had felt when Papa went to war, but this time he knew things would not return to the way they had been.

Peter didn't talk about his feelings very often at home, but he told Papa about the changes at school. Papa and Mama looked at each other, and Papa was angry.

"You just behave yourself, Petru," he muttered. "Follow instructions and don't give them any reason to pick on you or abuse any of you children."

Mama tried to make home a happy place, but it seemed to Peter that everyone had been sad for such a long time.

Peter and Ivan had become friends when they were very young. The war made the two boys even closer. There were Ukrainian families in Opaka, but of the few boys Peter's age, only Ivan was Ukrainian. Their shared heritage gave them an even stronger bond. With the surveillance of Ukrainians, Peter's little Polish friends played less and less with him, and there developed a definite split between them. Children often reflect the prejudices of their parents.

One day at school, during prayer, Peter made the sign

of the cross in the manner of the Byzantine Rite, with his thumb, forefinger, and middle finger pinched together to symbolize the Trinity. He touched his forehead, his chest, his right shoulder, and then his left. Voytek, a young boy Peter had known for years, watched Peter cross himself. After the class sat down, Peter glanced over at him and saw that Voytek was looking back at him with contempt. At recess Voytek came over to Peter and shoved him against the building.

"What did you do that for?" Peter asked.

"Do what?"

"Push me for no reason."

"It doesn't matter. You're just a Rusyn."

Peter looked at him in disbelief. Why should that be a reason today when they had known each other since they were babies? The teacher saw them and yelled from the doorway of the school to ask what was going on.

"Nothing, Madame Teacher," Voytek volunteered, glaring at Peter. "Pietro just tripped."

"Tri—" Peter didn't get a chance to finish the word.

Voytek stood between Peter and the teacher with his back to her. She couldn't see his face and was too far away to hear their conversation.

"Yes, you tripped. You Rusyns are clumsy. Or maybe you're just stupid." He smiled at his own words. "Yeah, stupid! You better watch yourself. You don't belong here. I saw you cross yourself today. You do it backwards, just like a good Russian Orthodox. We know about them. I bet you don't even belong to the true Church. You're so dumb you don't know your right side from your left."

It was Peter's turn to glare, but he was in full view of the teacher. She treated him and other "Rusyn" children very coldly. "Don't give them any reason," Papa had said. Peter forced his teeth to unclench and managed a sickly smile.

"Oh, I know very well what is correct," he said slowly, nodding his head like an old sage. "I won't be part of the harvest."

Voytek looked at him, puzzled. Peter stepped around Voytek and went back into the school. Recess was over.

Chapter 28

Wolves

Peter listened as old Baran told Papa the news from town. Some Ukrainian students in Lubachiv had gone to the mass grave on Sunday to hold a memorial for the fallen Ukrainian soldiers. They went because it was Pentecost, and it was traditional to visit the graves of loved ones on that special day. The Polish police arrested them. Now word came that they were being beaten and tortured in jail, as an example to others who might think about any display of nationalism or loyalty to anything but the current authorities. No one knew how long the students would be held or what would happen to them.

Torture? Beatings? Peter's brain repeated. *For singing and reading tributes to fallen heroes? For praying for the dead on a special Sunday?* He felt sick inside.

"Goodnight, my friend," old Baran said to Papa, and then with a slight bow, "and to you, Maria." The man stepped out into the mild evening and went home.

The house was quiet. Mama was spinning thread. Papa sat on the bench and leaned back against the wall with his eyes shut. He rubbed his forehead as if to rub away fatigue or at least the grievous things he had just heard. His face was ashen.

Daria and Myhal were visiting some friends. Oleksa was reading, and Kashia and Maryna were asleep. Peter looked at Papa and wondered if he should speak. He had so many questions again. Finally, he could stay silent no longer.

"Papa, how can this be? Before this last war, there were parades and speeches. Ukraine resurrected! The hymn said our fate was going to be happy. We were all brothers and free. Free, Papa! I heard it said that our land had been invaded by intruders, and now they would be gone. Then there were more battles. More war. Now the war is over again, and students are being beaten for praying at graves? Papa, why is this happening?"

Myhailo looked at the ten-year-old boy whose eyes were those of someone twice or three times his age. *Peter, the questioning one,* he thought. *The one who wants to know about everything. He's already seen and knows too much. No child should ever have to see what this time has brought to us. How do I explain now? My precious son has looked war in the face. He's also felt the exhilaration of freedom. How do I explain?*

"Petrush," he said wearily. "You know what wolves are, don't you?"

"Yes, Papa."

"They're God's creatures who are made to hunt and catch their prey. They're hungry and must eat. When they catch a deer, they rip it apart and consume it. It's their nature."

"Yes, Papa. You've told me."

"Petrush, there are other wolves on this earth. Not just the four-footed creatures we would expect. They also hunt and rip apart from hunger, but it isn't a natural hunger. It's a hunger of greed and hate. One that's never satisfied. They rip and tear at the hearts of men—at their faith, their identity, and their nation. We are not as helpless as a deer, but even we cannot always fight our attackers. Like deer we're unwilling victims, but we don't find peace in a speedy death. We're victims whose hearts and dignity are torn, but we continue to live. Those wolves who attack the identity of men are more vicious than those beasts who hunt and kill quickly. So, Petrush. That's what happened. We thought we were finally free, but the wolves came and tore us apart from three sides."

Peter listened to his father. The images in his mind were vivid and terrifying. He clearly saw "wolf-men" devouring other men and yet not killing them. It was a horrible picture. Even at his age, Peter understood what the images meant. After the parades and speeches, he had felt the invisible but real pride in his heritage. It was because he had felt it so strongly that he knew what was being ripped away. He understood.

Peter looked at his father's haggard face. Peter's face was so filled with sadness that Myhailo asked himself why he used the example he did. Wolves terrified children so much, but what had happened and was happening was more terrible. Peter, in turn, saw the pain in his father's eyes and shared it, and because it was so intense, he turned and ran outside.

The evening sky was deep and clear, and stars twinkled in the rich dark blue of space. Peter's heart was pounding, and his eyes were stinging. *I won't cry,* he told himself, *even though I'm all alone and no one will see.* He remembered the two soldiers by the roadside, on the way to school that day so long ago. He remembered how they rode off with bullets flying after them. He remembered the soldiers who were shooting. He looked at the ground beneath his feet and poked at it with a stick.

This soil, he thought. *This was ours and free. We still live on it, but it isn't free anymore. The wolves. Those wolves will never tear at me and rip out my heart. I'll never let them. I know who I am. I'll never forget who I am. They'll never take my heart and leave me to live without it. I'm not soil that can be walked on. I'm not soil where a border can be moved and then I'm different. I know who I am, and I'll be free even if no one knows it but me!* He thought about the police in the city, and his anger made him tremble. He shook his fist in the direction of the city and then stopped. *The evil isn't just there,* he thought sadly. *City, village, or field, the evil surrounds us.* The thought overwhelmed him.

The sky seemed to open wide above him like the gaping mouth of a monster ready to swallow him up, and he felt lost and small. Shadows moved and threatened him. The shadows looked like soldiers reaching out to take hold of him. Some of the shadows looked like the open jaws of attacking wolves, and tears blurred the beasts before they reached him. The night was sinister and evil, and he cowered and was deathly afraid. He sat with his knees drawn up to his chest and covered his head with his arms. His eyes began to sting with angry tears. His ribs felt like they were being squeezed, and it was hard to breathe. Peter swallowed down the lump in his throat and stiffened his body to stop his trembling.

"I know who I am," he hissed defiantly at the shadows. "I know who I am," he said, peering up at the cold, unblinking stars. "They will never conquer me. Never!" The words he uttered faded, and the wind seemed to die down.

Peter wiped off his face with the cuff of his sleeve. The sky seemed less cavernous, and the stars twinkled again. The shadows of the marching soldiers and menacing wolf heads became the windblown leafy boughs of trees silhouetted against the barn. The evil, dark shapes once more became the storage barn, the well, and the chicken coop. It was simply a quiet evening again. Peter's heart began to beat less violently, and he smiled to himself.

"I know who I am," he whispered proudly.

Peter looked back at the house. Papa was still sitting on the bench, but now he was watching Mama spin thread while he spoke quietly with her. Peter went back in to help with the spinning.

Chapter 29

Good-Bye

Peter sat up in the loft. It was cold. Colder for him than the chill in the early winter air. He had cried so much that he was exhausted. He felt so frustrated that life once more had done something to him that he could not control.

The funeral had been that morning. They had all stood near the grave in the churchyard. Now they were home again, but the bitter wind that had howled around them in the churchyard now howled through their hearts. Peter covered his ears, but the sound stayed. The noise of the howling wind was replaced by the thundering sound of the blood throbbing through his ears when he began to cry again.

"Oh, Papa," he wept. "What are we going to do without you?"

Papa had been weaker after the typhus, but still he had been able to work in the fields. The year that followed was so filled with disappointment over the new government that Papa's spirit seemed tired too, but his deep love for his wife and children gave him purpose in life. The cold winds of autumn brought sickness again. It was nothing as dreadful as the typhus, but Papa became sick. So very sick. Now he was gone.

"Oh, God, I can't stand this. I need him! Why did you take him? I had my Papa so little. What about Mama and the others? Kashia and Maryna had him even less than me!"

Bura moved in her stall. Her chain clanked against a metal bar. He'd heard the sound so many times, but this time it reminded him of the death bell. The palamar, the bell ringer from Peter's church, had rung it when he got word that Papa had died. It was rung to let the village know that one of their neighbors had died. He had rung it again for the funeral. Peter knew that whenever he heard it again, he would remember the times it had rung for Papa.

Peter continued to sit in the loft. Pundyk was getting older and found it hard to crawl up to the loft with Peter when the weather was damp. Pundyk also missed Papa. The dog finally stopped whimpering and walking listlessly around the farmyard. Now he kept guard at his post by the stable door. Pundyk looked old and weary that day.

Oh, Lord, Peter thought. *Papa looked old and tired too. Are all the ones I love so much just going to get old and tired and then die and leave me? Papa's gone. I want the world to stop for a while. I wish life changed more slowly. But no. We still eat supper. We still milk the cows and feed the animals. We still sleep at night. The Komars, next door, still fight. I even heard a man laugh at a joke while he walked down the road today. It's as if it didn't matter that my papa's gone. It does matter. We'll never see him again until we go after him. Papa, you must be in heaven like Mama said. You're with your parents now. You're a good man. If Mama says you're there, you are. Mama knows these things. You don't feel the cold anymore, and you won't be tired or sad. You're with God.* Peter felt calmer for a moment but then began to cry again. *Who'll answer my questions? Who'll teach me about the world and who I am? I miss you so much. I still need you.*

Peter thought of his father at work in the barn. He remembered watching his big, coarse hands gently brushing Brownie and patting Mama Cow while he talked to her and filled her manger. Then Mama Cow mooed, interrupting Peter's memories. Peter looked down. It was milking time. Mama was in the house and would not come to the stable tonight. Peter had come out to do the evening chores a little earlier than usual because he had wanted to be alone for a while and weep by himself. In the house he had to be strong for Mama. In the barn, with evening chores almost done, he could sit and think for a while. Now there was the task he left for last. He wiped his swollen eyes and crawled down from the loft. He picked up the clean pail and began to milk the cows. For a boy of ten, he did his tasks expertly. After all, he'd learned how to do everything from Mama and Papa. *Papa.* Peter could barely see the cow as he sat beside her. His eyes were full of tears. At one moment it felt good to do a familiar task. It made the day feel like any other. Then his heart reminded him of what had happened, and he wondered if any day would ever feel normal again.

Chapter 30

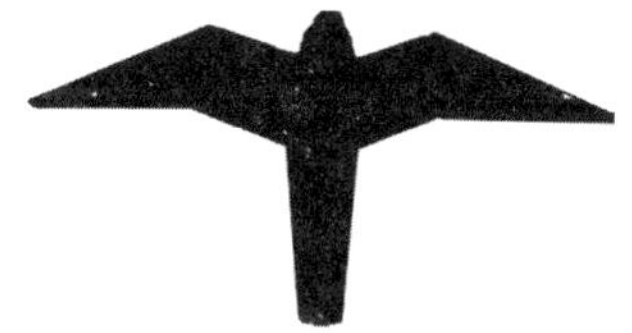

Hawks and Cuckoos

The pasture gently sloped up to meet the hardwoods and pines of the thick forest on its western edge. There beneath broad protective boughs of an ancient oak, Peter and Ivan sat to watch the road that stretched from Lubachiv to Opaka. It was market day, and the road was busy with horse carts and villagers on foot going to and from the city. The boys made certain that their cows were in their proper places in the pasture, but their attention was focused on the road. They waited for Daria to return from market with a promised surprise for both of them.

When they finally saw her, they ran down to greet her and help carry her basket up to the shade of the big tree. They all sat down on the grass, and Daria sighed contentedly.

"It's easy to see why you like this spot so much. It's the nicest in the whole pasture."

Neither boy said anything but sat there grinning and waiting. Daria's dark eyes sparkled. She didn't say another word before she reached into the side of her basket and pulled out something wrapped in thin white paper.

"This was supposed to be for your lunch, but I can see you'll never wait that long."

"Bublichky! Mm! Thanks!" Peter exclaimed when she unwrapped the yeast rolls.

"Oh, thank you very much!" Ivan added.

"May we please have them now?" Peter pleaded.

Chapter 30

Daria shook her head and smiled. "Go ahead. Enjoy them!"

The boys nibbled at the tender rolls. The treat was so wonderful, they both wanted to make it last as long as possible.

Peter sighed and repeated an old proverb. "When you have bread in your pocket, you can face anything!"

"What idiot wants to keep this in his pocket? I want it in my mouth!" Ivan said, laughing.

"So, Ivan," Daria asked, "When do you think we should all go to see your new nephew? Is Natalia ready for company?"

"She's always ready to see you," Ivan said happily. A quick movement in the sky stole his attention. "Look at that hawk," he said, pointing. "What kind is that?"

"Look, Petrush!" Daria said. "That's the one Papa used to tell us about." She and her little brother shared a bittersweet smile. Remembering things that Papa had told them made him seem very close by, but it also reminded them that he was gone.

"Papa told us that's a sparrow hawk. There's a legend about it. Some people say that it begins its life as a cuckoo, the kind we hear in the forest." The three friends sat and watched the bird beat its wings and then glide effortlessly on the wind. The fine black and grey striping on the breast of the bird was clear in the spring sunlight. "They say it lives as a cuckoo for three years, and then is transformed by some magic into a sparrow hawk to live out the rest of its days. Papa didn't think it really happened. He said the two birds have almost the same markings. Maybe they were easy to mistake for each other."

"What wonderful thing did the cuckoo do to deserve to be transformed into a hawk?" Ivan wondered aloud.

"I don't know. Papa said the cuckoo isn't a very nice bird. She doesn't tend her own eggs or babies. She lays an egg in the nest of another bird, usually a plishka, and the plishka hatches it and raises the baby as her own. The problem is that the little cuckoo is bigger than the plishka's baby when it hatches, and the baby cuckoo takes all the food the mother bird brings. The plishka's own babies usually die."

"That's cruel."

"Papa said nature can seem cruel, but creatures do what they are meant to do in order to survive."

"You would think that being transformed into a hawk would be a reward for something wonderful!" Ivan said dreamily. "I would love to be a mighty hunter like that. Just think! Strong wings. Keen eyesight. To be the hunter rather than the hunted!"

"Maybe the transformation isn't a reward," Daria offered. "Maybe it's a punishment."

"What do you mean?" Ivan asked. "The cuckoo has a good life. First to play and sing while someone else does her mothering, and then to be a hunter and not the prey."

Daria chose her words carefully. "I can't say how the cuckoo or the hawk would see it, but for a human being, it is terrible not to have babies of your own to raise. Mama says her greatest joy is in her children, even if mothering is full of worry. We were Papa's babies too. Once, when we sat with the cow while she labored to deliver a calf, he talked about the hardest thing he ever had to do. He said it was leaving us to go to war. He said the fighting and hunger were easier to accept than the fact that he was away from us. He had a duty to fulfill, but he resented being taken from us for those years. Those days were lost to him." She paused. "So. We were talking about the cuckoo. She doesn't know how empty her life is. She's ignorant of what she doesn't have. Maybe when she's transformed, she becomes aware of something she lacks and begins to search for it. The hawk always seeks. Perhaps the punishment is that she never finds what she really looks for."

The boys listened but said nothing.

Daria went on. "The cuckoo may be unaware of what she's missing, but not all animal mothers are like that. Poor Mama Cow is still grieving. She worries me."

The three of them looked at the bony creature in the distance near Bura and Ivan's two cows. Her movements seemed mechanical. She ripped up the grass and swallowed it.

"It's really hard for her, isn't it?" Ivan asked.

"Yeah," Peter sighed. "This is twice she's borne a calf and then lost it in a month's time. Each time, she and Bura had calves within a week or so of each other."

"Mama Cow was always so watchful and gentle with both new calves," Daria said softly. "She'd moo, and no matter which calf ran to her, she'd lick it and let it suckle. Sometimes she'd feed both at once! Then each time it was the same. After a few weeks, her calf died. The little ones never seemed to gain enough strength. If she were human, I think she'd kidnap one because she needs to love a calf so badly."

"Yes, and there's the other problem," Peter added. "You know how smart she is. And well, sometimes I wish she were a lot dumber. Something in her head told her that a week or two after she has a calf, the Jewish cattle dealer from Lubachiv comes to see it and estimate its worth... Then soon the calf dies. I don't know if she sees a connection or what, but now when she sees the dealer, she chases him. The last time he came into the barn, she went crazy. She broke her chain and chased after him like an angry dog. She chased him twice around the yard before Mama yelled from the house for him to come inside. Now Mama Cow gets nervous whenever she sees anyone with a long beard and a black hat."

"And our Mama feels sorry for the cow," Daria said. "She hopes the cow will calm down before she hurts herself or someone else. Last week, just before you came back from your grandma's, Mama Cow broke down the barn door. She heard a calf bawling in the Komars' barn, and she went berserk. She rammed the door so hard it broke off its hinges. Then she ran over to the fence and began to moo gently to the calf she heard."

"Does anyone know why she's lost so many calves?" Ivan asked Peter.

"Myhal said that after the war, it could have been from lack of feed, but now he thinks that we'll have to try a different bull. We've been using one the same breed as Mama Cow. She's a good milker, and we were hoping for another heifer like her, but maybe if she had other calves like our half-breed Bura, they'd be stronger."

"Well, you two cattle breeders can discuss your ideas, but I have to be home before noon." Daria laughed. "Be home in time for supper, Petru."

The boys thanked her again for the bublichky and walked her back to the road before going to check on their animals. After they led their cows to a place closer to the trees and left them to graze, the boys returned to their favorite spot beneath the oak.

"Look at this!" Peter laughed. He moved his jacket and found a little bundle there. "Daria left us another surprise!" He unwrapped two thick slices of a poppy seed cake.

"Daria is wonderful!" Ivan said happily. "Two slices of makivnek! When I get older, I hope I find a wife that's like Daria. She's nice!"

Peter said nothing and handed one of the slices to Ivan. *I wonder if Daria will be anyone's wife,* he thought. There weren't many young men left in the district after the wars. *Daria's almost twenty-two,* he told himself. *Maybe she'll spend the rest of her life as a spinster. A very nice, kind spinster.* The thought made him sad.

The boys ate the lunches they had brought from home and finished with cold water from the stream and the delicious slices of makivnek. They saw some other boys nearby.

"Do you think they'd like to play a game of 'Piggy, Piggy' with us, Petru?"

"Sure they would. They're not as unfriendly as they were last fall. Besides, Voytek was the one who kept them from playing with us, and he's not tending cows this spring. His little brother, Janek, is doing it now, and he's too small to give us any trouble."

The boys ran off to meet the others and began to organize the game. There were seven boys in all, so it promised to be a lot of fun. First, they looked for long sticks near the forest edge. Fallen branches were perfect. They had to be straight and as long as a walking stick. Two of the boys began to dig shallow, bowl-shaped holes in the ground. The holes were called "pens" for the piggy. Because there were seven boys, six pens were dug. Peter found a small chunk of wood about the size of his shoe.

"I found something to use for the piggy!" he shouted. "Let's play!"

A boy named Stash gave a friendly laugh and teased Ivan. "This was your idea, so you're the first piggy!"

Ivan smiled. "I won't be the piggy for long! Let's go!"

Chapter 30

The game was simple, but it had a definite ritual. Ivan stood off to one side with his stick and "piggy." The other boys each chose a pen to guard. Each boy began to walk in a circle around his pen, making certain that one end of his stick was in the bowl-shaped hollow. The boys all began to make a buzzing sound and then recited a nonsense verse.

Grey-brown kitty, one,
Grey-brown kitty, two,
Grey-brown kitty, *three*!

On the count of three, Ivan ran to guide the piggy toward one of the pens with great skill and agility. As soon as he neared a pen, the boy who stood guard tried to hit the piggy as far away as he could. Ivan used his stick to move the piggy and also to protect it from being hit. Ivan pretended to try for Janush's pen, but while he battled with Janush, he watched Stash out of the corner of his eye. Stash was so busy yelling encouragement to Janush and friendly insults at Ivan that he didn't tend his pen as carefully as he should. Ivan took his chance and batted the piggy expertly into Stash's pen. Then Ivan laughed.

"Now, let's see how long it takes you, Piggy Stash, to find your pen!"

Everyone had a good laugh, and Stash grinned good-naturedly. The game started again, and the piggy found its pen at least ten times more before the boys decided to rest.

Peter knelt down at the stream for a drink of water after the game. When he glanced at the cows, he froze. He sensed something was terribly wrong before he could figure out what it was. Mama Cow was running wildly toward the road. In an instant Peter knew why. There was a man on a small cart taking a calf to market. The calf was bawling loudly through the slatted sides of the cart, and Mama Cow answered it with an alarming cry.

Peter started to run before he stood up completely, and in his panic, he fell flat on his face. He scrambled to his feet and began to run as fast as he could toward the road. While he ran, he saw that the man had jumped off and was trying to chase Mama Cow away. Peter realized the man was a Jew. The long beard and the black hat triggered further frenzy in Mama Cow. She made wild, alarming crying sounds and began to chase the man. Peter finally got to the road just as the man dove under the cart to get away from her.

"Is this cow yours, boy?" the man shouted.

"Yes!" Peter answered.

"Get her out of here! What's wrong with her?"

Mama Cow had forgotten about the man for a moment and was standing near the calf and licking it through the slats of the cart. She made strange noises in her throat, and the calf answered her. Her cries of alarm had been heard by other cows in the pasture, and when Peter looked over his shoulder, he saw all the cows running toward the road.

"Come on, Mister! Get out of here! The other cows are coming too! There could be trouble. Somebody could get killed!"

The other children who tended cows came running across the field too, trying to stop their cows or at least turn them away from the road. Ivan ran up to Peter and handed him some sticks. The two of them hit Mama Cow's bony rump and shouted at her to move away. She felt the sting but was too concerned about the calf to obey right away. The man scrambled out from under the cart and jumped into the seat. He whipped his horse into a gallop.

"Go on! Get out of here!" shouted Peter, waving the horse on. The cart rattled and bounced down the bumpy road and in a few minutes was out of sight.

Peter stood near Mama Cow and talked quietly to her to calm her down. He and Ivan looked at each other and shook their heads. The other cowherds chased back their own animals, and the two friends stood there thinking about what could have happened.

Peter decided to go home with Bura and Mama Cow. "I'll see you tomorrow, Ivan. At least I think I will."

Ivan looked at his friend and gave him an understanding pat on the shoulder. "Don't worry about it. Any cow could've started it."

Peter just stared at Ivan for a moment. He shook his head again and began to lead his cows home.

Chapter 31

Old Krupka

Autumn came. With all the field work and pasture duties, Peter didn't get to school as often as he wanted. He missed his favorite lessons in geography and the parts of history that didn't have to do with Poland because he could get to school only one or two days a week. Even then, Myhal, who was the man of the family now with Papa gone, scolded him for sneaking off to school instead of helping with the farmwork.

It was the first harvest without Papa. Peter wondered if he would ever begin to think of events as just events again and not always with the added thought of something without Papa. There had been Christmas without Papa, Easter without Papa, field work without Papa, and questions without Papa to answer them. Soon the first year without Papa would be over. Mama didn't cry so much anymore, but she had not begun to sing again either. Her eyes had lost their sparkle, and she always stood for a long time by his grave after church or whenever she passed the cemetery. The only real laughter and song in her life came from little Maryna, who was too young to understand the sadness.

Maryna was a joy to everyone. She was three and a half years old and very talkative. She liked to listen to stories Peter told her and seemed to prefer spending most of her time with him. He taught her songs and was amazed at how she could listen to his changing, cracking voice and then turn around and sing the words with the clear sound of a lark. Her singing was so sweet, Peter called her his "little bird." He loved it when she sang to him or kept him company with her chatter while he spent long hours in the barn mending harnesses or building things with wood. She was dark-haired and dark-eyed like Mama, and her little smile seemed to make the sun shine on cloudy days.

Myhal closed the main gate to the farmyard one warm autumn morning and heard Maryna laughing and playing with Pundyk. He stood and watched her clapping her hands and chasing the old dog around the yard. Just as he turned to secure the latch, old Krupka, one of the village wardens, came up to him.

"Was your little brother pasturing cows near the hayfields?"

The question replaced Myhal's smile with a frown. "I don't know. I was out all night tending the horses at night pasture. I just got back this minute. I really couldn't tell you where he is right now. Why, is something wrong?"

"Is something wrong? Ah! I'll say there is!" The man looked a little dazed. "Either I'm cursed or my eyes are seeing things that aren't there. I went on patrol near the hayfield this morning. First, I looked out and saw something in the distance." He paused and muttered, "It was a little foggy then, maybe an illusion." Krupka looked at Myhal and began to wave his arms. "Well, I looked and saw two cows. Something like yours. One was sort of dark, and the other was patchy. Then I blinked my eyes, and there's nothing there! I stood on a knoll," he sputtered, "and looked in the direction of the eastern fields and saw one cow running along the edge. Never saw anything like it! A cow running that fast! I started to run after her, and when I got over the crest of the hill, there was nothing there. Then I stood near Brozyo's field and looked and saw something moving across the main road. I hollered for whoever it was to stop, and when I crashed through the field and got to the road, nothing was there!"

Krupka started to mutter something unintelligible, and Myhal tried not to give even a hint of a smile. He suspected it probably was Peter. It sounded like some of the mischief he liked to make, especially mischief that would drive a warden crazy.

"I can tell you this," Myhal began in a serious tone. "When I saw my little brother yesterday, I told him to pasture the cows up in the far section of my western fields. You know the area, up near where I'll be living after I get married next month."

"Ah!" the dazed man nodded. "Yes, congratulations to you!" Talk of the wedding distracted Krupka for a moment. "Heard your banns in church. So you'll marry that dark-haired Anna from the other side of town. Nice Polish girl. I'm surprised you won't be living at home with your mama."

"I wish I could. Mama has been widowed—it'll be a year in a few weeks. I feel I should stay to help her, but you know my mama. She insists that we go ahead with the wedding. Anna's mother is quite old now and a widow too. Anna's the youngest and the last one at home, so we'll have more room there. We'll live on her mother's farm."

"Yes, smart thinking." But then Krupka's addled mind wandered back to the business of being a warden again. "Well, if you told your brother to go to pasture up near your section, then he couldn't have been on the other side of the village trespassing at the same time. You have a red cow, don't you? Maybe it was red, maybe black. I don't know. Once I looked and there were these two cows, and when I looked again, there was only one. I thought I'd finally caught the little devil and had him in my grasp, and then he vanished like the fog. Frankly, I don't know *what* I saw. Two cows, maybe three ..." Old Krupka's eyes glazed over again. He turned and absently waved to Myhal and headed down the road mumbling to himself. Myhal stood near the fence and watched the man wander off.

Petrush! he thought to himself. *You're up to your old tricks! You were just telling me how bored you were. You slippery little fish. So far they haven't caught you.* He had to smile in spite of the fact that he had to remind himself to scold Peter. He remembered that Papa had been aware of Peter's antics and would wince at the thought of what could happen if his son were caught. But the boy had a mind that never ceased its plotting, and he had the cunning and speed of a weasel. Somehow Peter always slithered through, unharmed.

Chapter 32

The School Inspector

In spite of some changes, life settled down again to a slower pace with the coming of winter. Myhal and his dark-haired Anna married and settled in her mother's house. Myhal still came to help Mama as much as he could, but Oleksa and Peter usually took care of all the heavy chores. Myhal's wife was a kind, sweet girl and was very good to Mama. Mama often said how lucky she was to have such a good daughter-in-law. It was rare indeed to have a mother-in-law and daughter-in-law who genuinely liked each other.

After the holidays, Peter was glad that he could concentrate on his winter tests at school. With harvest work done, he was able to go to school every day. The school building in Opaka had been closed, and classes were now held in Felzendorf, where most of the students were either Polish or German. Peter and Ivan felt outnumbered but tried to behave and fit into the school's routine. The teacher was a young Polish woman who was very high-strung and nervous. She favored the Polish children in the school and was especially strict and sometimes cruel to Peter and the other "Rusyns."

Peter's nationalism had blossomed with the political demonstration that he and Papa had attended, and it had never wavered. He was proud of who he was and held his ground, but he also knew enough not to cause a great deal of trouble and create problems for Mama. His years of outsmarting village wardens had taught him the fine art of walking a tightrope: of holding onto beliefs and yet not falling into the temptation of openly being hostile.

Chapter 32

He didn't like his new teacher, but soon decided he was there to learn his lessons and not to learn to like her. She used lectures as the main teaching tool. There were very few books, and she expected the students to hear the lessons and absorb them in that way. No one was allowed to take notes. Peter wanted to learn as much as possible but didn't trust his memory without the chance to study facts over and over again. He always chose to sit in the back row of the class. Inside the shelf below his desktop he kept an open notebook, and with the broken-off stub of a pencil concealed in his hand, he took notes. His right hand appeared only to rest on the shelf, while his left elbow was propped on the desktop, and his left hand supported his chin. He would stare intently at the teacher, hanging on her every word. He had to discipline himself not to look down to check his writing. Some notes were illegible, but usually he could read dates and key words when he got home.

More than once, Peter was caught taking notes and was punished. The teacher took away his broken pencil stub, ripped his precious notebook in two, and then hit his hands with her long, hard pointer stick. Afterward, he was sent to stand in the corner for half of the day. The first time it happened, Peter felt humiliated. He prayed he wouldn't start to cry, and somehow he didn't. He never stopped trying to take notes. It became a game to see how long he could get away with it until she caught him again. As time went by, getting caught was no longer a humiliation, but a victory. He proved to himself that the rules and punishment could not break his spirit. He desperately wanted to learn, and he studied his notes every night that he had them.

He studied all he could. He loved geography and nature studies. He had always loved history, but now it had become mainly Polish history. He studied it anyway. Papa had always told him to learn about all he could because he could never foresee what he would need to help him in life. So Peter studied Polish history too, even though he felt bitter about it.

Finally the day of the examination came. Peter's teacher was more jittery than usual. She always wore her hair in a tight bun at the nape of her neck, but that day her hair was wound so tight that her face looked stretched. She kept pacing, adjusting the books on her desk, and smoothing back her hair. Pan Inspector was late. She couldn't concentrate on any new lesson, so the students were copying lists of words from the blackboard.

Pan Inspector, the one Peter thought looked like a turtle, arrived. The children were required to call him by his formal title: Pan (Sir) Inspector. They were never allowed to address someone with his authority by his real name. When he opened the door to step inside, Peter's teacher jumped and immediately developed a twitch in her left eye.

"Good morning, Pan Inspector. Welcome to our school. My students are—"

"Yes, yes, Madame. I am certain everything is in order. I have other schools to visit today. I would like to begin."

The teacher tried to walk gracefully to the front of the room, but caught her foot on the corner of the front desk, tripped, and knocked three books off of the front table. The inspector knew what she was like from past visits. He frowned and pursed his thin lips, and then with an intense effort to be polite, he spoke.

"I think the students will perform very well on their own. Perhaps they will respond better to my questions if I can put them at ease. Why don't you go out in the morning sun for a short walk, and I will take care of the class myself?"

His words were not a gentle suggestion. They were an order.

"Yes, Pan Inspector," she said, choking. "It is very kind of you. It is a lovely day."

She stumbled into her coat and scarf and headed for the door. She turned, looked at the class with a pleading face, and flew out the door.

All of the students had been standing since he arrived, to show respect for their visitor. He walked up and down the aisles like a general reviewing his troops. Peter kept fighting his mental images of Pan Inspector's shaved head retreating into his shoulder blades. Then again, without his shell, how could the turtle do that? Peter tried to clear his thoughts. His imagination would get him into trouble, especially if he smiled or laughed. "The turtle" walked by and stared at Peter for a moment before turning to go up to the front of the room.

"All right, you may all sit down." He held one end of the pointer stick in his right hand and repeatedly tapped the other end of it in his left. He looked at all the students one by one. He mentally noted the ones he would question.

Peter saw the back of Ivan's head and noticed that his young friend's ears were very red. *Ivan is really nervous,* Peter thought and shared his fear. Peter clenched and unclenched his fists. The tension in the room was almost tangible. Pan Inspector spoke.

"We will begin now. The examination will be entirely oral this time."

He began to question some of the younger children who sat in the front of the room. Each student he pointed to and questioned stood solemnly, answered the question, and sat down again. Some stumbled over their answers; others were a little more confident. Ivan was given a question about rivers from a geography lesson, and he answered it carefully. When he sat down, his shoulders slumped from relief. After a few more minutes of general questions, the inspector paused. He looked at the back of the room, and Peter felt the sharp brown eyes drilling holes into him. Peter swallowed.

Pan Inspector was now ready to question one student in depth to see just how well Madame Teacher was doing her work. He always liked to pick someone in the back of the room. Most of the mischief makers and daydreamers sat in the back. That was a fact of life. And there was that sandy-haired, grey-eyed boy back there. The one with the strange look in his eyes. Was it defiance he saw there, or what was it?

"You!" he said, pointing to Peter.

"Yes, sir," Peter answered and stood up.

Peter was too occupied with watching the inspector to notice the sympathetic look Ivan threw him. Pan Inspector walked down the aisle and stood in front of Peter.

"What is your name?"

"Petro Fedyk."

The inspector sat down at Peter's place and told Peter to face him. Peter felt a chill. If Pan Inspector was sitting down, Peter was in for a long siege.

The inspector asked Peter long questions about geography and nature study. Finally after Peter had had time to respond fully to each, the inspector began to drill him on Polish history. Pan Inspector named certain men and asked Peter to explain what government positions they held. He asked dates of wars, changes in borders, and even some questions about church history—based on the Polish point of view, of course. Peter answered all the questions fully and knew the answers were correct. Correct thanks to those forbidden notes and all his study. Throughout the interrogation Peter's teacher peeked through the window, from time to time, to see what was going on. She looked worried. Finally the questioning stopped. Pan Inspector looked pleased. He smiled with his thin lips, and Peter was certain that if a turtle could smile, it would do it just that way. The inspector stood up and looked down at Peter.

"You are a fine son of Poland, young man. You've learned your lessons well."

"No, sir," Peter responded calmly.

The inspector's face clouded, and his jaw clenched. He didn't understand the boy's remark. It wasn't said with disrespect. It was said gently and calmly as if it were just another answer to a question.

"You have indeed learned your lessons well!" the inspector insisted firmly.

"Thank you, sir," Peter said.

"You are a fine son of Poland."

"No, sir," Peter said simply.

The inspector bristled. He couldn't interpret the boy's meaning. Then he recalled Peter's last name. He wondered if this response was defiance or simple-mindedness. No, not simple-mindedness, not with answers like the ones he had just heard.

"Ah, I see. You are a Rusyn." Pan Inspector spat out the last word as if it were dirty and waited for a reaction.

Peter flinched inside but did not let his face betray him. He looked at the inspector intently as if waiting for the next question, but none came. The man walked quickly up the aisle, picked up his coat, and left the school room.

Peter sat down and took a breath. Ivan turned around and gave him a bug-eyed look that asked him why he took such a chance, but Peter just smiled at him. The test was over.

Later that day when the class was dismissed, the teacher told Peter to stay behind because she wanted to speak to him.

Uh, oh. Peter thought. *Maybe Ivan was right. Maybe I shouldn't have said openly that I'm not a son of Poland. But I couldn't agree with the turtle either. Oh, well. I may be in trouble, but Papa would be proud.* As he walked up to the front of the room, he noticed that the teacher was smiling at him. She looked almost pleasant, even with her missing front tooth.

"You have made me very proud today. Pan Inspector was very impressed. He told me that I must be a very good teacher." She smiled and for once didn't seem so nervous.

Peter thought, *Yes, a good teacher to be able to instruct even a Rusyn so well,* but he only said, "Yes, Madame Teacher."

"You are a good pupil."

"Thank you."

"Here, I have something for you," she said and handed him a new notebook. "Here's a little reward for your good study habits."

"Thank you very much!" Peter said with a sincere smile. Notebooks were expensive, and the family had hardly any money to spend on them. "I will always try to do my best."

"Yes, I think you will! You may go now. Tell your Mama how well you did!"

"Yes, Madame Teacher," Peter said and left school. Ivan was waiting at a discreet distance and was dying of curiosity about why Peter had had to stay behind.

From then on Peter was one of her favorite pupils. He always did well on important examinations and was always rewarded with a new notebook—or pencils and even cigarettes when she had them!

Chapter 33

Shame

Peter wiped off his forehead and replaced his cap. It had been a long day in the fields, and he led the horses to their stalls. He was fourteen now, finished with village school, and considered old enough for the field work a man could do.

"You worked hard today," he said, praising the horses and patting their haunches. "Enjoy your suppers!"

He turned to hang up the harnesses and stopped. He looked at Pundyk's guard post near the door, and a sad little smile appeared on Peter's face. He said quietly, "I miss you, old fella. That wagging tail of yours and that long pink tongue that hung out when you panted and made you look like you were smiling from ear to ear." Peter wasn't ashamed of the tears in his eyes. "Mama says we have to get a new dog to replace you. No one could replace you." Peter finished hanging up the harnesses, and his thoughts went on. *I'm thankful you died in your sleep right there by the door. Some dogs crawl off to die alone and are never found. You stayed right here at your post till the end. Always loyal.* Peter wiped his eyes. *I can't think of a new dog yet, ol' boy. I just buried you a week ago.* Peter sighed out loud.

As he turned to leave the barn, he heard an echo to his sigh. He stopped and listened. This time he heard a muffled sob. The sound came from the loft. He silently climbed the ladder, and when his head cleared the floor of the loft, he saw Daria sitting in one corner with her hands covering her face. He went over to her and gently touched her shoulder.

Chapter 33

"Daria, what's wrong?"

She hadn't heard him approach, and his touch startled her. She looked up, and when she saw it was Peter, she quickly wiped her eyes and tried to smile. "Oh nothing, Petru." But her red eyes brimmed and overflowed. "Everything!" she sobbed.

Peter sat next to her and hugged her. "Tell me. Maybe I can help."

"No. No one can help me."

"What's wrong? Are you sick? Did you hurt yourself? Why are you up here all alone? Mama's in the house. Maybe I should go and get her …"

"No. Don't call her," Daria said weakly. "She already knows and can't do anything."

"Daria, I don't understand you. You're scaring me!"

"Oh, Petru. I did something terrible."

"You couldn't! You wouldn't know how!"

"Oh yes, I have. I've hurt the whole family."

"Daria, you don't know how to hurt anybody or anything. What do you mean?"

She stopped sobbing and looked at her brother. Her voice was shaky, and she had to whisper to get out the words. "I've brought shame on us all. Look at me, Petru."

Peter frowned and didn't understand. She stood up, and his eyes glanced at her body. She looked just fine. She was even putting on a little weight. But she wasn't plump. She said she'd brought shame to the family. He looked up at her red-rimmed eyes.

"Oh, Lord have mercy on us," Peter mumbled. "You mean …?"

She nodded and covered her face with her hands and sobbed again. "Yes, I'm beginning to show. Mrs. Pohanka saw me today and called me a horrible name."

"Old Mrs. Pohanka is an old biddy."

"But what she said is true."

"Did you tell Mama? That's right, you said she knew. She never said anything."

"Mama has known from the day I first suspected. She said everyone would know soon enough. She wanted to spare me as long as she could."

"Who did this to you?" Peter was getting angry. "Tell me!"

"I did it too. I was a fool," she sobbed. "It was Viktor Holkavich," she whispered.

"Viktor … That scum? He's lower than spit! Oh, Daria, he chases every skirt in the district! The only one he's in love with is himself. All the boys listen to his stories of his conquests. He tells everyone he'll marry them if … Don't tell me you believed him? Daria, he's a snake in the grass! No, that's too kind. Snakes at least have backbones. He's a worm." Peter's head was spinning. "Did you tell him?"

"Today," she said, crying.

"Well, when are you going to see Father Ivan? You show already—you'd better hurry!"

"Viktor said he won't marry me. He said he isn't sure he's the father. He called me a tramp and said it could be anyone's. Petrush, believe me, he was the only one. I'm not what he says. I'm getting older and don't want to be a spinster. I thought …"

"He said … ugh! I'll beat him to a pulp! Oleksa will help me!" Daria looked even more frightened. Peter choked back his anger. "I'm sorry, Daria. I know. I believe you. I know how you are. Oh, God!" He hugged her. "Was Mama angry?"

"Mama cried when I first told her. She could've sent me away or thrown me out, but she didn't. She hugged me and cried and said I was going to suffer because of this, but that I have my family and my family's love no matter what."

"She's right."

"He won't marry me, Petru."

"Maybe that's God's blessing."

"But there's the baby."

"What did Mama say?"

"She said to pray and think about one day at a time. She wants me to see Father Ivan."

"Mama's a smart woman."

"Petrush, I want to run away somewhere, but I don't know where to go."

"We can live through it. Viktor Holkavich is the one who should feel shame, but he'd need a backbone and conscience for that. Worms like him don't have either." Peter saw that insulting Holkavich was of no help to his sister, so he hugged her and said nothing more.

After supper he went to Ivan Soroka's house. As soon as the two were out beyond the village road and cutting across the fields, Peter told Ivan about Daria.

"No!" Ivan said in a raspy whisper. "Daria? Daria and that vermin? Viktor Holkavich is scum." He spat on the ground. "I'm ashamed that his family is Ukrainian."

"Don't worry, that is the only thing he has in common with us." Peter gagged. "I guess the best tree can bear wormy fruit."

"So now what's going to happen?"

"He won't marry her. He said he isn't sure the baby is his."

Ivan whistled through his teeth. "Sounds like him." Ivan kicked a clod of dirt and sent dust flying. "What will Daria do?"

"I don't know. Mama says to live today, and tomorrow will be here soon enough. Daria isn't alone. She's got all of us to help her."

"I'm sure of that."

"It's the rest of the village that she'll have to face. She's not the first one this has happened to, but there are some tongues in this village that can lash like a bullwhip if they want to. Daria has given them cause for gossip." Peter sighed. "Mrs. Pohanka stopped in the middle of the road today and pointed her bony finger at Daria and screamed that she was a tramp and other names Daria doesn't deserve!"

"Mrs. Pohanka thinks she's holier than the Blessed Virgin Mary, but my mama could tell you stories," Ivan said to try to comfort him. "In spite of what's happened, Daria doesn't deserve any of the names. My mama often says how sad it is that Daria never had a suitor like Natalia did. Daria deserves a good man like Stephan."

"Yeah, and she'll end up with that bastard, Holkavich!" Peter recovered some of his good humor. "I thought your mama always calls Stephan a devil and a tease."

"She does when he's nearby, but she always smiles a little when she says it. When he's not around, she tells Natalia to be a good wife because she got quite a catch."

Peter smiled. "I like your mama."

"My family will help Daria as much as they can. Be sure of it."

"I know," Peter said. He looked over the fields at the last stripes of color from the fading sunset. "She did this just to get a husband and have a family of her own. She loves children. When Natalia had her first baby, I could see the longing in Daria's eyes. She was so afraid of being a spinster. But he's such a rat!"

"Can we talk about some other things before we go back?" Ivan asked.

"Sure. I think I need that too."

"Old Ihor came over last night to talk to my papa. The latest news is that the Poles are trying to pass new laws about inheritance rights and the possession of land. You know what else? It's rumored that they may try to colonize this part of Halychyna."

"Colonize? This isn't empty land or the big prairie of America or Canada."

"Too big a percentage of the population is Ukrainian. They doubt our loyalty."

"Yeah, not enough 'loyal sons of Poland.' Where do they plan to put colonists?"

"Some big parcels of land will be divided and made available only to Poles from the west. None of our people have a chance at any. You know why?" Peter looked at Ivan, and Ivan continued. "Because we're subversives," he said with exaggerated solemnity.

Peter snickered. "The village hall closed because gathering there was 'subversive.'"

"I guess dancing and flirting with girls is dangerous to the government."

Peter shook his head. "Maybe the government has a few brains we didn't bargain for. You can't swear that we met there to stand around and praise the Polish eagle."

Ivan smiled. "They want us outnumbered. Then, when they're in the majority, they'll swallow us up. Wipe away all traces of us. We won't even be 'Rusyns' then."

"So what's new? We can't speak Ukrainian at school. Copies of Shevchenko's poetry have to be hidden. He's subversive too—we're in awfully good company."

"Next just watch," Ivan added. "They'll go after the churches. And you know what else? There's talk that soon they'll start to draft Ukrainian boys."

"Into *their* army? Maybe I should take back what I said about them having brains."

Their walk brought them over to the fields where gentle slopes were planted in rye.

"See my mama's field over there?" Peter asked. Ivan nodded. "That's where I buried Pundyk. There, near the far corner." Ivan just looked and said nothing. "I buried him deep enough that no plow will disturb his sleep, and yet not so deep that his spirit would have trouble getting out to chase bunnies."

"I can almost see him now."

"Yeah, he was loyal to his animals in the barn, but oh, he loved to roam sometimes and come up here to chase rabbits. He never caught one, but he had a good time."

"Do you still need a new pup? Our dog finally had her pups last night. Looks like Koval's Luka sired them. All of them are black as coal except for one that's the same color as Pundyk was. That little tan one is a male too."

"I want a black one—a female."

"Sure, Petru," Ivan said, looking at his friend in the fading light. "We'll pick out the blackest and friskiest one in the litter. Mama will be happy that you'll take one."

"I'll see you tomorrow after chores."

"Good, but tomorrow Mama wants us to stay at the house and visit with her. She's baking a poppy seed cake and wants us to have some. She says all we do is take walks."

"It's the only way it's safe to talk about politics."

"Yeah, but she says if we keep taking so many walks, we're going to wear down our feet, and we'll be too short to get the pick of the pretty girls in the district."

"Your mama should be the local matchmaker."

"Who said she isn't?" Ivan grinned.

The boys came to the village crossroads and parted ways.

"See you tomorrow," Peter said softly, and his thoughts turned to Daria once again.

"See you."

Chapter 34

Grey Morning

Autumn came, and Peter's walks with Ivan continued. There was a little more time now for walking and thinking. With winter coming, most of the crops had been harvested. The grain either was in storage or had been sold through Hershko, the grain dealer in the village. Most of the potatoes had been dug, and Peter told Oleksa that he would go to dig the remaining ones near the area called "Opshar" where the rye fields were. Oleksa promised to bring the wagon later to help load them and carry them home.

It was a dull, grey morning. The air was damp and chilly and seemed unfriendly. Peter scowled at the weather because it seemed to scowl at him. The whole world seemed bleak. The talk he had had with Ivan the night before, the notice that Oleksa had received from the army—everything depressed Peter. He looked at the fields. Ivan had said the rumor was out again that some of the great land estates would be parceled out soon, but only to Poles. The law had not yet been passed, but it would be eventually.

"That's all we need," Peter said to himself, scowling again. "There are enough people here already. Land is scarce, and they want to colonize with Poles from the west! Colonize! To increase the number of Poles!" His mood became blacker. "And Oleksa. Now he's received word that he'll be drafted into the army."

Oleksa shared some of Peter's political beliefs, and after a quiet curse that Mama would not hear, he told Peter some of his thoughts: "Maybe I should leave this place rather than serve this government of thieves."

Peter listened to him and mentally added a few descriptive terms of his own. Peter knew that he would never obey the draft willingly. *I'll never be a Polish soldier,* Peter vowed silently. As he neared the field, his mind raced. *God! This is all so stupid! Our land and freedom stolen, and they want us to fight for them too! Don't they know we'd just as soon shoot their officers as shoot what they think is the enemy?*

He stabbed the earth with the digging fork and loosened the potatoes. He tossed the good ones to one side and moved down the row. Each stab gave vent to his frustration, and each jab matched a muttered curse at the indecency of it all.

I have nothing to look forward to now, he thought. *I'm a misfit on my own land with no hope of opportunity. I can't go on to school unless I renounce who I am and pledge loyalty to the Poles. Oh, Papa! Why aren't you here now when I need to talk to you? What should I do? Since the war they've tried to blot out everything that's ours. Our churches are suspect because they're not Latin Rite. Being Greek Catholic is "radical." Crosses! Even our crosses they change because they say three-barred ones are Russian Orthodox! Why should that bother them? They call us Rusyns anyway. The word "Ukrainian" doesn't exist for them. We can't speak our language at public meetings anymore. Why should they fear our language? They say it's nothing more than the babblings of some barbarian scum. Schools are closed.* Peter was almost in tears. *Lviv is a Polish city now. The university is Polish now too. Ivan said that all Ukrainian studies have been dissolved. No more studies, no more culture, no language. Nothing! Blot it out. Erase it so that anyone who comes after us will have no idea that we ever existed. Colonize as if this were empty land and we weren't even here. The wolves are at our throats, killing our pride and our identity. They made promises in treaties that we'd have our rights, but then they turn around and treat us as if we're dirt. No. Less than dirt. They fought a war to get our soil. They wanted that. But to them we're nothing. We're creatures so low, we need no rights!*

He stabbed angrily at the soil and began to feel despair. *Papa, I need you now! I can't trouble Mama with this. I told her several times how I feel, and she started to cry each time. She's afraid I'll join the Underground. I don't want to give her pain or fear.*

His arms ached from digging, and amid his feverish thoughts, he realized he needed to rest a little. Peter leaned on the fork and looked off in the direction of the empty grain fields. Just at the horizon, partially blocked by the low rise in the land, he saw whiteness. Large masses of white both on the ground and in shimmering waves low in the grey sky.

"The storks! It must be time!"

He dropped the fork and ran far over to the edge of the field of white. Just two days ago, when he was last here, there was nothing but a barren field. Now it was alive and full of dozens—no, hundreds—of huge white birds. The black-tipped wings and red beaks and legs gave the field an incredible mixture of color that was brilliant in contrasts. The colors looked like one of Mama's embroidered icon towels. The birds milled around and made low grunting and hissing sounds that gave a feeling of foreboding and anticipation.

One or perhaps two of the birds sounded a loud clacking noise, and suddenly the drama began. The birds began to take flight, and the sound of the hundreds of wide, beating wings covered all the other sounds of this world. They rose higher and higher, swinging in wide circles to gain height. They rose in a steady clustered stream and slowly separated into casual groups. They whirled higher still and reached a height that made Peter light-headed just to watch them. While he watched, Peter's spirit rose with the birds in the sweeping circles toward the dizzy heights. He felt the power of the huge wings, felt them almost lift him, and he felt the earth drop away from him as he rose and flew. When they reached the heights they sought, they turned southward to fly to winter havens.

Then everything was so quiet that the stillness had a sound of its own. The whispering of the breeze in his ears seemed to be a lasting echo of the rushing sound of the wings. Peter couldn't remember how long he'd been standing there. He was lost in the awesomeness of what he had just seen, and for an instant he was surprised to find that he, indeed, had not flown with them.

He suddenly came back to reality and looked around. The field was empty except for a few, distant, forlorn spots of white. Those would be the old ones left behind. Too old for the journey. Those who would stay behind either to die with the cold of winter or to be the prey of a fox or wolf.

"That's it!" Peter said aloud. His eyes widened at the abruptness of the idea. *That's it!* he thought. *I'll leave too. I won't be left for the wolves or the freezing of my soul. I'll fly too and face whatever I must. Then I can be free!*

The thought was implanted, and the commitment made. Peter would no longer be a prisoner in a forbidding land. He'd shed the boundaries as readily as those majestic birds, and he would fly to his freedom and a home where he could be who he was.

Oleksa arrived with the wagon. The fork was lying on the ground, and almost two long rows of potatoes were dug, but where was Peter? He stood up on the wagon and shouted. Off in the distance he saw the figure of his brother silhouetted against the sky.

"Off daydreaming again!"

Oleksa shouted again and waved his arms. This time the figure turned and began to run to the wagon. Peter was taller than Oleksa and quite thin. His jacket was unbuttoned, and it flapped around him as he ran. Oleksa watched him and thought, *He looks like a big, gawky bird about to take flight.* He smiled at the picture his words painted.

"Bird-watching, eh, brother?" Oleksa said as Peter came nearer.

Peter smiled and shrugged his shoulders. "They were leaving for Italy. The storks, I mean. I wanted to wish them God's speed!"

"You've always had a soft spot for wildlife, Petru. Too bad that spot is in your head." Oleksa had noticed that Peter was almost five centimeters taller than he and decided that some teasing would keep "little brother" in his place.

Peter said nothing, smiled, and went back to dig potatoes. He worked quickly and steadily, but the vicious stabbing was no longer necessary. A decision had been made, and the need for curses was gone.

Chapter 35

Sisters

Daria endured long months of gossip and insults while she waited for her baby to be born. It was the usual practice of most villagers to ridicule and condemn a girl in her situation. It was also common for the girl's family to do the same. But Daria's family was only saddened for her. Maria was a religious woman. Some religious people are very self-righteous and love to lecture anyone whose sin is exposed. Instead, Maria showed Daria compassion and love and wept quietly while she watched her daughter suffer public ridicule. In spite of what she endured in the months before the birth, Daria was secretly happy. She already loved the new life she felt inside her, and it made her smile.

One evening in early autumn, Daria, Kashia, and Peter were walking home from a visit with their cousins. Daria suddenly felt ill and turned very pale. Kashia helped her to sit down near the front gate of a farm and sat next to her to support her with her arms.

"I'll get you a cup of water," Peter said and ran to the nearby farmhouse.

A woman came to the door of the house, and he asked her for a cup so that he could get Daria a drink from the well.

"You want water for *her?* the woman said insultingly. "Hmph! Is the result of her fun making her a little sickly?" Her shrill voice carried easily, so Daria and Kashia heard each word. "When you make your bed the way she did, you have to be willing to lie in it."

Daria sat quietly and shut her eyes. Kashia felt sorry for her and was angry at the woman. "What a witch she is!" Kashia muttered and hugged Daria.

Peter tried to remember his manners in spite of the fact that the woman had none. "A cup, please," he pleaded. "Remember what they say: 'Deny a pregnant woman any of her needs, and mice will devour your harvest.'" He smiled, shrugged his shoulders as if to apologize for having to quote such a wise old truism, and extended his hand for the cup.

The woman sighed and gave him a ladle. Peter thanked her so graciously that the woman was embarrassed. Daria had her drink, and then Peter and Kashia helped her home.

Daria's baby was born that winter. She named her son Marko. Maria and Kashia were there to help Mrs. Gont during the delivery of the child, and he was fat and healthy. Daria adored her little boy and vowed to face the world with an illegitimate child as bravely as possible.

Little Marko helped his mother with her new role in life. He was a handsome little fellow, and each time Peter looked at him, he had to grudgingly admit that the child's father was good-looking in spite of his ugly soul. Little Marko was also good-natured and soon won the affection of the villagers. Daria was happy that her son was treated kindly as he grew and was not made to pay for her mistake. In fact, the spite and insults of the people soon shifted to Viktor Holkavich. Daria, after all, was doing a good job as a mother to little Marko. The wrath of the villagers turned on the man who refused to do the honorable thing.

Viktor Holkavich finally acknowledged the boy to be his. His mother, a woman who possessed all the charm of a shrew, decided to convince her son to marry Daria. She had two lazy daughters who were having trouble finding husbands, and frankly she wanted some help around the house. Viktor finally gave in to the nagging of the neighbors and his mother and decided to marry Daria one afternoon when little Marko was two and a half years old.

Daria prepared for her wedding. She didn't have the romantic dreams that Natalia had had with Stephan, but Daria was happy that she would be a wife and be able to give her son his rightful name. She knew she would have to live with Viktor's family. Life there would not be easy, but Daria felt that if she did her best, things would be all right.

On the day of the wedding, everyone was dressed for the celebration. Little Marko even had new woolen pants and a linen shirt. His father carried him to church and held him during the marriage ceremony. Peter watched and tried to sort out his thoughts. He recalled Natalia's wedding with all the holy mystery and billowing incense. He had hoped for the same for Daria. He looked at Daria's face and saw her gentle smile. She looked at Marko with the quiet pride of a young mother. Viktor held the boy haughtily, as if to say, "Yes, he's mine. Didn't I make a fine son?" He held the boy like a banner—or was it a cross—to show the real reason why he stood in front of the priest that day.

The prayers Peter offered up in church that day intertwined with those of his mother, his brothers, and his two little sisters. Before they left for church, Kashia stood and waited with Peter and Maryna for the procession to begin. She hugged Peter and whispered, "I'm going to pray with my whole heart that Daria will have the strength to put up with her new life and somehow be happy." He and his sister shared sad smiles, and he nodded.

It wasn't long after the wedding and after Daria had moved to the Holkavich household that little Marko started to appear on Maria's doorstep. Her house was the only home he had ever known in the two and a half years of his life. Now, not only was the Holkavich house a strange building, but life there was very different as well. Viktor's mother and sisters found fault with everything Daria did. Viktor either said nothing or sided against her. Marko wasn't used to all the fighting and would become frightened and run home to his grandmother and his other family. Peter wanted to let the boy stay, but his mother always told Marko that he had to go to live with his own mama and papa. She also told him to help his mother as much as he could. He went home crying, but his grandmother's advice stayed with him. He tried very hard to comfort his mother and to be a good boy.

Sisters

One day a few months after the wedding, Peter was hoeing in the late afternoon sun when he saw Daria running over the fields toward him. He waved to her and began to walk to her. Even from a distance she seemed upset. He felt his stomach tighten. Something was wrong. He ran back, got his hoe, and then ran to meet his sister.

"If that rat beat her, I'll …" he mumbled. Something was very wrong. *Why is she running to me now in the afternoon? Old Viktor usually waits till he's good and drunk in the middle of the night before he decides to have one of his tantrums.*

Daria neared, and he saw her face was red and streaked with tears. She was crying and wringing her hands. "Petru, come now! It's Maryna! She was in the barn." She gasped for air. "Kashia heard a scream and ran to find Maryna on the floor behind Old Grey. The horse kicked her in the forehead. They can't get her to wake up!"

Peter broke into a run and left Daria behind. His mind raced too. *Old Grey. A strong, sensible horse. The only one with enough sense to keep control of the wagon even in mud. But she's a twitchy, ticklish thing sometimes. I was afraid that someday she might hurt someone. But why Maryna? My little bird.* He could see her playing in the barn and remembered her singing in her high sweet voice. *God, how I love to hear her sing.*

He ran all the way to the house, and when he came inside, he saw her lying on the bed. Mama and Kashia were bending over her. The little girl's forehead was deeply gashed and bruised. Mama had cleansed the wound and was just beginning to bandage it.

"Mama, what can we do?"

His mother's voice was hollow and weary. "Only wait and pray."

Mrs. Gont came with a pan of some herbal solution and handed wet cloths to Maria. "Here, bathe her head with this before you bandage. It soothes," she said.

Peter hugged Kashia, who cried silently. "Has someone called the doctor?" Peter asked. The only doctor in the area was the one who treated both farm animals and people.

"He said that only time will show what will be," Mrs. Gont said sadly.

It was a few days before Maryna regained consciousness. She was very weak. Finally, she began to grow stronger, and her wound began to heal on the surface. After a few weeks, she could sit up in bed and talk, but Peter's little bird never again fluttered around the room helping Mama and Kashia. Her beautiful, sweet singing came back, but she was never able to walk again.

Chapter 36

Argentina, 1927

"Petru, I tried everything I could think of to get a deferment. It didn't work. You have to try to get one for yourself. They'll be sending you notice next spring when you turn eighteen, and you'll have to go in for basic training."

Peter and Oleksa were walking in from the fields. The boys were taking care of the harvest by themselves because Mama had stayed at home to take care of Maryna. She was feeling better but still needed Mama at home.

"I know I want to try," Peter said. "I just don't think there's much hope. You'll have to go in if you're needed. They let Myhal off because he's the oldest, and he heads our farm with Mama and his wife's farm too. If they wouldn't give you a deferment, why do you think they'd give me one?"

"Maybe one son is all they want."

"I doubt that," Peter snickered.

"Try, Petru. There isn't enough land for all of us. Maybe they'd defer you if you started in a trade. Maybe you could go on to school. There has to be something. You know that being a farmer has no future for you. Mama told us about Papa's land. When they married, his older half-sister was a spinster. She kept telling him how much land Mama had and how he would have more than enough to work. He signed over his inheritance to his sister so that she'd have land to sell for income in her old age."

"Papa was kind."

Chapter 36

"Yeah, he didn't know he'd have sons to leave it to. Most of Mama's land goes to Myhal and Daria under Polish law. Mama said it bothered Papa to think what he'd done after we were born, but then it was too late."

"Maybe if he had been able to leave it to us, the Polish inheritance laws would have fouled it up anyway. Besides, Papa gave us other things," Peter said, defending him.

"Well, I've been thinking about learning a trade. The village cobbler said he'd take me on as an apprentice. Since the last war, he's had all the boot-making work for this region—especially since that old traveling cobbler died. Remember him?"

"I haven't thought about him in a long time," Peter said, remembering years past. There had been a Jewish man who came to the village once a year with his son. The son had a deformity—what people in future years would call a cleft palate. He couldn't talk clearly, but he was always happy to show Peter how quickly he could cut and shape leather for boots. Peter could watch the whole process because the cobbler and his son would stay at the house of the people who hired their work. They stayed sometimes for as long as a week, sleeping in the barn and getting meals from Mama, while they fitted and measured the family for shoes and boots. Oleksa broke into Peter's thoughts.

"Your only real hope is to marry a wealthy girl." Oleksa's tone was serious, but his eyes teased his younger brother.

"Don't talk like an idiot. The ones who have land and would marry a village boy like me are either fat or ugly or both. Besides, I don't want an arranged marriage. I'll find my own wife when I decide I want one. I haven't got time to chase girls."

"Come on now, Petru. You must've noticed the girls around here. You want to be an old bachelor?"

"Would that be so terrible? Papa took his time. He was in no hurry to be married. And look, he found Mama," Peter said with pride. Then he chuckled. "You're the one who has his eye on someone. Your Anya? As for me, I have other things on my mind."

"Like what?"

"Well, you said yourself that there isn't enough land for all of us. I've been thinking about leaving. I've been thinking about it for a long time. Until now, I saw no way of getting out. Now there is one. Have you heard about what Voytko Kucharski is doing in Lubachiv?

"Voytko? What about him? Last I heard, his mother was trying to find him a bride."

"He's organizing a group of young people to go to Argentina."

"Argentina?"

"To be farm laborers."

"Argentina?"

"Yes, remember what little geography you learned? Argentina. Has a nice sound … Ar-gen-tina. Remember? In school we learned that some of the land there is like the steppes in Ukraine. It must be beautiful." Peter's tone became wistful.

"Voytko's older than you. Does he want a puppy like you tagging along?"

"Watch who you're calling a puppy!" Peter punched Oleksa in the arm. "He's not much older than you are!"

"Then I know exactly how he feels," Oleksa laughed.

"I'm going to sign up with Voytko and then try for a deferment."

"First you have to wait until winter when you get your fancy invitation to join the army."

Chapter 37

The Straw Wedding

After Sunday liturgy, the villagers mingled in the churchyard. Autumn was at its richest, and the leaves on the beech trees in the cemetery were a golden yellow. The whole village was transformed by the fall color, but Peter and Ivan Soroka had other things on their minds.

"Come over to my house tonight after chores," Ivan told Peter. "You know Janush has been drafted. He leaves for training at the end of next week. We have to make plans."

"Can he come over tonight too?" Peter asked, searching the crowd for him. Janush had been in church that morning.

"I saw him a few minutes ago, but he had to leave with his father to take care of something at home. He'll come tonight. He wouldn't miss it."

The two boys laughed softly and knew the plans they would make would be pure mischief. Whenever a young man left for the army in peacetime, it was almost a matter of tradition that he and some of his more fortunate friends would indulge themselves in a few harmless pranks in the village. Perhaps it was a way of releasing some of the draftee's frustrations at being taken away from his happy life. Or perhaps it was a farewell signature—something to remember him by until he came home again. In truth, it probably was a glorious excuse just to get into trouble and blame it on someone who had left town and couldn't be punished in the near future.

The usual pranks were innocent enough. Real vandalism

wasn't tolerated. Innocent as the acts were, however, they were always performed in the middle of the night under the protection of darkness. One favorite trick was to steal a farmer's long front gate, carry it all the way to the other end of the village, exchange it for the front gate of another farmer, and then carry the second gate back to the first farm and hook it to the hinges there. It didn't seem to matter that the pranksters ended up doing an awful lot of hard work. Farmers awoke to find a few gates rearranged, there would be some good-natured cursing to clear the morning air, gates were carted back and forth, and life would continue.

After a while some more creative mischief makers tried to vary the methods used. Instead of exchanging gates, more inventive young men disconnected and transported a few of them to the railroad tracks at midnight. When the one o'clock freight came by and began to slow down as it approached Lubachiv, the gates were flung onto a passing flatcar for a ride to the city. At dawn, word would come that several long gates were awaiting their owners at the rail yard.

When the boys met that evening, they wanted to come up with something unusual.

"Janush, we'll plan something you'll be remembered for," Ivan promised.

Janush looked a little sheepish. "My papa told me not to send anything to Lubachiv by train. My uncle lost his gate like that, wasted a whole morning going to find it, and then broke an axle on the wagon coming home. Papa said if I'm responsible for anything like that, he'll come to army camp after me to teach me the error of my ways." Janush smiled but was genuinely afraid. His father was not a big man, but he was built like a bull with powerful shoulders. He had some of the best-behaved sons in the village.

"We won't do anything like that," Ivan said confidently, even though he had no idea of what they were going to do.

Peter smiled. "That nonsense with the gates is common mischief. We'll be truly creative." He had been hatching ideas for weeks. He looked at Janush. "Who should the victim be?"

Janush paused a moment. There was someone he would love

to bother. He'd had his eye on a young village girl named Irena Koval. Her father was pleasant enough but made it understood that Janush wasn't wealthy enough for his daughters. Then, too, those were still troubled times. The Kovals were Ukrainians, and Janush was considered Polish. Janush went to church every Sunday in the village church, knew all of the songs and responses to the entire Ukrainian liturgy by heart, and even sang in the choir. He also spoke perfect Ukrainian, which he'd learned from his grandmother. Peter told Janush more than once that Janush was a much a Pole as Peter was. Peter considered that a great compliment and one he didn't give often. Janush appreciated Peter's feelings and wished that Irena's father felt the same way.

"Well, who is it?" Ivan asked.

"Mr. Koval."

Peter and Ivan smiled at each other. They knew all about Irena and their lovesick friend.

"I hear they're planning a wedding soon," Ivan teased.

Janush's face turned bright red. He hadn't heard anything. He hoped it wasn't Irena.

Ivan saw the effect of his words and went on. "My mama was saying at supper that Irena's older sister is going to marry a young fellow from Lubachiv. The wedding will be in about a month."

"I won't be here." Janush frowned. "I'll miss the party and all the food."

"And the chance to flirt with Irena in public," Ivan grinned.

Janush reddened even more.

"All right, Mr. Koval is our target." Peter stared at Janush. "And because you'll miss the real wedding, we'll put on one of our own."

"What do you mean?"

"We can take some straw and twine and make small haystack figures. Nothing fancy—just figures that can be set in a wagon like a whole wedding party going to church. We can even decorate them a little for appropriate people. Like stick a pipe in the face of the one who represents Mr. Koval."

"Hey, we can even have a bride!" Ivan added. "Mama has some ribbons that are left over from a wreath she made, and we can thread them into the straw of the bride figure."

"No, just use paper ribbons. The dew might ruin the real ones," Peter offered.

"Yeah, and Mama would have a fit," Ivan agreed.

"Take an old scarf for the head of the bride's mother and an old jacket or something for her brother," Janush suggested.

"That would be easy enough."

"Where are we going to do all this?" Janush asked.

"Why not in one of Koval's own wagons?" Ivan laughed.

"Good idea," Janush smiled. "But let's try to use the smaller one, especially if we have to pull it far. Maybe we should do this right in his own barnyard."

The boys stared at each other and then laughed and slapped one another on the back. If they could do it right under old Koval's nose, it would be spectacular! *If* they could do it.

"What about their dog?" Ivan asked. "He yips at his own shadow."

"You mean Luka?" Janush smiled. "He shouldn't be a problem. Even if he was, my papa is going to help my Uncle Vytol butcher a cow next week. Maybe I can get some bones, and we can bribe Luka to be quiet."

"Not a bad idea," Peter said, nodding. "See if you can get a few extras for the neighbors' dogs on each side."

"What about the straw for the figures? Where do we bring that from?" Janush asked.

"Mr. Koval's barn?" Ivan suggested.

The three faces broke into evil grins, and they all cackled like old witches concocting some wild brew.

"If we get away with this, the whole village will talk about it for months."

"For years!"

"We'll be legends," Ivan said dreamily.

"Let's not get carried away," Peter cautioned.

"Too bad we don't know if the family plans to be away some evening next week."

"That wouldn't be any good. They might use the smaller wagon."

Chapter 37

"You're right. We'll have to do it with all of them at home and asleep."

"Too bad we can't slip them all some brandy so they'd sleep more soundly. It would help me breathe easier," Janush muttered.

"Listen, Janush," Ivan said seriously. "With what we're planning, you can't breathe anyway. It'd make too much noise."

All three boys laughed nervously.

"Let's go for a walk past the Koval farmyard on the back road and take a look at what we have to do," Ivan suggested.

"Good idea," Peter said. "We'll plot our strategy right there."

The three of them walked casually down the lane that ran along the back of many of the village farmyards. The property was laid out like almost all the others in the village. The house was at the far end of the long rectangular piece of land, near the village road. The boys stood by the gate at the other end. That gate opened to let out the farm wagons on their way to the fields beyond the village. Scattered between the back gate and the house were two barns, a chicken coop, the outhouse, storage buildings, and the well.

"Let's hope no one has to use the outhouse in the middle of the night. It could ruin our plan if we're seen," Janush said.

"Not to mention how seeing us would scare the unfortunate soul. Might never make it to the outhouse in time!" Peter chuckled softly.

"Shh! Here he comes. Hi, Luka. Hi boy! Nice dog!" Janush whispered.

The dog barked once but then recognized Janush and quieted down.

"Oh, that's good! He knows you," Ivan said approvingly. "With a few bones to help that along, he shouldn't give us any trouble."

They looked at the two farm wagons sitting in the yard.

"We will use the smaller one."

"What if it isn't in the right place that night? We'll have to move it."

"Then we will definitely use the smaller one."

"I'll bring some grease," Janush offered. "We don't want any squeaky wheels."

Above their heads an owl sounded in the enormous oak tree.

"Too bad that big old tree isn't between us and the house. It could shield us a little and maybe even muffle some noise," Ivan murmured.

Peter looked up at the ancient oak with its thick spreading boughs and said simply, "Yeah, too bad."

They leaned on the fence in the dark and looked at the yard.

"What phase of the moon will it be at the end of next week?"

"Almost a full moon."

"Oh wonderful. We may as well do it in broad daylight," Ivan said sarcastically.

"Pray for clouds," Peter muttered. He stopped a moment. "Janush, do you have any long lengths of heavy rope? Any kind of rope at all?"

"I think so. I'm not sure if it's at our farm or at Uncle Vytol's."

"Good," Peter whispered. "Let's go back to Ivan's and make our plans."

The three went back to the house and plotted for another two hours. For the next week and a half they slyly studied Koval's farmyard whenever they passed it either on foot or in their farm wagons heading out to the fields.

The big night finally came, and all the planning was worth the trouble. The dogs quietly enjoyed their bones, greased wheels and pulleys moved noiselessly, and even the moon and clouds cooperated. The meter-tall, cone-shaped straw figures took shape and were arranged in the wagon. The figure holding the reins had a pipe stuck in it where a face would be, and Janush added some grass blackened with soot for a moustache. That figure was definitely Mr. Koval.

When they were done, the boys surveyed their masterpiece and almost forgot the need for silence while they admired everything.

"They won't believe it!" Janush chuckled.

They all wanted to laugh out loud but only shook hands and disappeared into the black night, each finding his own way home.

Chapter 37

The next morning Mr. Koval arose before dawn and went out to the barn to do the milking. As he walked back to the house, he glanced over the fence toward his neighbor's yard and saw Myhal Mlodjinski, Peter's brother, coming in from his milking chores.

"Nice morning, isn't it, Myhal?"

"Yes it is! A good day for bringing in crops. Which field will you work today?"

"Thought I'd go out to my north field. I'll hitch up the small wagon and head out to dig potatoes." When Koval mentioned his wagon, he pointed over his shoulder to where he had left it the night before.

Myhal looked at him and beyond his shoulder and asked, "Where is your wagon?"

"It's right there!" Koval said, turning. It wasn't.

His eyes ran the length of his farmyard, and then his mouth dropped open. He set down his bucket and rubbed his eyes. There was his wagon. The straw figures of the mock wedding party sat there quietly. There was even a bride with paper ribbons on her head, and as he walked closer, he saw that the driver of the wagon had a pipe and a black moustache. It was all very cleverly done. The crowning touch to the entire spectacle was the incredible fact that the entire wagon, complete with passengers, was perched five meters above his head, on two broad boughs of his stately oak tree.

Chapter 38

Fortunes and Fate

After the Christmas holidays passed, both Peter and Oleksa talked to Mama about the need for a deferment for Peter. She was more than happy to try to petition for it, but the reason made her very sad.

"Argentina is on the other side of the world," she said with tears in her eyes.

"Mama," Oleksa said softly. "You know how Petru feels about the government. He'd never make a good soldier. This may be a way out."

She looked at Peter. After a moment she said simply, "I'll go see a woman I know."

The woman was the wife of a draft board official. They lived in Lubachiv, but his office was in Jaroslava, thirty kilometers away. When Maria went to see the woman, she took two prize chickens, some fresh eggs, and other gifts, or bribes, depending on your point of view. The woman was sympathetic because she knew Maria had bargained twice before. Her request for Myhal's deferment had been granted, but Oleksa's had been denied.

After a month went by with no news, Maria went back to the woman, who reported that Peter's chances for a deferment appeared to be good. Her husband was due to come home at the end of the week. He was expected to bring the necessary papers at that time. Peter waited anxiously for that Friday to arrive, and when it did, the papers were waiting for him.

Chapter 38

"Mama!" Peter cried when she brought the documents home. "You did it! I have the deferment! Now I can go!" Peter was laughing and dancing around the house. "It wasn't that hard! It wasn't impossible! It all went so smoothly! I'm so lucky! Thank you!"

Maria smiled when he hugged her and thanked her, but her smile faded quickly. She thought of how hard it really had been to apply for that deferment, how very hard for her, but all she said was, "We'll go to town again on market day, Petru. We'll see what arrangements you can make with Kucharski then."

On market day Maria and Peter walked on the side of the main road that ran to Opaka from Lubachiv. They had been to the city and were returning with their packages. Peter carried most of the parcels, but his biggest burden rested on his mind and in his heart. The news they had heard in town changed everything.

"What do I do now? You got me the deferment, and now what use is it?"

His mother walked in silence. Peter didn't know if she was sorry for him or glad about how events had changed. Finally she sighed deeply and decided to speak.

"Son, they're older than you are, and without Kucharski they don't want to go. Would you want to go by yourself?"

It was Peter's turn to be silent, but Maria knew that he would go if he could. *Yes, you'd go, Petrush, even if you went alone,* she thought. *How many times have we been through this? If I think about it too much, I cry all the time.* She looked at him and saw the determination on his young face. *My dear son,* she thought. *So like your papa. So determined. A dreamer. An idealist. And yet I know what it costs you. You dream your dreams, but you suffer for them because you worry about your duty to your family too. God forgive me, I know I'll cry rivers if you go, but I know in my heart it's right. You have no future here. Your dear papa ate himself up with worry and guilt when he realized he had nothing to leave you. What you'll inherit isn't enough to support a lame horse. Myhailo had such hopes for you. You were our little scholar. "Our little professor," he called you. For me, I'd sign a paper telling the Poles that they were all saints, just so you could go on to school. But you'd never do that. Too much of your papa's spirit in you. The only other route would be the Underground. God forbid!* She bit her lip. *Idealism is so expensive. Sometimes one pays with his life.* She looked at her son again as he walked beside her. *I want you near,* her thoughts continued. *But to love you the way you need to be loved, I must let you go. I must help you get out. I'll die a little when you do, but if I don't, either your spirit or you yourself might die.*

"Yes, Mama. Yes, I'd go alone if I could. But without a ship? It's too far to swim." His voice was heavy with frustration.

Maria was silent. An image flashed into her mind and cut into her heart like a knife. *So long ago I began to call you my little fish. Now you talk of going on the ocean and swimming so far away. It's a bitter thing that your sweet nickname was really a prophecy.*

As they neared Opaka, they approached the house of old Hershko, the Jewish grain dealer. Some Jewish merchants in Lubachiv had cheated Maria in transactions, and she had no trust in them. But Hershko was different. She respected him. He was always kind to the family and gave them good prices for their grain.

Hershko respected Maria too. He always thought of her as a strong woman, twice-widowed, who went on with her life and raised her children to be fair in their dealings with people. She was a small, slight woman, but strong. Very, very strong.

Hershko stood in his garden, enjoying the pleasant evening. The soft fragrance of his first spring flowers drifted on the breeze, and he savored it. He saw Maria and Peter nearing his property, and he nodded to them.

"Good day to you, Hershko, and how is everything with you?" Maria said.

"Nu, nu, everything is fine." He had a funny habit of starting sentences with "nu, nu." It somehow gave emphasis to what he said. "And what can you tell me that is good?"

"I want to thank you for the advice about getting those rabbits. They're a good source of meat for my family, and our little Maryna delights in watching them."

"How is the poor child?"

Chapter 38

"She does as well as she can. She can spend time either in bed or sitting in a big chair, so she has a little more variety now."

"I understand," Hershko said kindly. "And with the rabbits … Do you still have the same grey female you started with? She was very tame."

"Yes. It's hard for me to use her little ones for food. I find I can't eat rabbit meat."

"Somehow, Maria, I am not surprised. You are always very sympathetic toward your animals. That can be good and bad."

Maria smiled and was a little embarrassed.

"Nu! What else can you tell me that is new?"

"Well, today I have a problem."

Hershko came closer to the fence. He peered over the little round glasses that he wore and looked at her. "Nu, nu! That's not good. Let's see if we can find a solution."

She paused a moment. "You know, Hershko, I'm having some trouble with him," she said and tilted her head in Peter's direction.

"What kind of trouble?" he asked with a frown. "With the wardens? Police? Or does he want to get married?"

Maria laughed softly. "No, nothing like that. He's much too young for marriage."

"Nu, what then?"

"Go ahead, Petrush. You tell him."

"Some young people became organized with Voytko Kucharski to go to Argentina to be farmworkers. I wanted to go with them. Now, today, we found out that he changed his mind and decided not to go. Without him as a leader, everyone else has resigned. No one is going. I got my papers from the army for the deferment, and it's all for nothing."

Hershko listened to every word and then stepped closer to Peter while he slowly studied his face. The old man thought for a while and then carefully chose his words. "Listen to me. I'm an old Jew, and I know a good many things. If you want to leave home, then go to Canada. And soon!" He paused for a second and muttered as if to himself, "For soon it may be too late." He stared at Peter again. "As for Argentina, my young man, forget about it. It was a blessing those plans dissolved. It's too far, and that is not where the future lies. Go to Canada. Canada! I know someone who can inquire for you."

"Do you think I could get permission from the army to go to Canada?"

Hershko peered over his glasses again. His look was intense. "Listen to an old man who has seen a great deal. You have to try!" Hershko searched in his coat pocket for a pencil and then reached for one of their parcels wrapped in paper. He wrote down a name and address. "When you make your decision, this man will help you."

Maria looked at her son and then smiled at Hershko. "Thank you for your advice, Hershko. Good evening to you, and give my greeting to your kind wife."

"Thank you, thank you. Nu, nu, and you my young man," he said, shaking his finger at Peter like a wizened old schoolteacher, "Heed my advice."

Peter and his mother followed the road home. Maria kept her eyes fixed on something far ahead on the road. Finally she asked the question she had to ask.

"You're going to try for Canada, aren't you?"

Peter looked at her and said, "Mama, please go to that woman again and ask if perhaps it might be possible to get permission to go to Canada."

She looked at him and shook her head. "Oh, son, son."

Peter opened the wooden gate for his mother. They were home.

Ivan and Peter still met for walks. The two old friends trusted each other and shared their news and fears during the long walks when they were certain they weren't overheard.

"I miss being able to talk as much as we used to," Ivan said one Sunday afternoon when he and Peter stood on a rise near the Opshar.

"You've got two farms to work now. It isn't easy. How's your grandfather?"

"His hands are very bad. I've never seen them so swollen. Papa needs my help on the farm, but he sends me to my grandpa as much as he can. I'm going to start going there to stay for a week at a time instead of just a day or two. I wish his village wasn't so far. This wet weather has been hard on him, and he needs my help even more."

"I'm sorry. Send your grandparents my greetings, will you?"

"Sure!"

The boys were quiet for a while.

"You know Argentina fell through."

"Yes, I heard. Does that mean you'll stay now?"

Peter looked at his friend. "Oh, Ivan, how can I? I told you when I first got the idea to leave a couple of years ago." Ivan nodded. "I didn't know how I'd do it, but I knew I had to somehow. Argentina fell through, but the other day, Mama and I talked to Hershko. He told me to go to Canada. He gave me the name of a man to contact."

"You're going to do it, aren't you?"

"Yes."

Ivan's head dropped, and he kicked at the dirt clumps at his feet.

"Why don't you try too, Ivan? We could go to Canada together. We had a lot of adventures when we were little. Think of what an adventure Canada would be!"

"I thought you liked farming. You love your family. You have friends here. The church. Opaka. Can't you stay and be happy here? We can grumble all we want about politics when we're on our walks. Maybe we could even get into some mischief."

"No," Peter said quietly.

"I can't leave," Ivan said. "Sometimes I tell myself that it's because Grandpa and Papa need me, but really Bohdan could help them too. He and his wife aren't that far away. And there's Stephan. I guess I can't leave because I don't want to. I love the land. I hate the same things you do, but I guess I feel this is fate. What happened happened, and I have to live and make the best of it. Maybe by staying, I can make things better."

"I understand."

"Do you? Sometimes, I look at you, and I wish I could be like you. I wish I had your ideals and nationalism. I do feel those things, but not like you do."

"You don't have to," Peter said gently. "I'd love it if you could come to Canada too." He laughed softly. "Listen to me! I talk as if I had my papers already. I hope to go, but maybe I won't be able to. Maybe you'll have to teach me how to stay here. Ivan, you're my best friend. I won't tell you how to think or feel. Sometimes I wish I could be like you! I wish my love of this land and my family was enough to keep me. I look at Mama and Maryna, and a knife cuts into me. Maryna needs so much care now. Mama is getting older. I wish I only wanted to stay here and take care of them. In some ways I do and would do it gladly. But there's something in me that won't be still. My papa told me that we're all destined for something. We must go where God points, or we won't find peace in ourselves. Right now I think I'll never know what peace inside feels like. I feel like I'm reaching for something, but I don't know where to reach, or if it's even there."

Ivan sighed, and then looked at Peter. "Now it's time to say I understand. We've been friends since we were babies, Petru. We both wish we could be like each other, and yet we know we can only be ourselves."

Peter smiled sadly. "Sometimes I wish we didn't have to grow up. I wish life was like the party after Natalia's wedding. A time to stuff ourselves on good food and have fun!"

"Instead there's pain and suffering too. My mama still cries over Maryna's accident. What's it been, ten months now? And she cries over Daria too, when Viktor beats her."

"Your mama is a kind woman."

The boys started to walk back to the village.

"I have to leave this evening for my grandpa's farm. Because his hands are so bad right now, I'll be there for a couple of weeks. After that I'll try to get home every weekend."

"If I didn't know you better, I'd say you found yourself a pretty girl in your grandpa's village," Peter teased. When Ivan blushed, Peter laughed, "Oh, ho! You *have!* Well, good for you! Tell me all about her!"

The two friends walked slowly back to their homes, finally sharing happy news.

Chapter 39

The Test

Peter's head was filled with thoughts of Canada. He went to the village school and asked the teacher if he could look at a geography book. It was Saturday afternoon, and she was there cleaning out the classroom. He found a map of Canada and saw how large the country seemed. It looked as though it wrapped itself around half the earth. Below it was the United States of America. That too was large, but not as large as Canada. He read the description of the endless prairies and forests. He felt his heart pound as he read.

I wonder, he thought, *will Canada ever be a real place for me, or only a distant, foggy dream? It's so far away. Will I ever be there? Or will it be beyond my grasp?*

His finger traced the possible route he might take. The thin German atlas the teacher had given him had maps of northern Europe. He found the port of Danzig and followed the Baltic Sea to the North Sea, through the English Channel, and out to the Atlantic beyond.

What must the ocean be like? Water as far as one can see. What about monsters of the deep? He chuckled softly. *What of monsters around here? An even trade, I'll bet.*

His finger moved across the Atlantic, and then on another page he found again the dreamland called Canada. "Canada," he said softly. It had a beautiful sound. Almost like a prayer. Perhaps it was. He stood up and closed the atlas.

He thanked the teacher and left the school to head for the

crossroads and home. He looked at the fields, the distant forests, and the greening of the pasture along the river where the geese were. The white birds clustered on the banks and gracefully gliding on the water reminded him of clouds in a gentle wind. This was the only land he had ever known. A journey to Canada would not bring him back to Opaka the way the wandering during the war had done. It would be years, not weeks, before he might come back.

Evening was not far off, and as Peter neared his house, he heard the village church bells ringing. The palamar rang the bells to tell the villagers there would be a liturgy the next day. Peter saw his mother sitting on the long bench near the side of the house. Smoke, the tame grey mother rabbit, was in her lap, and Mama stroked the soft fur on the animal's back. Maryna was in a chair nearby and called to Peter when she saw him. Mama smiled at him when he bent to kiss her cheek, and then he turned to his littlest sister.

"It's such a beautiful day, Maryna. I thought I'd hear you singing with the birds."

"Oh, Petrush," she began. "Mrs. Gont has a wild bird of her own! A goldfinch! The little thing flew into the window a few days ago and was stunned. She caught it and put it in a cage. The bird began to sing today. It sounds so beautiful! She feeds it millet and seeds from wild grasses. I could never sing as prettily as that finch. You should see the colors it sports! Brown and orange and black and yellow and white too! I thought they were pretty in the trees, but up close the one she has is beautiful!"

Peter listened to his sister chatter while he washed at the well.

"Supper will be ready soon," Mama said as she stood up and turned to go in.

After he finished, he went over to Maryna. "Are you ready to go in the house?"

"Please, can we wait till the geese come home? I like to watch them all marching down the road together and see each little group go into their yards. They make me think of little fluffy angels out on patrol."

Peter smiled at the images she painted with her words and sat to wait with her. Soon the birds appeared. The village geese no longer needed anyone to tend to them. Each morning at some secret time they knew, they all filed out of the many farmyards and met in a long stream of white that moved down the road toward the pasture near the bend of the river. Each evening the entire flock came back together, and it was fun to watch how tiny groups would break off and go into their own yards as each farm was approached. They were intelligent birds. They never made a mistake and went to the wrong farm.

After their geese were home, Peter lifted his sister up in his arms. "You were talking about how nicely Mrs. Gont's wild finch sings. It could never sing my favorite songs for me the way you can."

She wrapped her thin arms around his neck and hugged him as he carried her.

"Mmmm," Peter hummed approvingly as he entered the house. "I knew we were going to have something delicious. I could smell frying onions." Peter put Maryna on the big bed and helped her arrange her pillow so she could sit up.

Kashia turned from the stove. Her pretty face was pink from the steam from the big pot she'd been tending, and she laughed. "Varenyky tonight! Maryna and I helped Mama to make them while you went to see Pan Hershko."

Mama looked at Peter when Hershko was mentioned but was afraid to ask anything.

"Well, Mama, I found that I have to go to Lubachiv tomorrow after church. I'll meet the man Hershko suggested."

"On Sunday?" Mama asked.

"The man is a Jew and wanted no appointments today."

"Oleksa and I will go with you."

The next day the three of them went to meet the agent who arranged all papers for passage to Canada. He took all the information that he needed from Peter and sent it on to Peremyshyl, to the Canadian Pacific Steamship Company office.

"I can tell you no more than this right now," the man told Peter. "You'll have to face an examination board in a few weeks. You'll receive word soon as to the exact date. The examination will be here in Lubachiv."

The Test

"Examination?" Mama asked.

"Yes," the agent answered. "Canada wants only strong and intelligent laborers. Before your son can go, he'll have to pass some tests."

Four long weeks went by before Peter received notice that the special agents were coming to Lubachiv to interview all applicants interested in becoming farm laborers in Canada. A list was enclosed of the names of young people from villages and towns all around Lubachiv who wished to be considered. Eight of the young people were from Opaka. One of them was Eva Zuravel, Peter's cousin. Mama said that Evcha's parents did not approve of her wanting to apply. Aunt Pashia was against it. But Eva's name was on the list, so they must have granted their permission.

The day came for the examination. Peter went alone to the office in Lubachiv. There were at least thirty young men and women already there. Some had come with their fathers, who wanted to see just what kind of organization this Canadian Pacific was. Uncle Stepko was there with Eva. Peter spoke to them briefly and then went to read the notice board outside the main door. The white paper tacked to the board explained that applicants would be called according to their respective districts. All morning Peter watched as one by one the young people went into the building to be interviewed.

Finally, at 11:30 in the morning, a man stepped out of the building and announced that applicants from Felzendorf were next. Four young men about Peter's age stepped out from the crowd to show that they were present. Peter recognized two of them from the years he had gone to school in Felzendorf. The first name was called, and one of them went into the building. After two of the applicants from Felzendorf were finished, the same spokesman stepped outside to speak to the crowd.

"Attention, everyone! Attention! The examining board will now take some time for lunch. In one hour we will resume conducting the interviews."

Most of the people walked to the main street to get something to eat at one of the inns or restaurants there. When the crowd thinned out, Peter decided to stay around the building. He had very little money and had been so nervous when he left home that he had forgotten to bring anything to eat. He looked at the notice again and walked casually around the corner of the building because he was tired of standing in one place. Pacing gave him something to do. The hour seemed like it would never end. The clock on one of the government buildings kept time, but Peter looked at it so often, the hands never seemed to move. He was certain it was broken.

"Nothing that has anything to do with this government works properly," he muttered to himself. *Oh,* he thought, *how I want to be rid of this government!* Then he remembered the test and became nervous again.

He saw that he was near the window on the side of the building where the examinations were being held. There were two men in what looked like the examining room. One man was Uncle Stepko, and the other was one of the officials. Peter moved a little closer to the window. A tree grew there next to the building, and he felt that he could casually lean against it and appear to stare off into space while he caught what was going on inside from the corner of his eye. The men talked and took no notice of him. They both gestured a great deal, but Peter couldn't hear what they were saying, so he wasn't certain what was discussed. After a few moments, they walked over to a long table near the window. The official began to look through a stack of papers and finally pulled some out from the bottom of the pile. He made notations on them and replaced them almost on the top of the stack. The men continued to talk and left the room.

Peter frowned. *What was that was all about? Maybe Uncle wants special consideration for Eva.* He stood quietly staring at the pile of papers. *I wish I had someone shuffling papers in my favor right now.* His stomach growled. He looked down at it and slapped it with his hand. *Nervous or not, I better get something to eat,* he thought. *I want only my mouth to answer the official's questions today.*

Peter bought a hard roll with butter and a cup of tea for his lunch. Finally it was one o'clock. He headed back to the building. The last two applicants from Felzendorf were called first. Then after what seemed to be forever, the official stepped out.

"From the village of Opaka ... Eva Zuravel!"

The Test

Eva walked in briskly and closed the door. Peter watched her walk in. *Evcha will be picked to go, for sure,* he thought. He clenched and unclenched his fists. He was so nervous he could hardly stand it. He began to intertwine his thoughts with a prayer. *Oh please! Mama says what is meant to be will be. Please let this escape be meant for me. Please! Make my thoughts clear and guide me through this test!*

"Petro Fedyk!"

Peter heard his name and walked toward the door. He took a deep breath and walked into the examining room.

Three men sat at the main table with their backs to the big window. As Peter faced them, he noticed that the face of the man on the left was set in a permanent scowl. He was fat and greying and looked bored. The man in the center was younger and more trim. He hardly looked at Peter at all when he came into the room and seemed more interested in the forms in front of him on the table. The man on the right had a tanned, craggy face. His features were rough-hewn and weathered like someone who worked outdoors, but he looked comfortable in a business suit. He did most of the talking. Peter looked around, but there was no chair to sit on. He was expected to stand.

Because this was an official event, everything was to be conducted in Polish. As a matter of principle, Peter never used the language unless he absolutely had to. Now he was glad that he had learned it well while he was in school. It would not have been good for him, a "Rusyn," to speak the language of his official "mother country" poorly.

Anything, Peter thought. *I'll put up with anything—just let me do well.*

The two men on the left were busily writing while the third man began the interview. He also took notes, but not as many.

"You are Petro Fedyk?" he asked in Polish.

"Yes, sir," Peter answered politely.

"Do you know how to work on a farm?"

"Yes, I've lived and worked on a farm all my life."

"Do you know how to plow?"

Chapter 39

"Yes."

"Do you know how to sow?"

"Yes, but not too well yet."

"What do you mean?" the man snapped.

"It takes great skill to be able to scatter seed evenly throughout the field. I do much better now than when I was younger, but I still don't possess the skill at sowing that my father had. He could sow a field so evenly that the crop—"

"Fine, fine." The man smiled. He didn't look so stern anymore. "How deep do you make furrows in the fields?"

"It depends on the time of the season and the soil. We plow sometimes twice a year in the same field."

"Yes, but how deeply?" he asked and shot a look to the other men.

Peter saw it and knew his nervousness was making him talk too much. *Answer only what they ask,* he told himself. He looked at the craggy-faced man. "We plow from five to twenty centimeters."

"What kind of work will you do in Canada?" the official on the left asked.

"Farmwork. I want to do farmwork in Canada."

"How old are you?"

"Eighteen years old."

"Do you know how to read and write?"

"Yes."

The official on the right opened a large book and pushed it across the table toward Peter. "Read here," he said, pointing at the beginning of a paragraph.

Peter stepped forward and lifted the book. He tried to concentrate and was relieved to find that he could read it easily. It was a geography book. He read aloud about the types of soils around the region where he lived. Peter finished the page and was about to turn it to continue. The official stopped him.

"That's enough. Do you understand what you just read?"

"Yes."

"And what does it mean?"

"It was about the soil. The color and texture of it."

"Do you consider that in farming?"

"Yes, always."

"What about springtime? How do you know when the soil is ready for planting?"

"My father taught me to test the way it feels when I squeeze a handful of it. The feel of it can tell you much about how wet it is and whether or not it's ready to be worked."

"Write down what I dictate to you," the man on the left said.

The official in the middle said nothing but handed Peter a pencil and a sheet of paper. The official on the left read a short list of words. "Print the first two words, write the next two, and the last word I want you to print in capital letters." Peter did as he was instructed.

The man on the left asked him again, "Do you want to work on a farm?"

"Yes. I was raised working in the fields, and that's what I want to do when I go to Canada. I want to work on a farm."

"Are you in good health?"

"Yes, I think so."

"Do you have problems with your eyes?"

"No."

"Do you think you'll be able to obtain a deferment from the army?"

"I hope so. I applied to go to Argentina and was granted a deferment for that, but the group that planned to go disbanded. I hope the draft board will consider that and grant me a deferment to go to Canada. I've already applied."

The men paused and consulted the papers in front of them. They set down their pens, and all of them looked at Peter.

The man on the right side spoke. "Well now, everything is in order. You may leave now. Your examination is over."

"Thank you," Peter said and walked outside. There was nothing more to do but wait. The men had to complete the interviews and decide who would be accepted and who would not. The deliberations would take a few days, and applicants were told to return to the agent in Lubachiv. The list of those who passed the examination would be posted at that time.

Chapter 39

The next days were unbearable. Peter worked in the fields, tended the animals, and sat with his family in the evening. He tried to become immersed in what he was doing so that he could forget time, but by concentrating on the need to forget, all he did was think about the results of the interviews.

The day came. The office opened at nine o'clock in the morning. Peter rose early that day, tended to chores, and was at the office in plenty of time. When the agent arrived, he tacked a sheet of paper on the outdoor notice board and went inside the building. One by one, the young people who had gathered read the list and turned away disappointed. When Peter finally came close enough to the board, he could not believe what he saw!

For the villages of Opaka and Felzendorf, and in fact for the entire district surrounding Opaka, there was only one name listed. Only one. That name was not Eva Zuravel. The one name listed was Petro Fedyk.

Chapter 40

Papers

At the moment Peter saw his name, his mind began to race. Canada! It was within reach. He had the chance to get out. His name was the only one from his village and the other settlements in his area. It was odd. It was wonderful! But what of Eva? He had seen the official make notations on what was probably her application. He wondered what it was all about. He shrugged his shoulders and wondered what he should next.

The agent can tell me what to do now, he thought and went into the building.

The man who sat behind the table was the same one Hershko had sent Peter to the first time. The man looked up as Peter walked in and said, "I was expecting you."

"Good day to you, sir!" Peter said. "I'm here to ask what steps I must take now!"

"Well, young man. First, secure your deferment. Perhaps now when the draft board hears of your status with us, they'll take it into consideration. When you get those papers, go to the Canadian Pacific agent, in Lviv, to register and give him a deposit for your passage. It would be best if you could do all this within one month."

"I'll try my best."

The man nodded.

"How much of a deposit do they want?"

"Oh, take about ten dollars. By the way, the only currency the company will take is American dollars. They do not want Polish money."

"United States of America dollars? Where can I get them?"

"Through the bank, or try some of the wealthier landowners. They deal in dollars sometimes. Good luck, young man," the agent said and gestured for him to leave.

Peter stood there thinking. "Yes, thank you," he said, distracted by his own thoughts. The agent returned to his paperwork, and Peter turned to leave for home.

Peter was amazed to find himself at his front gate. He had walked all the way back to Opaka with only a passing notice of where he was along the road.

How do I tell Mama? he wondered. *Will she be happy? No. Not happy. She wants to help me, but at the same time, she doesn't want me to leave. How can I tell her?*

Peter didn't need to wonder how he would break the news. The village grapevine had carried his news back to Opaka at least an hour before Peter reached home. Eva had already stopped by to share her disappointment. She had not been accepted and made it clear that she was going home to sulk and cry for at least a week. With Peter it was another story.

When Peter walked into the house, Mama's face was wet with tears. She knew already. Peter went to her and hugged her. He said nothing. Maryna sat in bed and was spinning thread with a hand spindle, but when she saw Peter, she stopped. She tried to smile at him but didn't say anything. He tried to comfort Mama but began to feel so depressed that he helped her to a chair, kissed her on the cheek, and left the house.

Peter tried to find something to do. He cleaned out soiled bedding from the stalls in the barn and soon tired of doing that. He worked on broken harnesses. After a short time, he put that aside too. He couldn't concentrate on anything. Finally night came, but he couldn't sleep at all. He got up before dawn, ate breakfast, and went out to the fields.

At noon he came home for lunch and looked around the house. Everyone was gone, except, of course, little Maryna. She sat in bed and occupied her time with spinning.

"Where's Mama?"

"She went to the city."

"Are you hungry, Maryna?"

"No, Petrush. I had lunch with Kashia. She left to do some errands for Mama."

His little sister followed him around the room with her large, sad eyes but said nothing about Canada. Peter poured a bowl of soup for himself and took a large piece of bread and butter. He ate and thought to himself, *I wonder if Mama went to see about my deferment.* He looked at Maryna. He didn't feel like talking about it with her.

"Do you want to go out and enjoy the sunshine? I can take you outside."

"No, Petru. Not today. I have some spinning to do, but I'm tired. I thought after I finished this floss, I'd sleep a little bit. Outside, I can't sleep."

"Fine. I'll be back from the fields for supper." He went over to her and gave her a cup of cool milk. He helped to smooth her pillow and hugged her before he left.

As he walked out to the fields, he was troubled with thoughts of his littlest sister. *Since the accident, she's been confined to the bed or a chair. My little bird will never fly again. His throat tightened. Who will carry her about when I'm gone? Should I go? Should I stay? Who but God knows what I must do? In my prayers I beg for direction. I thought I had it when my name alone stood on that list. It was like a great big sign post pointing out. The way out! Are Maryna and Mama other signposts showing me that I should stay?* Peter agonized over his thoughts while he weeded.

When he came home to eat supper, his mother was there preparing the food. No one said much at the table that night. Oleksa had worked with the cobbler that day, and after the table was cleared, he shared the news he had heard in the shop.

"The news is all over the village, you know, Petru? You're quite a celebrity," Oleksa said, almost teasing.

"I know. That's something I didn't want."

Chapter 40

"Well, most of the people old Medvid has talked to are happy for you. Old lady Komar is her usual charming self. She said, 'Oh, he'll go. Go to Canada! Hah! He'll get as far as Danzig and be sent back again.' She had a nephew who went that far, and at the physical examination, the doctor found something wrong with his eyes. They sent him home again."

"I don't think that'll happen to me."

"That's not all. Old Tenuch is telling everyone that first you sailed off on your adventure to Argentina and suddenly were home again. He says your holiday to Canada will be just as brief."

"Old Warden Tenuch always underestimated me," Peter said with a secretive smile. "Besides, if the good people of this village are having a good laugh on me, let them. Everyone needs a good joke now and then to sweeten life. I'm doing them a service." Peter tried to speak lightheartedly, but the effort was lost on the family.

All through supper Mama said nothing. After the last of the bowls were washed and put away, she sat down and listened to what the boys were saying. Finally she spoke.

"I went to ask about your deferment today. The officer was in Jaroslava as usual, but his wife listened to me patiently. She had already heard about the results of your interview. I think everyone has. She told me to come back and see her in two days. Her husband was waiting to hear whether you had passed. By then she'll have word from him and will be able to tell me something."

"Thank you for going to her, Mama."

"Go do chores now. I have spinning to do."

"Yes, Mama," Peter said, and left with Oleksa to go to the barn.

The day came for Mama to return to Lubachiv. Peter came in from the fields as the sun was setting and was surprised to find that Mama had not returned. Kashia prepared supper for him and Oleksa, so they ate. Still Mama did not return. The brothers did the chores and returned to the house. Mama had not come home.

"It's getting dark, Oleksa. Let's walk to the city and meet her on the road."

Just as they went to the door, it opened, and Mama came inside. She said nothing, but it was clear she had been crying.

Papers

"Mama, why are you crying? What's wrong?" Peter said softly.

"I don't know myself. I don't know if what I'm doing is good or bad."

"Mama, will I get permission to leave?"

She looked at him and wiped her eyes. She handed him a kerchief with something wrapped inside. Her hands were shaking, and after he took it, she turned away. Peter untied the cloth and found several sheets of folded paper. He opened them and quickly read what they were. Two papers were from the army, and the third was a travel permit.

"Here, Oleksa," Peter said. "Read these for me, out loud."

Oleksa took the papers and read the most important word on each sheet. "Canada … Canada … Canada."

The next day Peter bought a train ticket to Lviv. He passed the exam and had his deferment, and now before anyone could change his mind, he was on his way to the agent in Lviv to secure passage on the ship. He found the Canadian Pacific office near the train station and gave the agent a deposit of ten American dollars. In return, he was given a receipt and an information sheet about the cost of his ticket and what it included.

"Come back in two weeks with your birth certificate and be prepared to have a physical examination," the agent told him. "Come to this office and we'll direct you to the doctor. Be here soon after we open up for the day."

To get his birth certificate, Peter had to go to his parish priest in Lubachiv. Father Ivan was not always an easy man to find. Unless it was time for liturgy or confessions or vespers, he was rarely at the church or in the rectory office. In a moment of panic some people would run all over Lubachiv looking for him with no success. When he had to be found to help someone near death in the village, it was Peter who was usually sent to bring him. Peter did not panic. He simply took the time to think about where the priest might be. He first considered the time of day. With that in mind, he remembered that Father Ivan, or as Peter secretly called him, "Ivan the Bald," was a troubled man. He had to care for two parishes, the one in the city and the one in Opaka, with no help from anyone. For years, he had worked with his father, who was the first parish priest Peter could remember. Now that the old man had died, Father Ivan had to do it all by himself. He also had to put up with harassment from the Polish priests who belittled him because his rite allowed him to marry and have a family. Maybe the Polish priests were just jealous. Father Ivan knew the joys of being a family man, but he also knew the trials. He had a good wife, but their three daughters were no picnic. It was not surprising to Peter, therefore, that this man who had to suffer so much in silence would sometimes try to drown his problems in a strong drink at some local inn. Peter usually started his search at the less expensive but respectable places and worked his way up from there. Most of the time, after two or three tries, Peter would find him downing a very small snack and a very large bottle of wine or something stronger.

It was Friday afternoon, and Peter tried the church and rectory office. The priest's wife came to the door. She was a woman of average height and features. She always had a serene smile on her face, and this time was no exception. Adversity didn't seem to affect her. Two of her girls were shrieking at each other in the other room, and there was a loud crash. She seemed to take no notice and remained smiling and calm. She told Peter that her husband was out for the afternoon. She didn't say anything about him being called to tend to the sick or dying, so Peter decided the priest was making a short retreat at some tavern. Peter went to Father Ivan's favorite place, which was a hotel owned by a Ukrainian man in Lubachiv. Success! He was sitting near a window, and the afternoon sun fell softly on him. His shining head reflected the sunlight with a pink halo, and Peter smiled at the picture he saw. The priest was eating fish and bread and drinking something clear and colorless. Peter was certain it wasn't water. The bottle next to him on the table was two-thirds empty. Peter noticed that and thought, *Looks like Father is providing a place for the fish to swim inside him.*

The priest saw Peter with his cap in his hands, as he waited for permission to speak.

"Glory be to Jesus Christ!" Father Ivan said.

"Glory forever."

Papers

"What is it, Petrush? Does someone need me?"

"No. It isn't an emergency, Father. I'm the one who needs something from you. I passed the test for Canada. Now I need my birth certificate in order to get my passport."

"Indeed. Yes," the priest said as he wiped his chin. "I heard about your tests. I've almost finished my lunch. Why don't you run along to my office? I'll meet you there in a half hour. I have to find the records in the church."

Peter did as he was told. He went to the rectory, and the priest's wife let him into the office to wait. He saw her face again. She always looked the same, no matter what happened. At first, it would seem a blessing to have such a serene wife. Nothing rattled her. Fighting children, doorbells, nothing broke her composure. Peter wondered if it was such a blessing.

Father Ivan arrived and wrote out the papers Peter needed. His pen scratched on the paper, and the large clock ticked on the mantle. When he finished, he did not hand the papers to Peter. Father Ivan leaned back in his chair and folded his big hands over his chest. He looked at Peter.

"So. You're planning to go, are you?"

"Yes, Father, I am."

"Your mother is saddened by this."

"Yes, I know."

"With things the way they are, you're probably the wisest of us all. Your mother knows that. That's why she has done so much to help you. You should be very grateful."

"I am. I'm very thankful for the way she's let me try."

"You'll find a lot of our people in Canada."

"Yes, I've heard that."

"In Canada, I've heard a man can be Ukrainian. None of this 'Rusyn' nonsense. You can use the language, practice your faith, and even openly promote your culture and traditions—all without the government sticking its nose in to tell you that you are undesirable. Our traditions give us strength. I've heard that in America you can do these things too, but there you must try to be an 'American' too, like everyone else. Canada understands us a little better."

Chapter 40

Peter said nothing.

"You realize that for the first time you'll be traveling far without your family. But remember you won't be completely alone. We're all weak because we're human, but if you have faith, it will sustain you. You must draw your strength from it especially when you feel alone. I admire your mother. She has strong faith. I hope you've inherited her strength. I know you were close to both your parents, and now, of course, the bond you have with your mother is very great. Go with God now and turn to Him when you're alone. Go find your new world, but never forget your faith when you're far from home."

"I'll try not to, Father."

"Here are your papers, Petru."

"Thank you, Father."

The priest extended his hand to Peter, and Peter shook it.

"I'll see you in church on Sunday. I'll be coming to Opaka for Divine Liturgy."

Peter smiled and nodded. "I'll be there."

Peter left the rectory and walked down the street and around the corner and disappeared from view. Father Ivan watched him from the window in silence. He raised his hand and blessed the boy quietly as he walked away. Whatever thoughts he may have had about the young man who was about to travel so far were shattered by a crash, thud, and shouts. His two youngest children were at it again. Father Ivan wore no mask of serenity. His face was a picture of parental anger as he hurried off to administer some penance while the sins were still fresh.

Chapter 41

The Physical

Two minutes after the office opened on the appointed day, Peter was at the front desk of the Canadian Pacific agency. In a few minutes, the agent he had seen during his first visit came to talk to him.

"Here's the doctor's address. Just take the tram. You can board it around the corner, and it will take you right to the doctor's office. Have the doctor fill out these forms."

Peter took the tram, found the office, and stepped into the waiting room. The room was stark white, with a creaky, polished wooden floor. A few straight chairs were set against the wall. At the far end of the room, near a door leading deeper into the office, there was a desk. A woman dressed in black and white sat there with a stack of papers in front of her.

She must be the nurse, Peter thought.

She looked up at him and smiled. "Yes? What may we do for you?"

"I've been sent here by the Canadian Pacific office. They told me to bring these forms to you. I'm supposed to see the doctor for a physical examination."

"That's fine. Sit down. We will be with you in a little while." She took Peter's papers and disappeared behind the door near her desk.

Peter sat down. *I'll get this over with,* he thought, *and that'll be all I have to do. The final step before I can get passage to Canada.* He felt relief that his dream was finally becoming real. Peter began to read some of the papers the agent had given him.

Chapter 41

The nurse returned and spoke to him. "Follow me, please." She led him through the door near her desk and down a short corridor where he saw several other doors. She opened one of them and motioned him inside. "Please go in here and strip to the waist. The doctor will be in soon."

Peter stepped into the little room and took off his shirt and undershirt. He sat down on the chair and waited. The room had a table in it with a surface that seemed higher off the floor than normal tables. There was a small chest of drawers in one corner, and on top of it were some odd-looking instruments. The door opened, and in came a different woman wearing a long white coat.

"Good morning, young man, I am Dr. Marenyak."

Peter's eyes opened wide. *The doctor?* he thought. *A woman doctor?* Peter blushed. His face was the color of one of Mama's Easter Krashankas. He felt his face and neck burning. All he could manage to stammer was "Good morning." The only females who had ever seen him even partially naked since he had become a young man were his mother and his sisters. Peter was raised to be comfortable with the functions of the human body, but he was also very modest. He was horrified to think that this woman, this stranger, was going to examine him. He tried to stand up straight and follow her instructions. She checked his eyes, ears, and nose and made notations on a sheet of paper. She told him to open his mouth as wide as possible, and she looked at his teeth and throat. She felt his neck and had him turn his head from side to side.

"Now I'm going to listen to your heart," she said and picked up a stethoscope. She listened carefully as if trying to hear a distant sound.

Peter stood there staring over her shoulder and thought, *Why does she need that thing? My heart is pounding so hard everyone can hear it out on the street!*

She wrote something down and said, "Make a fist and then open your right hand."

Peter did as he was told.

"Now your left. Fine. Roll your head to the front, side, and now back, and to the other side. Good, good. Bend forward from the waist." She walked in back of him and pushed her fingers against his spine to check the alignment at the shoulder blades and near his waist. "Now bend to one side, yes, and now to the other."

Peter did exactly as she told him. She wrote something down and left the room.

Peter sighed. *Well, I survived that,* he thought. *Examined by a woman doctor!* He shuddered and jumped as the door opened again. She came back into the room.

"Now we shall complete the examination," she said in a matter-of-fact tone.

Peter stood there puzzled. *I thought I was done,* he thought. Peter froze. She had begun to talk again, and he could not believe what she was saying.

She repeated, "I said stand here wearing nothing more than you did when you were born."

Peter felt his face burn again. It was flaming. *Oh my God,* he thought. *I'm going to die or faint or I don't know what. Maybe I'll just turn blue and pass out. But with my luck, she'd still be here when I came to.* Peter didn't know that his eyes were as big as saucers. The doctor saw this but kept a straight face.

"Do you hear me, young man?"

"Yes, doctor," Peter stammered and took off everything except his underpants and his socks. He looked at her again.

"Take off your socks and pants," she said patiently.

Peter's mind went blank, and he wanted to run and hide, but there was nowhere to go. He did as he was told and prayed he would fall unconscious any minute.

"Swing your left leg front to back." Peter did as she ordered. "Rotate your foot. Make circles with it! Good. Now do the same with your right." Sheer terror made Peter sweat. He stared straight ahead and wished he was finished or dead, whichever could come first. "Turn your head and cough," she ordered.

When he did as he was told, she pressed her finger into his groin. He choked.

Oh my God, he thought.

"Now the other side," she ordered. "Fine, fine. That's all, young man. You may get dressed now." She turned and left the room.

When she closed the door, Peter's shoulders slumped, and he covered his eyes with one hand. Then he looked at his nakedness and hurried to get dressed and cover up his body again. He was finished when she returned.

"Take this sealed envelope to the agency," she said with a pleasant smile.

But Peter saw no smile. He couldn't bear to look at her. He stared at the envelope and murmured, "Thank you." He left the examining room and almost ran past the nurse. She smiled and said good-bye to him. Her smile only embarrassed him more. *She knows,* he thought. *She knows what I just had to do.* He practically flew out to the street. He took a deep breath and waited for the tram. When one arrived, he boarded and sat down. He was too embarrassed to look anyone in the eye. He felt certain that anyone who looked at him would know in an instant what he had just endured. He stared at the envelope. He wished that it wasn't sealed. He wanted to know whether he had passed. "Well that's done now too," he told himself and began to feel more at ease.

At the office, he stepped up to the front desk and gave the envelope to the young woman who sat there.

"What do I have to do now?" he asked.

"Wait here for a few moments, please," she said and went into an inner office. She reappeared a moment later with a sheet of paper.

"Everything seems to be in order, sir," she said with a pleasant smile. "This paper lists what you'll need to take with you for your journey. It also shows the date and hour of your departure for Vyhorova from Lviv."

Peter stared at the paper. "I leave Lviv on Monday, August 13, 1928. August 13. Two weeks from today!"

The young woman nodded and smiled. Peter's face broke into a wide, happy grin, and he almost laughed out loud. "Two weeks!" he shouted. "Thank you! Thank you very much!"

Chapter 42

Arrested!

Peter felt so light-headed! He couldn't believe his dream was finally within his grasp. People stared at him as he headed for the train station, and he wondered why. He saw himself reflected in a window while he ran along and realized that he was grinning like a fool. He tried to keep a straight face, but he couldn't help it. He felt like laughing out loud, dancing, and thumbing his nose at anything that had to do with the government. The laughing and dancing he had to avoid on the street, but he couldn't resist wiping his nose with his thumb while he stared at a government insignia near the train station.

"Here's to you!" he said to the Polish eagle. "You old buzzard. You're one bird who won't get his talons into me!" He was thoroughly enjoying himself and ran up to the ticket window at the station. "What time does the train leave for Rava-Ruska?"

The ticket agent looked at him. "You missed it." The man was in a disgruntled mood and enjoyed giving bad news. "You just missed it by ten minutes."

Peter's broad grin shrank only slightly. "When is the next one?"

"The next train leaves at sixteen-twenty. You'll have to wait until then."

Peter looked at the clock. That was almost four hours to wait, and with the delay he would miss his connection for Lubachiv and probably not make it home by nightfall. Peter felt bad about that, but his smile stayed. When the train finally pulled in, he boarded.

Chapter 42

There were only four people in the car, all peasant farmers. They sat on the bench along one wall. The bench on the other wall was empty.

This will be a safe group to travel with, Peter thought and sat down. When the train pulled out, the steady rhythm of the wheels on the rails and the warm afternoon made him sleepy. Joy was invigorating, but after so many weeks of restless sleep, the relief of finally knowing he would be able to leave allowed him to relax. He fought to stay awake, but the clackity-clack of the train as it moved along became a lullaby, and Peter fell asleep.

"Sir, get up! Get up, sir! You are under arrest!"

Someone was shaking Peter and shouting at him. Peter woke up. A young uniformed policeman stood over him and roughly shook Peter's shoulder.

"Get up, I say! You're under arrest!"

Peter wasn't certain if he was dreaming some terrible dream or if it was real. He stared at the policeman in disbelief. "Why am I under arrest? I'm on my way to Lubach—"

"The train from Lviv arrived hours ago. This is an empty car. You're sleeping here. Vagrancy is an offense!"

"But I fell asleep on the way here from Lviv. Where are we?"

"You are in Rava-Ruska, and you are under arrest!" The policeman took Peter by the arm and pulled him up. "Go to the station now!"

He made Peter walk in front of him. Peter was directed into the station and to a room located off to the side of the main lobby. There was a step up, and then narrow double doors opened into the room. The room was empty. There were long benches along all four walls. It was probably some sort of waiting area. The doors had long narrow windows in them, so Peter could see out into the larger waiting room. The policeman left, and Peter sat and stared at the buff-colored walls. There was nothing else in the room except the benches and the light overhead.

Now what? That dumb eagle must have heard me and decided to sink a talon into me after all. This is so stupid! What did I do? I committed the horrible crime of falling asleep. Wait till I tell Mama. Arrested for being a vagrant! All those years I got by the wardens without once getting caught, and I'm arrested now! It's so late. I must have missed the last train to Lubachiv. The next one isn't until morning. I wonder what's going to happen now. I hope I can get everything cleared up by then. What a mess!

Peter wasn't certain how long he sat obediently in that room. He stood up and walked over to the door and looked out through the glass. There was no one around. He wondered if the doors were locked. When he tried the handles, they opened. He stepped down into the short corridor leading to the waiting area and looked around. No one came to stop him. He looked toward the main waiting room where a few people moved about. Peter went to the waiting area and looked up at the clock, which showed it was 22:45. There weren't too many night trains left to catch, and the station was quiet. There were some benches along the walls, but the corners and far walls were dimly lit, and Peter wasn't sure if he'd be safe there. He needed to sleep and had to spend the night in the station. Pickpockets and thieves were common, and he wanted to spend the night without any trouble. In the middle of the room was a big, low, round table. Above it was a large chandelier. It wasn't the elaborate kind you would find in a palace, but it was a nice, bright collection of lights that lit up most of the room. The low table was used by people as a seat while they waited, or as a place to rest a valise or suitcase. Peter decided to lie down on it and spend the night under the light of the chandelier.

When he awoke, the clock on the wall declared that it was four o'clock in the morning. It was still very dark outside, but people were beginning to arrive to catch early trains. Peter sat up, stretched, and walked over to the ticket window.

"What time does the train leave for Lubachiv?'

"At five."

Peter yawned and went back to sit down and wait. He felt hungry but didn't trust food sold in places like train stations, so he tried to think of one of Mama's breakfasts and the fact that he would be home in a few hours.

He saw the strange little side room where he had been held. *Was that a bad dream?* he wondered, yawning. *He told me I was under arrest but never took my name. I escaped but stayed here, and no one came to get me. So either I'm free without trial or I'm a fugitive from justice. I guess I'll just keep on going.*

Chapter 42

The hour slipped by, the train for Lubachiv pulled in, and Peter boarded. After a while he noticed that dawn was starting to break across the sky. First the sky turned a pale grey, and the blackness was pushed back from the east. Villages and fields were silhouetted briefly against the birth of color in the sky, and finally shapes were illuminated by the growing light. The fields and foliage Peter saw from the train glistened with a heavy dew. He saw people traveling along the roads. Life was awaking for another day.

This will all go on each day, even when I'm not here to see it. He imagined himself gone from that place, as if his eyes stared out from an invisible body. *This is how it will be when I'm not here. Life will continue. Dawn will come, and my eyes will see something different. Things I can't imagine because they've never been before my eyes. Two weeks.*

The conductor announced Lubachiv, and soon the train slowed to pull into the station. Peter hopped off at his first chance and ran for the Blensky Street door and out onto the road that led to the city market. He turned in the direction of Opaka. Blensky Street eventually ended, and he came out onto the field roads. In the distance the gentle rays of the risen sun fell softly on his village.

"Opaka," he said softly, "you've been my cradle all these years. Two more weeks in you and then what? What will it be like not to see you anymore? I know how the sun plays with your rooftops and the domes of the church. What will it be like to leave and to know another place as I've known you?"

Peter reached home, and Mama had breakfast waiting for him. She had kept supper for him the night before until she was certain he must have missed the train. He was too late for morning chores, so he stayed a while longer after he finished eating and told her and Maryna everything that had happened to him. He showed Mama the information sheet and read her everything that was on it. When he came to the date he was to leave, she whispered it to herself and then said nothing else. Peter went to help Oleksa in the fields, and Mama stayed behind in the house and wept.

Chapter 43

Two Weeks

The two weeks he had left seemed to fly in comparison with the months of waiting for that final permission to go. There was so much to do and not enough time for everything. The sun seemed to race across the sky and mark off each day. Peter tried to continue to help in the fields as much as he could. It was August, and some of the crops were beginning to ripen. There was work to be done, but each time Peter met a villager in the fields or on the road, the person wanted to stop and ask about his plans. Most wished him well. Some of the older women who had known him as a child even cried over him and said they would remember him in their prayers. There were a few who openly laughed at him and pointed as he went by.

"There goes Petro Fedyk!" they'd yell. "The big dreamer! Have a good voyage from here to Vyhorova and back again!"

Peter was irritated at first but then would tip his cap and give a deep bow and wave to his hecklers before he continued on his way. The smile he wore could not be erased by their remarks. His thoughts merely repeated what he felt so strongly. *Laugh. Go ahead and laugh at me. I'll get out. Nothing will hold me in this country any more.*

Mama carefully washed and ironed all of Peter's few clothes. Daria wanted to help and insisted she would iron his shirts. In the meantime, Mama sewed a new shirt for him and mended his older ones so that they would last a long time. She bought a wicker suitcase for him from a neighbor in the village. One made of leather or cloth would have been stronger, but she had no money for such luxury.

Chapter 43

Twice Maria and Myhal went to a wealthy German landowner who sold timber in Felzendorf. He promised to loan them the money for Peter's travels at a reasonable rate of interest. He assured Maria that he would have the money in time for Peter's departure. He also agreed to keep it for her until the day of Peter's departure because she was afraid to have that much money in the house.

The last few days spun by with dizzying speed like the swirling spindles Peter had used when he helped Mama spin. Now that the time was coming closer, Peter began to try to remember all the details of daily life that he had taken for granted for so long. He wanted to remember everything everyone said to him.

One evening the family was together at home. Maryna sat in bed while she spun thread and chattered about things she had seen outside that day. Kashia talked with her and Peter as she washed dishes, and Mama sewed the last few stitches on the new shirt. She had used some of her own woven linen for it. The fabric was a soft white, and Peter remembered how he had watched Mama make the cloth.

I watched Mama spin that thread, he thought. *I watched her weave it on those winter days. I saw her soak it in the river and lay it out on the grass to bleach it. I saw her freeze it in the winter on the snow to soften it. I never dreamed she'd use some of it for a shirt that I would take with me to Canada.*

"It's finished," Mama said and shook out the shirt before she held it out in front of her. "Put it on and let me see how it looks."

Peter put it on and admired it. "It looks very nice, Mama. I'll take good care of it. Thank you!" He hugged her and kissed her on both cheeks.

She didn't look at him or smile. She went over to the wardrobe and opened it. She took out something wrapped in a handkerchief and handed it to him. "I want you to take these with you," she said simply.

Peter opened the cloth, and inside it he found a small dark metal crucifix on a chain and a thin book that was so small it fit in the palm of his hand. The cover was hard, black paper, and inside he read, "МОЛИТВИ." It was a prayer book.

"This is all I can give you when I send you off into the world. I wish it was more."

Peter looked at the cross and the little book because he couldn't look at his mother without beginning to cry. *You're giving me a chance for a new life,* he thought, *just as you gave me birth. How do I tell you that you've given me what is most important in this world?* He didn't know how to tell her all the things he felt. He stared at the crucifix and the prayer book. Finally he found he could speak.

"You've given me life, Mama," he said softly. He felt that in a moment he would sob and start to cry like a child, so he stood up and went out of the house.

It was a warm evening, and he gazed out beyond the farmyard to the fields. He held the cross and the little book tenderly, kissed them, and put them in his pocket.

"Be with me, God," he prayed softly.

When the last night came, Peter wanted to do the night chores by himself and say good-bye to his friends in the stable. Before anyone could say anything, he announced, "I'll do the chores myself tonight, Mama," and quickly stepped out of the house.

The warm smell of animals and hay met him as he entered the barn, and he stopped for a moment to look around him. This was the barn Papa had built after he came home from the war. They'd lived in it for a short while until the house was rebuilt. He'd been in it thousands of times to tend to animals, to read or sleep in the loft, or to listen to Papa's serious talks with old Baran and others. Peter's eyes began to sting.

He set down the milking pails and filled the manger for the cows. He pulled the stool over to the side of Bura. He cleaned off her udder and milked her carefully. She stood quietly in her stall. Peter moved the milking stool over to Mama Cow's stall. She was getting so old that her hooves were curling, and her red and white hide seemed to hang on her bony body. Peter teased her lately that at her age he ought to call her "Grandma Cow." Tonight he said nothing. He cleaned her off and milked her. He stopped to marvel that even at her age, she still gave so much milk.

"You're a good old girl," he said softly while he gently patted her bony rump.

He carefully carried the milk pails to the house, gave them to Kashia, and then returned to the barn. Now he could begin the chores and take his time with them. He fed all the animals and gave them fresh water. He cleaned out the stalls and gave the cows clean straw bedding. He paused in the loft when he was throwing down the hay and looked at the barn again from that familiar view. The animals hardly moved. Everything seemed so quiet. Even Mooshka, the little black dog who had come after Pundyk, sat quietly by the door.

Peter hopped down. The chores were done. Now the hard part came. He visited all the animals and stood silently by them for a moment. He touched each one on the neck and whispered a soft farewell.

The horses were not yet old friends of his. Brownie was now living on Myhal's farm on the other side of the village. He had seen her earlier in the day and had said good-bye to her then. Old Grey had been sold soon after Maryna's accident. The two horses that stood in front of him now didn't have the spirit or character of the two who had once inhabited the stalls, but he patted them and encouraged them to work hard for Mama.

"Bura," he said softly when he came to her, "look after your mother."

Then he came to Mama Cow. "Well, old girl. You may show your age in some ways, but your milk is as sweet now as it was for your first calf, and your eyes are as bright as those times we outsmarted the wardens. Those men have gotten fat and lazy since we stopped our adventures. They never really caught us, did they?" He laughed softly through stray tears, and the old cow mooed. "You never really got too old for that, you know. I just got too tall to hide behind the rye. I hope you didn't mind. I think you miss those times as much as I do. I feel guilty now, old girl. I'm going on an adventure soon, but this time you can't share it. I'll bet you'd love the pasture grass in Canada. I'll bet it's as sweet as that lush, soft stuff on old Kazhanko's paths." He paused. Peter put his arms around her neck and began to cry. "Will you wonder what's happened to me when my face doesn't appear in front of you every day?" He petted her velvety nose and said softly, "I hope your days will be quiet and easy. I won't be here to say good-bye to you when you finish your life. Maybe the rye in heaven is taller than here on earth, and it'll hide me when I get there someday. Then we can have our adventures again. That is *if* old Kazhanko or the wardens ever get there. Otherwise we'll have to go and pester them in Hell… just for a visit, mind you. Good-bye, old friend." He sobbed and then patted the old cow again before he left the barn.

He rubbed his eyes and almost fell over Mooshka. "Be good, little one, and guard this part of my family for me." He cradled her little head in his hand and smiled at the shining black eyes. The dog licked his hand and followed him toward the house. "No, Mooshka, you stay in the barn and guard my dear ones there." The dog obediently went back to her place by the door.

"Petru!" a voice called softly.

"Ivan, is that you?"

Ivan stepped out of the shadows. "I just got back from my grandpa's farm. I'm sorry I couldn't get back sooner. He's been quite sick."

"I'm sorry. Is he any better?"

"He seems to be. I'll see you at church, but I wanted to come tonight too."

"Thanks," Peter gulped. The sadness he felt was hard to swallow away. His throat seemed constricted, and he could hardly talk.

"I'll only stay a few minutes."

"No, Ivan. Stay as long as you like," Peter protested.

"I know you want to be with your family tonight," Ivan went on. "God's speed to you. We've been like brothers all our lives. We've had some good times, haven't we? We're so alike, and yet you've always been braver than me. Willing to risk so much more."

"We all have our destiny, Ivan. Papa used to say you have to listen to your heart."

"I guess your heart is stronger than mine. You won't compromise your ideals. I wish I had your will."

"Who's to say who's stronger? You always said it would be too hard for you to leave. I can't find the strength to stay and put up with the government. The only other choice is one I promised Mama I wouldn't make."

"Thanks, Petru. I didn't want you to think I was a coward."

"I'd never think that!" Peter was quiet as he stared over the fields behind the farm. "Ivan, I have something to ask you."

"Just ask, and I'll do it."

"Keep an eye on Daria for me. You know that monster she married beats her when he's in the mood. She may not always tell Mama, but she may tell Natalia."

"I'll do what I can."

"I don't really know what you can do about it. He's such a jackass!"

"Who knows, Petru? Nights here are dark, and no one knows who shares the road with him when he walks home drunk." Ivan smiled. "Besides, with you gone off to Canada, I'll need to think up my own mischief."

Peter smiled. "I didn't mean that, but by all means, follow your conscience!"

"Natalia sends her farewell. She wasn't sure if she could come tomorrow. In case she doesn't, she told me to remind you to be careful on the high seas. You used to fall in the river so much when you were little, she's afraid for you on the ocean."

Peter laughed softly. "She'll never let me forget, will she? She never saw us take the horses swimming in the lake, or she'd know that I'm sure of myself in the water."

"She better not have seen us! We all went skinny-dipping when we took the horses for their swim!" Ivan smiled, but his laugh died in his throat.

Both stood silent. Finally Ivan spoke. "It's time for me to go."

The two old friends looked at each other.

"Ivan, I wish you all the goodness that life can offer."

"I wish you the same."

The two boys hugged and parted.

"З Богом," Ivan whispered, meaning "Go with God."

"З Богом," Peter answered.

Ivan walked away, glanced back, waved, and then disappeared into the darkness beyond the gate.

Chapter 44

Leaving

The night was a restless one for everyone. Finally the last morning came. Myhal came early to help Oleksa with chores while Peter went to church with Mama and Kashia. At liturgy, Peter saw most of the villagers he had known all his life. Many of them came over to him after church to wish him well.

Old Mrs. Gont came up to him and cried for a while. She hugged him several times and scolded him, "You behave yourself, or you'll break your mother's heart. Do you hear me, boy?"

"Yes, ma'am, I do. I'll be good."

"I wish you had a sweetheart here. Maybe then you wouldn't be so eager to go."

"Mama says I'm too young for such foolishness," Peter said, blushing.

"It doesn't matter," the old woman wept. "You're going so far away! I helped bring you into the world just a short time ago, it seems. If you're too young for a sweetheart, then how can you be old enough to leave home? You were always your Mama's 'little fish.' I never thought you'd want to swim so far."

Mama stood nearby and said nothing. Her eyes glistened with tears, but she smiled quietly at Peter. Father Ivan finished in church and came outside. He walked over to Mama and took both her hands in his. He gave her a small comforting smile.

The priest turned to Peter and shook his hand. "Well, the next time I come here for Divine Liturgy, you'll be off on your journey.

Chapter 44

You know the litany where we pray for those who travel?" Peter nodded. "I'll make certain to mention your name each time until your traveling is finished. Your mother will let me know." He smiled and looked intently into Peter's eyes. "God is with you. Remember that."

"I will, Father, thank you," Peter said solemnly.

Ivan came with his parents and Natalia. Mr. and Mrs. Soroka embraced Peter and wished him good luck. Natalia hugged him and gave him one of her sympathetic smiles.

"Petru, we'll miss you. Don't forget us."

"I won't. I know you live on the other side of Lubachiv, but stay in touch with Daria."

She smiled again. "Daria is like my own sister, Petrushu. That won't change."

Ivan looked at his old friend and gave him a brotherly hug.

"Listen to me," Ivan grinned. "If there's good pasture grass in Canada, let me know. Don't try to outsmart any wardens over there without advice from me!"

Peter smiled, but inside he wanted to cry. The sick feeling he had from so many good-byes was not something he had anticipated.

Just before they left the churchyard, Peter stepped away from his family and walked over to Papa's grave. The simply carved white headstone read only, "Myhailo Fedyk, 54 years." Peter stood there as he had so many times before. He felt his father's spirit with him no matter where he was, but at the grave there was a special feeling. "Well, Papa, I'm leaving today. I guess I inherited your father's love of wandering. I wish I could talk over everything I do and see with you. I'll carry you with me in my heart." Peter said a prayer, crossed himself, and turned to leave. He touched the headstone one last time, to feel the rough texture of it and the warmth it had absorbed from the sun, before he rejoined his family.

After they returned from church, Mama finished packing Peter's suitcase. Daria came with his ironed shirts, and Mama tucked them into the wicker case. Peter brought her the little prayer book and cross she had given him, and she packed them tenderly with his clothes.

Little Marko came with his mother and entertained Peter with a song he had learned. Everyone tried to be cheerful, but it was difficult with eyes full of tears. The Zuravels came by to wish Peter good luck and a safe journey, and before they left, Evcha whispered to him that she was so envious she had to go to confession. When all the visitors left, the family had a quiet lunch together.

After dishes were cleared and the packing was done, Peter heard Myhal drive the wagon up to the house. It was time to leave. Peter had hoped and prayed so hard that he might be able to get out of Poland someday. He had suffered through the days and weeks after the examination that finally determined who would go to Canada. But he hadn't thought of these endless good-byes and how painful they would be.

Peter walked over to Maryna's bed and knelt at her side. She looked so pale and thin that he felt if he looked at her for more than a moment, his heart would break.

"Little bird, behave yourself. Don't forget to sing for Mama and help her spin." Peter said the words but thought, *Good God! Why do I sound like a big brother when all I want to do is cry and hold her in my arms?*

"Take care of yourself, Petru. Mama worries you won't eat properly and that you'll get a chill or something. Write to us and tell us all about the ocean. Tell us about what it's like to be in Canada. I wish I could go with you. We could have good times." Her eyes began to fill with tears. Her smile stayed, but her tears showed her sorrow. Then she wrapped her arms around his neck and hugged him. "I'll miss your strong arms, Petrush."

He held her tightly and wondered if he had the strength to let go of her. Oleksa knocked at the door. Maryna smiled again.

"Write us about everything, Petrush. Everything." Tears streamed down her face, and she held onto his hand when he stood up.

Kashia hugged him tightly. "Come back to us someday," she said gently and then turned away to wipe her eyes.

Daria came up to him and embraced him. She tried several times to speak, but each time her words ended in sobs. Finally she held him by the shoulders and looked into his eyes. "Don't worry about us," she said. "Take good care of yourself."

Marko stood next to his mother and held out his small hand to shake Peter's. Peter gathered the little boy into his arms for a tight hug and then gently handed him to Daria.

Peter couldn't speak. His throat was so tight he could hardly breathe. He picked up his cap and went to the door. He looked back at his sisters and the place that had been his home for so long. He wanted to save the image of it, but all he saw were blurred colors.

Mama was already sitting next to Myhal on the wagon. Mooshka stood near the wagon, and Peter bent down to pet her and give her a little hug. He jumped on the back of the wagon and sat near Oleksa. His bags were behind him. Mama said nothing. Myhal clicked his tongue and the horses began to pull out of the yard. Daria, Marko and Kashia waved from the front door of the house, where they were staying to be near Maryna.

Peter looked around the farmyard. Mooshka sat forlornly by the stable door. Some of the chickens and rabbits ran about. On the barn, near the broad empty nest, stood a stork. The bird gazed at Peter, and Peter tipped his cap to the majestic creature.

Peter jumped off to close the gate after the wagon passed through. He had done it hundreds of times, and yet he wanted to cherish each detail this time. This last time. The simple act of closing the gate became so precious and almost more than he could bear.

What am I closing in my life? he thought.

They drove down the lane and out to the main road to Lubachiv. Oleksa sat with Peter and watched the village slip away.

"Oleksa, give special attention to Maryna for me."

"You know I will."

"Take care of Mama and Kashia."

"Petrush, don't worry about us. We're all here together. We're the ones who need to worry. You're going off alone. You have no one to watch out for you but God. Mama's faith in Him is deep, but she's still worried sick about you. We'll take care of each other. Who'll take care of you? Remember, little brother, if you meet any bandits or bullies now, you'll have to take care of yourself. I won't be there to defend you."

Oleksa smiled as he teased Peter, but the smile was thin. Peter was silent. He listened to Oleksa, but stared at Opaka as it drifted away from him.

"I wish to heaven I were an artist."

"What does that have to do with defending yourself?"

"I wish I could draw or paint all that I see right now. Each leaf, each twig, each stalk of wheat. Oleksa, I never want to forget anything that I've loved so much."

Oleksa looked at the same dwindling view of the village. "That's where you were born and grew up," he said softly. "But you and I knew it couldn't keep you. I wish we could leave together. Go with God, Petru. Don't worry about us. We'll be all right." Oleksa looked at his brother for a long time. It was his turn to try to record each detail.

When they pulled up near the train station, Peter helped Mama step off the wagon. Oleksa carried Peter's bags, and Myhal found a place for them to wait. No one knew what to say. As the train pulled in, Peter hugged Oleksa and then looked into his dark, sad eyes. Oleksa hugged his younger brother back and went to tousle his hair the way he had so many times, but the playful gesture ended in a clumsy hug and a shuddering sob.

Peter embraced Mama. She was crying very hard, and her small body was shaking. He couldn't say anything. He couldn't let go of her. His mind raced with thoughts of staying. He couldn't remember why it had seemed so important to leave. How could he leave Mama? It was time to board. She tried to give him last-minute advice, and he reassured her that he would be careful. Oleksa gently pulled him away from Mama and then put his arm around her and held her close to his side. Peter and Myhal boarded the train. Myhal planned to take the train with Peter as far as Rava-Ruska before returning to Lubachiv, so he arranged Peter's bags while Peter stood at the window as if in a stupor. Peter looked at Oleksa as he held Mama tightly and comforted her through his own tears.

My God, Peter thought. *I'm leaving the people I love most in this world.* A chilling thought pierced his mind. *I'll never see them again in this life.*

Chapter 44

He felt very cold and tried to fight that thought. How could he think such a thing? He couldn't bear it. Peter gazed at them and felt their eyes returning his look. The train groaned and then slowly began to move. The image of Mama and Oleksa began to slide away. Peter felt as if he was staying in one place while the world spun away from him. He had no control over it. He felt panic. He leaned out of the window and watched them as long as he could until they disappeared behind some trees. They were gone.

Myhal touched his shoulder. "Sit down, Petru."

Peter wondered if he shouldn't go back. He knew that he could never be happy living in Poland, yet how could he ever be happy without his family? He checked his papers, felt for his money, and looked at his bags. Everything was there. He sat there forcing himself to remember why he was leaving. He had to remind himself of the reasons, or he would jump off the train and run along the tracks back to Lubachiv. Peter looked out of the window and watched houses and trees slide by. Myhal sat and watched his brother.

"We'll all take care of Mama and the girls."

Peter continued to look out the window and blinked away tears.

Myhal continued, "I think you were destined to leave us. After the last war, you seemed to be suffocating here. You never wanted to practice shooting or go on maneuvers with the other boys who looked forward to joining the army. You may not think I knew why, but I did. You couldn't stand the thought of becoming a soldier for Poland. I don't understand your need to leave. I only know that you have to do this."

Peter prayed silently that he was doing the right thing. On the way to Rava-Ruska, they talked very little. When they did, it was about the weather or the train.

Once in Rava-Ruska, Peter and Myhal went to check the time of the connecting train to Lviv. The schedule had changed, and it was not due until four o'clock in the morning. "That's fine," Myhal said. "I'll wait with you. There's a train for Lubachiv at five. I promised Mama I'd stay with you until you got on the train to Lviv, so don't argue with me. I'd rather have you disagree with me than Mama."

Leaving

The two brothers had something to eat and sat quietly for most of the evening and through the night. Both of them slept a little, and finally the time came. The train for Lviv pulled in, and Myhal helped Peter lift his bag onto the steps.

"Well, now it's our turn to say good-bye," Myhal said. His dark brows were pinched in a frown. They hugged each other, and Myhal looked at Peter. "Have a good life, little brother," he said. "I will miss you, Petrush."

"Thank you for staying with me. Watch over everyone." Peter's throat tightened. He couldn't say anything more.

Peter boarded the train. He held his suitcase and stood near the window as the train pulled away. He waved until Myhal faded from sight. *Now,* Peter thought, *I'm alone.*

Chapter 45

The Ten-Dollar Bill

Peter turned to look around. The train car was full of people even at that early hour. In the last month, Peter had traveled to Lviv twice, but this time was different. He was carrying over two hundred and fifty American dollars for his steamship ticket and expenses. It was all the money he had in the world, and he was afraid of being robbed..

What do I do now? he wondered. *Where can I sit to be safe?* He saw some women with baskets of vegetables. They were going to sell produce at the market in Lviv. "Excuse me please, ladies," Peter began politely.

"Hey, Veesha, the young man just called us 'ladies,'" the woman with the basket of onions said. Her pleasant face had sunburned cheeks and a smile showing several missing teeth. She was broad and round and would be a nice grandmother for children who needed to be hugged. The woman she called Veesha was younger, but just as plump.

"Yes, Auntie, I heard. Too bad he's such a skinny thing. I like mine healthier."

"Go ahead, young man," a third woman said, when she saw him blush.

"Please, ladies," he began again. They giggled when they heard his polite words. "I'm just a village boy …"

"And I'm a prince's wife!" the fat lady laughed.

"Quiet, Helka!" the third woman said. "He'll think we had

slivovitz for breakfast! Go ahead, don't let her bother you." The woman had dark eyes like Mama's.

"I'm on my way to Lviv. From there my journey just begins. I'm afraid of being robbed before I even get on my way. I know there are thieves on trains ... could I sit near you? I don't want to travel alone."

"Of course you can," the dark-eyed woman said. She nudged Veesha, who wanted to make a remark. "Travel with us. We'll protect you. If anyone comes near you, we'll send Helka after him!"

"I'll grab the thief and sit on him! He won't bother anyone again!" Helka said, laughing.

Peter imagined that her victim wouldn't do much of anything ever again, but he only smiled and was too nervous to really enjoy her joke.

"Thank you, thank you very much," he said in Polish.

Veesha moved her bulk over a little to let Peter pass by. "Here, you sit behind us near the wall. We'll all sit around you, and you'll look like a sultan with his harem."

The women laughed loudly while Peter did as he was instructed.

"Now we have you surrounded," old Helka cackled. "How would you like to meet my other niece? She's a healthy girl who could fatten up a little rooster like you in no time. She's a good cook. As soon as you get back from your little trip?" she said, tilting her head in the direction of his suitcase. "You'll let me know? Are you spoken for?"

Peter blushed again, and the women giggled. "My mama says I'm too young to think about marriage," he said quietly.

"I thought that was all young men and girls ever thought about," Helka laughed.

All the women laughed again, and Peter settled back against his suitcase. He had to put up with their teasing, but he was grateful for the market women. With them he could travel in safety. If they didn't kidnap him and hold him hostage for some desperate niece, he would arrive in Lviv with all his money intact.

In Lviv, Peter walked with the women as far as he could, and then, after thanking them many times, he turned off to go to the Canadian Pacific office. The last block seemed so long this time. He was certain some thief would spring from a doorway and rob him on the spot.

"I should've asked old Helka to walk me here," he muttered.

Peter finally saw the office and ran to the door. It was still locked, but some of the clerks were inside.

The young woman at the front desk looked up at the clock and saw that it was almost a half hour until the agency officially opened, but Peter looked so flushed and worried that she opened the door for him.

"I'm Petro Fedyk," he told her breathlessly. "Thank you for letting me in. I want to buy my ticket."

She smiled and told him to sit down and wait until the office really opened for the day. He was happy to rest and feel secure that he had protected his fortune. Twenty-five minutes went by, and the woman went to unlock the doors for the day. She returned to her desk and called Peter.

"Sir! You may go to the cashier now to buy your ticket. He'll answer any questions you may have."

Peter stepped up to the cashier's window and reached inside his shirt. Mama had sewn a little pocket into the hem of his undershirt. He pulled out the money and began to count out the bills. The agent took the stack and began to recount it. He counted each bill singly, and when he came to one of the ten-dollar bills, he looked at it carefully and set it aside. He counted the money again and looked at each bill.

"This ten-dollar bill is counterfeit."

"Counterfeit?" Peter gasped.

"Yes, do you have more money?"

"Yes," Peter stammered and gave the agent another ten.

"Don't worry son, counterfeit American money is quite common. I'm afraid there are some people who think they can make their own money, and no one will ever notice. Don't worry, I don't think you did this on purpose."

"What will happen to the bad ten-dollar bill?" Peter asked.

"I'll keep it here. This has to be investigated. Give me your name again and your home address." Peter gave him the information. "Now where did you get this money?"

"My mother borrowed it from a landowner in a neighboring village."

"What is your mother's full name?"

"Maria Fedyk."

"Who is this landowner?"

"He's a German man. His name is Schelimberg."

"Does he live in Opaka?"

"No. His estate is in Felzendorf."

The agent wrote everything down. "The rest of the money is good. I don't think this Schelimberg is a thief. He probably got this as payment and never even noticed."

"He sells timber," Peter volunteered.

"Don't worry. This is a common problem, but one that must be checked. I'll send this ten-dollar bill to the government bank in Warsaw. They'll go to the bank in Lubachiv, and then there'll be an investigation. Probably even a lawsuit. It will involve your mother and this Schelimberg. The loss will go to the one who cannot trace where he got the money."

"Would it be possible to have some paper and a pen? I want to write home so that my mother will understand what has happened."

"Certainly. You'll also need an envelope," the agent said, handing him the supplies. "You can leave your letter at the front desk. Leave some money for the stamp, and we'll take care of it for you."

"Thank you," Peter said. He was grateful that the agent was so understanding.

"All right, Petro Fedyk. Everything is in order. The train leaves Lviv tonight at 23:00. You'll be going to Dvige."

Peter spent the day seeing some churches and parks near the train station. He knew about the university and the museums, but his eagerness to leave filled his head, and he couldn't concentrate on anything very scholarly. Besides, Lviv was no longer Ukrainian. He didn't want to see what it looked like when it was Polonized. He had ten dollars less than he had planned, so he ate very little and tried to find something to read.

Chapter 45

Evening came, and Peter was already at the train station. He found the correct platform and waited. Other travelers began to arrive to wait for the train. He recognized some of them from the steamship office but knew no names, and no one spoke.

The train pulled in, and Peter found the proper car. He found an empty compartment, put his suitcase on one of the benches, and sat down next to it. After a few moments, the door opened, and a man stepped in with two valises.

"Are you alone?" he asked. When Peter nodded, the man said, "Good. Sleep if you like. I have to go out to check on a few things. I am an agent for the steamship company. I'm going to lock the door. Don't let anyone else in until I come back."

Peter didn't sleep. He couldn't. He was tired but very excited. There was nothing to look at out of the window because it was dark, so Peter decided to read for a while. After a half hour, the man returned.

"Still awake? Well, I suggest we both get some rest. This is just the beginning of your journey. You'll need your sleep," he said while he put his valises overhead and curled up on the opposite bench. "Good night," he yawned and was snoring in a few minutes.

Peter opened his suitcase and found the little cross Mama had given him. He remembered how she'd looked as the train pulled away. He crossed himself and said his prayers. He kissed the cross and hid it again among his clothes, and after he closed the suitcase and slid it under the bench, he went to sleep.

The agent delivered his travelers to Dvige and went on to another assignment. Peter and the others expected to board the ship right away, but another agent came and told them that there was a minor delay. They were told that they would be housed in some barracks in the city of Vyhorova. Some trucks came and loaded all the travelers and then transported them to the new waiting area.

The barracks at Vyhorova were a dismal sight. They were long, unpainted buildings with rows of metal cots inside. The thin mattresses on the cots were old and damp. Peter remembered the cherished benches with the down-filled coverlets at home. He thought of his family and wondered what they were doing. He chose one of the cots and stowed his suitcase under it. Then he sat down on the lumpy bed, looked around the room, and sighed.

The "minor delay" stretched to two weeks. During that time the company had to house the travelers and feed them each day. The "food" was tea and marmalade sandwiches. One of the young men in the group muttered that the reason for such a generous menu was that the steamship company didn't want heavy travelers who would load down the ship. There were a few thin laughs when he said that, but laughter didn't chase away hunger.

The two weeks of waiting gave the company plenty of time to conduct more physical examinations. A regular series of showers began too. Sometimes twice a day, Peter and the others were instructed to shower and clean off with a strong disinfectant. It was feared that these peasants carried their own passengers—body lice—and the steamship company sold tickets only for humans, nothing else. At some of the physicals, Peter felt embarrassment again, but at least in Vyhorova, the doctor was a man. But here Peter had to endure a new indignity. All his hair, all over his body, was shaved off as an added precaution against lice and other parasites. When that was over, the boys in his barracks looked like convicts.

Peter saw himself in the mirror and was ashamed of how he looked. With all his hair gone, the bumps and contours of his head showed. His ears looked big, and his cheekbones seemed to protrude to emphasize the weight he'd lost on his meager diet. The eyes that blinked back at him from the mirror seemed too big for his face.

I'm glad Mama isn't here to see this, he thought. *Look at me! I could scare someone with this face and not even have to try. I look like a plucked chicken. Canada will take one look and send me back.* He shuddered. *I guess I have to be stripped of everything they can think of before I can leave here. All I have left is what's inside.* His reflection gave him a secretive smile. *What I have inside is me.* He rubbed his head and felt the stubble. *This will grow back, I guess. I swear I'll never wear my hair short again! Even if I begin to go bald, what little I have left will be long enough to toss in the wind.* He shook his head, and his reflection shook back. *They photographed us like this! And gave us copies for our traveling papers! I'll get rid of them as soon as I can.*

Peter turned from the old, speckled mirror and went to the cot he occupied in the barracks. He took out a sheet of paper and began to write a letter home.

"Glory be to Jesus Christ! Dearest Mama and dear brothers and sisters …"

What do I write about? he thought. *I can't tell Mama I'm hungry. She'd worry more. If I tell her about this damp place, she'll have a fit. Can I tell her I have a bald head? Oleksa'd love that. If he could see me, he'd never stop teasing.* Peter tried to begin the letter several times, but nothing seemed right. "I'm too hungry to write," he sighed.

He put away the paper and pencil and reached inside his shirt for his money pouch. He counted the coins and decided it was time to go to town to buy something to eat. He returned the pouch to its place under his shirt, but left a few coins out and put those into his pocket. He feared losing anything that was his, so he took his suitcase with him. If he lost that, he would lose everything he owned except the clothes he wore.

Peter found a bakery and bought two large loaves of dark brown bread. They were solid and hard. He carried the loaves and his suitcase to the edge of town, where he sat down by the side of the road. He opened his suitcase and wrapped one of the loaves with a clean shirt, and then closed the case. The other loaf he broke in half and ate one of the pieces hungrily. The second half he intended to save for late in the day, but while he walked back to the barracks, he gnawed on it like a dog with a precious steak bone. By the time he reached the low building, the rest of the loaf was gone. Peter smiled to himself.

"Blast you, hunger!" he cursed softly. "You won't defeat me!"

Chapter 46

The Voyage

Peter jumped. He was sitting on his cot, thinking about home and wondering if he would ever get to Canada, when he heard someone call his name in Polish. He turned to see one of the other young men from the barracks coming toward him.

"It's a telegram! From the shipping line. We all leave tomorrow morning at six!"

The next morning, trucks did appear, and the young future farm laborers for Canada were transported to the docks. After embarkation, Peter stood near the rail and watched as the ship began to cut through the harbor to the Baltic Sea to begin its journey.

"Good-bye, Poland," he muttered with a little smile. "I wondered if I'd ever get to leave, especially during these last weeks of waiting. Good riddance. I'll miss dear Opaka, but never you." He turned his back to the shore and went to the other side of the ship.

When the ship reached Liverpool, England, there was another four-day delay. Peter didn't mind it so much because the food was better and more ample, and the place where he had to stay was clean and almost pleasant. Finally he and the others embarked on a ship called the "Montroyal" for the voyage to Canada.

The weather was good during the first two days at sea, and Peter enjoyed the chance to stand on the decks and watch the empty horizon. He carried his suitcase with him all the time. He was constantly afraid of his things being stolen. Each evening he would watch the sunset and would think about so many things.

Chapter 46

There's nothing here but water and this ship. No land, no birds. The only thing that shows we're moving forward is the white foamy water that spills off the sides of the bow. He paused and thought how the white froth reminded him of the white apron Mama usually wore as she cut through the many chores of the day. He tried to push aside some of the thoughts of home. He couldn't think about it too much. It caused too much pain and doubt to spring up in his mind. He knew that what he was doing was the right thing for him, but the pain was always there. It hurt to be away from all he had ever known and the people he loved. He had been told as he was growing up that he needed faith to carry him when he was uncertain or afraid. Papa always said that in hard times, if he waited long enough, he would see some good come too.

Someone on the sea must have great faith, he thought. *We chase the setting sun each day, and there's nothing to see but water. Will we come to land, or will we fall off the edge of the earth like people once believed? Have I ever really met anyone who has been there and back?* He shook his head as if to clear it. *I've got to stop thinking like this, or I'll go crazy. Canada has to be there! Somewhere this ocean ends, and land begins again.*

Peter went down to his crowded quarters where there were rows of bunk beds. He found his and went to sleep. The next day, a violent storm hit, and Peter felt as if he were in the belly of a raging monster rather than a ship. The creaking and moaning sounds of the seams of the ship were frightening. He tried to get up and find the toilet, but the ship was being jolted so violently that he could barely stand. He'd grown accustomed to the rocking back and forth, but now the ship was pitching. The bow lifted high in the water and then came crashing down again to meet the next swell. Peter didn't know what was happening, but when he tried to walk as the bow lifted, his legs felt like they were filled with lead, and he could hardly move. Then, when the front of the ship fell back into the water, he would take a step and fly forward as if he weighed nothing. He blessed the handrails that were mounted halfway up all the walls of the ship's corridors. Without them to hang onto, Peter envisioned himself being tossed around like an apple in an empty crate.

The pitching and tossing of the ship would have made

walking a game if it weren't for the nausea he felt. His stomach hadn't felt this terrible since the time he and his family had had typhus. He tried to get to an outside rail before he added to the pools of vomit he tried to avoid in the corridors. The doors to the outside were tied shut with rope. The wind and rain were so strong that no one was allowed on deck. Peter finally stumbled into a restroom and found relief from his nausea.

The days that followed were only a blurred memory. He stayed in his bunk and tried to sleep. His stomach and his head seemed at war with the rest of his body, and the moaning of the ship only made him sicker. Peter had no appetite, but he vaguely remembered someone telling him to try to eat something. Every day he bought some oranges because they were the only things that sounded good to him. He found the hard, dry loaf of bread that he had stashed in his case in Vyhorova. It wasn't moldy, but it was as hard as a rock. He gnawed on it, and the dry crumbs tasted good to him. The sound he made while he his teeth scraped at it reminded him of old Pundyk gnawing on bones.

Finally the weather broke, and the sea began to calm. He crawled up onto one of the lower decks and saw a lot of the other passengers lying on the open decks. They looked like they had spent the last few days the way Peter had.

They look like pickles lying in a field, he thought, but he didn't find his own joke funny because he noted that most of them were quite green, and that made him sick again.

The air turned fresh and clear, his head felt better, and he spent the morning watching enormous animals in the ocean. He never saw the entire beast, but he did see huge wet backs as they plunged into the waves followed by the paddle-shaped tails.

"Whales," he marveled, hypnotized. *So many things I only heard of in school, and now I see that they're real! I see them with my own eyes, and I still can't believe that all this existed while I lived in my little Opaka. I wonder if it's all a dream and I'll wake up and find that I'm still in Poland. Oh, that would be worse than seasickness!*

By noon the ship had entered a fog bank. *The fog is like a dream. It's as if we've sailed into a magical world where nothing else exists, not even the sea,* Peter thought.

He leaned over the rail and couldn't see the water below. He turned and saw that the deck had disappeared beyond the limits of his view. There were voices from other people on the deck, but he couldn't see them. Suddenly the fog became cold and frightening. His eyes struggled to see farther into it and couldn't.

How can we continue safely? he wondered. *The ocean is so big, but we could run into another ship or even the land and never see it.*

The cold mist clung to him like the cold sweat of fear, and he shivered. He noticed that the ship's engines had died down to almost no sound. Some women started to wail. Bells began to ring, and a fog horn blew. Some people screamed with the sounding of the horns and began to panic. One woman began screaming in Polish that death was coming.

"The fog is a shroud," she cried. "It wraps us all to make us ready for the tomb!"

Peter crossed himself and considered going to his bunk, but the thought of going inside the ship was suffocating. *I'll stay out here and face what comes rather than run down into that hole like a scared rabbit. My journey can't end like this.*

The wailing and crying continued on and off for the next several hours. The fog horn was deafening, but Peter simply clamped his hands over his ears. He wondered if the ship could bump into a whale. He tried to think of fog at home and how he had used it sometimes to outsmart the wardens. He was far from the rye fields here, and Mama Cow wasn't around to help plot maneuvers. He found comfort in memories and thoughts of home. Time passed slowly, but it did pass.

After several hours, Peter realized that the engines had slowly started up again. He had been sitting on the deck, huddled against his suitcase and leaning back against the metal wall that held up the rail. His clothes were damp and cold, and he noticed how stiff his knees were when he tried to stand. He peered over the rail and saw waves down below. The fog was thinning enough to see the water again. He stared toward the horizon but still saw nothing more than murky grey light. After a few moments, though, he could see farther!

He heard some crewmen call to each other, and then more passengers began to come up to the rail. The crying and scattered sounds of hysteria ceased.

Someone behind Peter said, "See, Stashia? I told you it would pass in time. You've always been afraid of the sound of your own breathing!" Some unseen Stashia still whimpered slightly and then was quiet.

Peter stood transfixed, staring into the fog. He saw a darkening, shadowy line on the low horizon. *Oh no! More fog?* he wondered. He was frightened again. *Fog in the night will be so much more horrible. It really would be like being in a grave!*

Someone shouted, "Canada! Canada!" and Peter realized that the shadow was land. The fog lifted more, and he could begin to see the outline of the coast as it touched the sky. Far off in the shadow, a light twinkled. A lighthouse?

Peter crossed himself again, not for protection this time, but in thanks. His throat knotted up, and he couldn't swallow. His eyes burned with tears. "Canada!" he whispered in awe. "Even if the ship sinks now, my arms can pull me there through the water. My God, You brought me to the shore!" He forgot everything else for a few hours while he stood and leaned against the rail studying the coast. *It's real,* he thought, grinning.

It grew dark, and finally Peter pulled himself indoors. He had something to eat and then went to his bunk to try to sleep. He thought about what would happen the next day. "Tomorrow my feet will touch Canada," he told himself and smiled in the dim light of the sleeping quarters.

At breakfast Peter found he had an appetite. He ate two herring and some bread and drank down some strong, hot tea. He grabbed his suitcase and climbed up to the top deck. The ship was nearing the port of Quebec. He had never seen any of it before. There was not one familiar face or tree or building or rock. Nothing. All new. Peter shivered a little in spite of the warm sun. He disembarked with the others and moved with the crowd, but when the moment came for his feet to leave the ramp and step onto the dock, he looked down at his shoes.

I'm really here! he thought and felt like cheering.

Chapter 47

Going West

After his papers were checked so many times that Peter feared there was something wrong with them, he was herded into a holding area with some of the other passengers. The ticket he had paid for in Lviv included two more things before his journey with Canadian Pacific officially ended. He was entitled to a train ticket to Winnipeg and a box lunch. After he received those two items, he was on his own.

The train left in the early evening, so Peter decided to spend some of his time investigating the box lunch. There were sandwiches and some fruit. The apple he readily recognized, but there was something in his lunch he'd never seen before. It was long and yellow with big brown blotches, and it came to a point at each end. The skin of the thing was firm, and the smell wasn't unpleasant. Peter rubbed it on his shirt as he would an apple and decided to take a bite. The skin was waxy and bitter. He spit it out, disgusted by the flavor. He squeezed the two ends together and the skin split in several places. He thought that maybe it had to be peeled like an orange, but the inside pulp began to ooze out, and he noticed tiny black specks in the cream-colored interior. He tasted a little of the pulp, but the black specks bothered him, and he spat out everything, thinking it was probably spoiled. Peter's introduction to a banana didn't discourage him. He just muttered philosophically to himself, "So many strange things to learn."

The train ride to Winnipeg lasted three nights and two days.

Going West

Peter was certain that they had traveled far enough to go all the way around the earth, across Siberia and Russia, and finally back to Opaka. He saw mountains, waterfalls, lush green forests, cities, farmland, villages, and pastures and all sorts of people. When the train stopped in one of the many stations along the way, he sat looking out the window and was startled by a man he saw. The man's skin was black as soot, and not just on his face the way little devils were from night pasture. Anywhere his skin showed, it was a shimmering, jet black in the hot sun. Peter couldn't help himself. He just stared at the man until he turned and walked away into the station. The man had been dressed in a plain shirt and trousers and shoes, just like anyone else. He had seen a full-sized, real black man, not just a little sketch of some native in a geography book.

The world is so incredible! Peter murmured.

After the train reached Winnipeg, Peter and some of the others were counseled to go farther west. Some chose Edmonton or Regina. Peter and a few other workers chose Saskatoon, Sasketchewan, because it was the closest of the choices to Winnipeg. Peter had barely eight dollars left, and he was afraid he couldn't afford many more train tickets. Another day on the train brought him to Saskatoon.

As the train cut through the province, Peter looked out over the prairie. From the deck of the ship, the dark ocean had stretched as far as he could see in all directions. Now on the train, he saw a sea of grasses waving in what seemed an endless wind.

"The steppes!" he whispered in awe.

He remembered the writings of Taras Shevchenko and remembered what he'd learned about the wheat-producing steppes of Greater Ukraine. This was what it had to be like. He wanted to stand and sing the Ukrainian National Hymn. He didn't, but he felt his heart pound with a joy. Father Ivan's words came back to him: "In Canada, you can be who you really are."

In Saskatoon the young laborers were sent to an employment agency to register. Once again Peter had to sit next to his suitcase and wait until someone was ready to talk to him. He sat with dozens of other young men, all seeking work.

Chapter 47

A man of about fifty years came up to where Peter sat. He had an absurdly curled moustache that was stiff with wax. His clothing was very different from any Peter had seen. He wore a plaid shirt and had a little kerchief tied around his neck. His trousers were of a strange cut and made of dark blue cloth, and his boots had high heels that were curved in the back. The man smoked a cigarette in a long slender holder, and the smoke curled around his face, repeating the same silly curve of his moustache. He snickered at the young immigrants and in a clear, distinct Ukrainian began to drawl.

"And so, you greenhorns, what did you come here for? Winter is on our backs out here. What're you gonna do? The growing season is nearly over. You're gonna die out here like a bunch of field mice!"

Peter and the others who could understand him looked at each other. The words shocked them, and they wondered who appointed his man as the first greeting committee at the agency. Then one of the agency men stepped up and told the moustached man to leave. The agent smiled and began to speak in broken Ukrainian and Polish.

"Please ignore what this 'fine' gentleman has said. You'll all be able to find plenty of work. He was an immigrant himself a few years ago and now resents any 'foreigners' who come in after him. He likes to come here and cause trouble."

What a strange place and strange people, Peter thought.

After some talks with the employment agent, Peter and four other boys agreed to get on another train the next day and head for a small town called Prud'homme, where some work was available. On the train ride to Prud'homme, Peter had only one thought.

This traveling has to end soon. I've used up my money on tickets, and the coins I have left can't buy enough to feed a field mouse! Maybe the 'moustache' was right.

The train slowed, and Peter read the town sign as they neared the station. Prud'homme. After the train stopped, Peter and the other four boys hopped off carrying their belongings. There really wasn't much of a station there, and for that matter, Peter wondered where the town was. At home all the farm buildings and houses were clustered together, and the farm fields were beyond the village. Here the village center consisted of a few buildings and that was all. A man near the track saw them and knew by their clothes and bewildered looks that they were immigrant workers, so he pointed toward one of the buildings.

"Panko! Go see Panko!" he told them and pointed up the street.

Maxim Panko was the man who helped place the immigrant workers with local farmers. Peter remembered the name from the sheet of paper at the agent's office in Saskatoon. None of the young men spoke any English, but they all walked over to the building that had been pointed out to them. Above the doorway was a sign.

GENERAL STORE
M. Panko, proprietor

"Panko" was a Ukrainian name, and all of them hoped to find someone there who spoke a language they could understand. When they stepped into the cool, dark building, a thin man of medium height was sitting near a desk on one side. He smoothed his sandy brown hair, and when he approached them, he extended his hand in greeting and smiled.

"Welcome, my travelers! I had word that some of you would be arriving." His words flowed in a gentle, easy style of Ukrainian. "Welcome to my place of business. I'll show you where to put your things and where you can wash up after your journey. If any of you are thirsty or hungry, I can get you something to eat. Lunch will be ready in about two hours. There are cots in the back where you'll sleep while you're here, and don't worry, I'll keep accounts for you. You can pay me once you get work."

It was so good to hear the familiar words and to feel a little more secure in this strange new land. Peter felt himself relax. He remembered Father Ivan's words about the freedom in Canada where a man could exercise his own culture and traditions.

After Peter washed up and stashed his suitcase under a cot, he went back into the store. Panko was seated on a stool near a table where he was writing in a ledger, and when he saw Peter, he asked him to sit down and talk. Peter told about his family and his village, and Panko listened politely. He had a kind, friendly manner.

Chapter 47

Peter liked the store. He had always loved to visit the shops in Lubachiv when he was little. Papa would show him all the bins and shelves filled with such fascinating things and smells. The chances for exploring in those places seemed endless, but of course Peter had to stay by Papa's side and resist temptation.

Panko noticed him looking around.

"Yes, I have a nice little store here. It's good to be able to run your own shop. Would you ever want to own a business?"

Peter thought for a moment. "No," he answered politely. "I love to work on the land, and I also love to read. Right now I want to be a farmhand, and then in the future, I don't know where life will lead."

Panko smiled again. "I have some paperwork to finish here. If you like, you can go for a walk before lunch. As for a job, well, the local farmers come into town on Sunday morning for church. Maybe one will come looking for some hired help after Mass."

Peter thanked him and went out. His walk took ten minutes. There wasn't much to see. Peter spent most of the time reading signs and trying to decide what they meant. There was a post office, a drug store, a gas station, and Panko's store. Beyond that was the vast, almost treeless prairie. It reminded him of being on the ocean again. A golden ocean under a deep blue sky.

A few days passed, and Sunday arrived. Peter put on his cleanest clothes after he washed up. He saw his reflection in the mirror. He was glad that he'd been en route for over a month. His hair had begun to grow. It still looked funny, but at least it softened the contours of his head, and he didn't look like a convict. Peter had a late breakfast and then sat quietly and waited in Panko's store.

At noon a car drove up, and a man with dark brown hair stepped out. He was no more than ten years older than Peter. He was lean but strongly built and looked like he would be at ease with heavy farmwork, even though he was presently dressed in a suit. Panko was out in front of the store, and Peter watched while the young man spoke to him. Panko nodded and pointed to the store. Panko called Peter's name, and Peter stepped outside, smiling to cover his nervousness. Panko said something to the farmer. The farmer had a pleasant, open face and smiled easily. Peter thought he resembled Myhal with his dark hair and thick brows, but this man was much taller.

"This is a French farmer," Panko said to Peter in Ukrainian. "His name is Joseph Grimard. He's a good man and wants workers for his farm."

"Good," Peter answered. "I'd like to work for him."

"He doesn't speak our language, but he is a patient man, and I think you'll understand what he wants you to do. Just remember what I taught you."

Peter smiled, and the farmer smiled back. Peter remembered the coaching he and the other boys had been given by Panko in the past few days. He had taught them to say, "Yes, yes, Mister, yes, yes"; "Good, good"; and "Thank you." Peter found the "th" sound a hard one to say because there was no such sound in Ukrainian. Panko assured him that if he said "tank you," it would be understood and appreciated.

The young farmer extended his hand, and Peter shook it. The man spoke to Peter and smiled. Peter understood nothing but the tone of voice. It was pleasant and friendly. Panko told Peter to stay where he was and stepped off to the side with the farmer. They continued their conversation while Peter's thoughts raced.

Mister Joseph Grimard! I didn't know the people I was coming to in Canada. Now I know your name. I have my first job in Canada! Peter grinned. *Wait till I tell Mama and the others. They'll be so happy!*

Panko called out another boy, a young Carpathian, and told Peter that both of them would go to work for the farmer. Everything was settled. The boys got their suitcases, put everything into the young farmer's car, and went home with him.

Chapter 48

The Grimards

When Joseph Grimard and his two workers arrived at the farm, Peter was very impressed. As he had noticed from the train, settlements in western Canada were different from those he had known at home. In Canada each farmhouse sat on the edge or in the midst of its owner's huge fields. The house was a nice farmhouse by Canadian standards, but to Peter it was a mansion. It had two stories and was so large! Compared to the one-room house where he had grown up, it was enormous. It was painted a beautiful, gleaming white. Paint was so scarce at home. Papa used to whitewash the walls on the inside, but the outsides of the buildings were weathered wood. This roof was shingled, not covered with straw. The barn and other outbuildings were large and new and well kept.

Grimard led the boys into the house, and they found themselves in the large farm kitchen. Peter was overwhelmed by all the cupboards and the sight of the huge table all set with individual plates and glasses ready for a sumptuous meal.

A young woman was there waiting to greet them. Mr. Grimard pointed to her and then to himself while he spoke, and although Peter couldn't understand the words, he knew that this slender, fair-haired lady was the young farmer's wife. There was an older couple there as well. Peter noticed that their last name was different. It was Brisson, so he thought they were probably the parents of Mrs. Grimard. Peter's limited understanding of the language prevented them from ever explaining that they were really Joseph Grimard's foster parents. A little boy stood by his mother and looked shyly at the two strangers. He was about two years old, and his name was Johnny. Peter gave him a sly little wave and a smile and noticed that in spite of the shyness, the child smiled back before moving to hide behind his mother. Mrs. Brisson held Johnny's little brother, a smiling pink baby, about six months old. The baby was introduced as Gerry, but Peter wasn't certain if the name was one for a boy or a girl.

Peter and the young Carpathian boy, Yuri, were motioned over to a bench where they sat politely and watched the women complete preparations for the meal. The boys were amazed by the amount and variety of food being put on the table.

When the meal was ready, everyone sat down at the table. Mrs. Grimard said something to the young men and smiled. They understood nothing. She smiled again and then frowned. They didn't understand her invitation to dinner. Both Peter and Yuri were used to customs in their own villages. Back home, the host or hostess would grab the newcomer by the arm and energetically propel him to the table along with a spoken invitation. They misinterpreted what was happening and sat smiling on the bench.

Maybe we eat later, they both thought.

"Maybe Panko fed them dinner already." Mrs. Grimard suggested to the rest of the family and smiled at the two young men. They heard the familiar name, and both nodded and smiled and said, "Panko, Panko." They hoped their stomachs wouldn't growl too loudly.

The rest of the day, Mr. Grimard showed them around the farm. He showed them the fields and the tools and machinery. He explained how everything worked and pointed to either Peter or Yuri to indicate what their tasks would be. The boys understood none of his words but answered, "Yes, yes, Mister, yes, yes" to everything. The young farmer smiled and nodded his head when they repeated the newly learned phrase. He looked at the two boys trying so hard to please their employer and spoke to them good-naturedly.

"I could be talking to you in Eskimo, and you'd understand as much as you do in English or French. Isn't that right?"

Chapter 48

The boys listened, and then when the farmer paused after his question, they both nodded and grinned and said, "Yes, yes, Mister, yes, yes!"

Laughing, young Grimard patted them both on the shoulders and pointed them in the direction of the stable. He showed them the livestock, and finally, as if to save the best for last, he showed them his horses. Again the farmer's tone of voice and smile spoke loudly to Peter. The man obviously loved his horses and took great pride in them.

"You know," Grimard said softly, as if he were telling something more to himself than to them, "I had a young mare who was the most beautiful buggy horse I ever hoped to have. I lost her last winter to a fever." He remembered his grief, and his eyes glistened for a moment. "I tried so hard to save her."

He patted the firm, sleek side of his favorite riding horse and was silent. Peter had listened to Mr. Grimard and had heard the sadness and pain; he saw it in his eyes and watched how he gestured and lovingly touched and patted his horses. The way he handled the grooming tools as he showed how the horses' shimmering coats were to be brushed reminded Peter of other hands that had taught him how to care for these wonderful creatures.

Here is a man who loves and respects these animals, Peter thought. *Papa would have liked and respected this young French Canadian farmer.*

That night at supper, Yuri and Peter needed only a nod of Mrs. Grimard's head to show them the way to the dinner table. The young men had decided between themselves that customs were different in Canada and that these good people intended for them to eat.

The meal was heavenly. There was so much food! Creamy mashed potatoes, lots of butter and fresh bread, vegetables, roast chicken, hot coffee, and sweet, cold milk. Then dessert was something exquisite. It was round and cut into wedges. The pastry shell enclosed a mixture of sliced apples and sugar and spices. Peter experienced his first apple pie. His mouth watered at the mere thought of it for days afterward. One thing was certain. These

Canadians ate very well.

After supper Peter and Yuri enjoyed the Canadian evening. The wind had picked up and was beginning to be quite strong, but there didn't seem to be a storm on the horizon. Peter wondered if strong winds were part of the vast prairies of Canada. Forests were scattered sparsely, and the huge flat fields did little to slow down the winds that blew.

In a short while Mr. Grimard motioned to the two young workers to come over to him. He took off his wristwatch and showed it to them. He pointed to the number nine and then put one hand over his ear, tilted his head and closed his eyes. The boys nodded and grinned. He wanted them to go to sleep at nine in the evening. Then he pointed to the three. He opened his eyes wide and stretched his arms out into the air.

"Get up, get up!" he shouted energetically.

"Get up, get up!" the two repeated enthusiastically and understood.

Grimard led them to a small building, a bunkhouse, and showed them where to store their things. He smiled, wished them a good night, and left.

The boys were exhausted. It had been a long day, and they were more tired than they could ever remember having been in their lives. It was a weariness that did not come from hard physical work. It was from trying to absorb and understand everything they saw and heard. It seemed as if every bit of strength had been used up listening and watching their new employer explain their work and the new world around them. They both wanted so desperately to please the farmer and to do well, and yet they understood not one word of what he said. The customs and language were so different that they might as well have come from another planet, rather than just from across the ocean. They wasted no time in getting ready to sleep. The little building that enclosed them was sturdy and sound, but the howling and moaning of the wind made the dark bunkhouse eerie. Finally the wind blew so violently that the walls rattled. Peter pulled the blanket up to his ears.

"Are you asleep?" shouted Yuri from the bunk overhead.

Chapter 48

"No, I can't!" Peter screamed back, trying to be heard.

Neither could remember falling asleep that night, but they must have because a loud knock at the door before sunrise awoke them.

"Get up, get up!" a voice called through the door.

"Get up, get up!" the two answered in chorus. The new day began.

Chapter 49

Canadian Life

The boys came to the farmyard and saw that the horses were harnessed and ready. Mr. Brisson motioned to Yuri to follow him, and they went toward the barn to tend to the livestock. Mr. Grimard called to Peter and motioned for him to take the reins of the team and drive the wagon. Peter was to follow the young farmer, who had climbed up into the seat of his tractor and headed off down the road. As Peter drove the horses, he noticed there was some sort of machine attached to the back of the tractor. It was probably for threshing because they were on their way to another farm to help in harvesting wheat.

When they arrived, the farmyard was filled with wagons and machines. Peter helped unhitch the horses and led them into the barn before hurrying into the house. The kitchen was filled with men sitting and eating breakfast around an enormous table. Happy shouts and greetings were directed at the young farmer and his helper when they stepped inside. Grimard's face broke into a happy grin, and he introduced Peter to the men. Peter politely shook the hands that were extended to him in greeting. He smiled and felt very stupid.

I wish I understood something … anything, he thought and tried to grasp each word to see if any sounded at all familiar. None did.

They were shown to their places, and once again, Peter was astounded by the variety and amount of food heaped on platters on the table. He filled his plate with eggs and ham that looked familiar. He also tried a big helping of flat round things called pancakes. He watched what other men did and imitated them. He put butter and a brown sauce called maple syrup on top and then tasted a little of the creation. Peter thought he had died and gone to heaven. He concentrated on the delicious flavors and the feeling of pleasure that filling his stomach gave him. His thoughts drifted homeward to Mama and his family. They'd never believe this abundance. Peter was jolted back to the present by the sight of the last farmhand leaving the kitchen.

Oh! he thought as he gulped down his coffee, *I'll be late before I even begin!*

Peter took the rest of his sweet roll and stuffed it in his pocket. He scooped the last of his eggs and ham into his mouth and ran to the door. He mumbled "tank you" to the lady of the kitchen and bowed slightly while he tipped an invisible hat and ran out.

Joseph Grimard waited for him and shouted, "Petru, go!" and pointed to the fields. Peter jumped into the wagon and followed his employer out to the fields to help with the threshing. Peter was told to fill the wagon with wheat and then drive it to the machine for threshing. Mr. Grimard stayed by the machine to run it and feed in the grain. The young farmer was so quick in his movements that sometimes he fed the wheat too fast and clogged up the machine. Peter had never worked harvest that way before, and his movements seemed awkward and clumsy. He had grown up on a farm, but these methods were more modern and so fast. The older, experienced workers were already bringing in their second wagonloads to the thresher, but Peter hadn't finished his first load. Finally, Mr. Grimard came over to Peter and gestured for him to watch.

"Look, this is how you do it," he said.

He took the pitchfork and loaded the wheat with powerful, smooth movements. Peter watched intently, feeling even clumsier and foolish.

He'll wonder why he ever hired me, he thought glumly.

Grimard looked at him and smiled. "All right, Petru, all right," he said and pointed to the wagon. He went back to the thresher.

Peter took the fork and began to load again. He tried to imitate Grimard's style, and it seemed easier this time. He tried to move with the same sweeping strokes and saw that he moved more quickly. He glanced over to Grimard and saw the farmer watching him with a wide grin. Peter smiled sheepishly and worked as hard and as fast as he could.

An hour or so after noon, a horn sounded. Peter had never heard anything like it. He looked around him and saw all the other workers jump on the horses and gallop off across the fields. Peter wasn't sure of what to do, but he unhitched the horses and began to walk them back to the farm house. He looked for Grimard, but he was gone. When Peter finally reached the road, he saw Mr. Grimard sitting in an automobile waiting for him. Peter waved, and Grimard motioned to Peter to mount one of the horses to ride it back to the house. Peter did as he was told. After he passed the car and the farmer was behind him, Grimard began to blow the horn. The horses were afraid of the car, so they broke into a run and galloped back to the farmyard. The farmer was right behind them. Peter helped water and feed the horses in the barn, and then the two of them went to get their own lunches.

In the house the men were devouring still another enormous meal, and Peter knew that he would have to hurry up and eat if he hoped to get any food for himself.

Things happen so fast in Canada! he thought. He looked at the men at the table and saw that the food disappeared so quickly, it was as if it was being inhaled. When everyone was finished, all of them left to return to the fields.

Peter got the horses, mounted one, and prepared to return to his place in the fields. Just to make certain that Peter was getting used to the fast pace, the farmer followed Peter again in the car and once again encouraged the horses to move by blowing the horn at their heels.

That night in his bunk, Peter reviewed his lessons for that day, much the same way he used to review what he learned in school at home. *Life in Canada is good. Mr. Grimard is kind and is a very patient man, but he teaches me that the pace of life is much quicker than what I ever knew at home. The fields are bigger, the volume of work so much greater, and there's no more time to do it in. Each meal is a feast and so delicious! But that feast is meant to fuel workers that must work at a feverish speed.* Peter smiled. *Mama and Papa always taught me to work hard at home. But now. Oh, yes, now, I must learn to work much, much faster!*

The threshing went on for weeks because the area on Grimard's farm and the neighboring farms was so large. The only thing that delayed the work was rain. It was a nuisance to the farmers because it meant that the enormous amount of work to be done was interrupted. Still, after days and weeks of exhausting labor, a day of unexpected rest was welcome too.

Peter, Yuri, and a third boy who had been hired found themselves idled by the rain one day. They helped with the livestock, but there wasn't much else to do. At breakfast that morning, they noticed that Mrs. Grimard was preparing to do some laundry in spite of the rain. After the meal, she carried in water, heated it on the stove, and then filled the washtub. It was impossible to do the regular wash because she couldn't hang the clothes outside to dry, but the two children needed some clean clothes. Gerry needed diapers and fresh sleepers, and Johnny, who was into everything, always needed a few clean shirts to make it through the day. The needs of little ones didn't wait for nice weather.

The young woman sighed quietly. She was tired. The baby had been up several times the night before, probably because the little fellow was teething. The gloomy day made the long hard task seem dreary. She was determined to find something good to think about. Gerry was napping, and Johnny was happily playing with a little wooden bowl and his favorite toy dog on the floor. Now was her chance to get some work done. After an hour of scrubbing on the washboard over the steamy water and soap, the last of their clothes was done. The young mother straightened up and felt the knot of tired muscles in her back. She brushed away a lock of hair that kept falling down over her forehead and smiled.

I've done this in record time today. Now I'll rinse it and hang everything near the stove and have plenty of time to spare to start lunch!

She hummed to herself and talked to Johnny, who was

now playing with some pot lids he had found in a low drawer. The kitchen door opened. She turned to see the three hired hands standing there with pleading looks on their faces and arms full of heavy homespun shirts and underwear. They said something to her in their own languages. She didn't understand their words and at the moment wished she didn't understand what they meant for her to do, but she did understand. The sight of the stack of heavy homespun material made her wilt. She looked once more at the pleading faces and sighed. She pointed to a chair and gestured for them to leave their things there. They all began talking and gesturing again in what must have been gratitude for her kindness. All she understood was "tank you."

"Tank you, tank you," she said with an exasperated but sympathetic smile and waved for them to leave so that she could get on with her work.

Still another day of threshing was interrupted by rain. They were able to work for two hours in the morning, but then the skies opened up again, and heavy rain fell. When Peter and young Grimard came into the kitchen for some coffee, Mrs. Grimard was there. In a few moments Mr. Brisson came in, followed by another young farmer. The men sat and made plans to go to a neighboring farm to catch a young bull to take to market.

Peter understood most of what they planned to do, but chose to concentrate on the aromas drifting from the oven. It was the day Mrs. Grimard baked bread and other pastries. He was quite distracted by the desserts those smells prophesized. Mr. Brisson pointed at Peter and said something about the wagon. Peter nodded. He had always been used to the methods of the Jewish cattle dealers in his own country. He was about to see how things were done in Canada.

As they prepared to leave, Mrs. Grimard pointed to a pile of ironed and folded shirts and other clothes on the bench. Peter recognized his things and gathered them up. Everything looked so fresh and nicely ironed that he wanted to thank the young woman. He was frustrated that all he could say was "Tank you verrrry much!" His r's were rolled and pronounced the Ukrainian way. He bowed slightly while he repeated the phrase a half dozen times more. He meant the words sincerely, and after a moment the young woman was embarrassed and smiled. She waved for him to go, to get ready to leave with the men.

The rain began to lighten as the four men headed for the neighboring farm. Peter rode in the wagon with Mr. Brisson and two of the farm dogs. Grimard and his friend rode on fine, sleek horses. They came to the appropriate field and stopped at the gate leading into it. Peter was told to position the horses and wagon in such a way that the road would be blocked just beyond the gate opening. This way, if an animal came galloping out of the gate, it could only turn one way to run down the road in the direction of the Grimard farm. Peter did as he was told but did not know what was going to happen.

Young Grimard and the other horseman galloped off toward a woodlot on the edge of the huge field. Before long they disappeared among the trees. The dogs ran off ahead of the horses, and everything became very quiet.

Peter and Mr. Brisson sat silently in the misty rain and waited. Peter had a chance to look around him at the endless open fields. The woodlot was one of only two that he could see anywhere in the distance. He continued to be amazed at the size of fields and the farms around Prud'homme. It was so unlike home. For once, even under the grey, dreary skies, the prairie winds were almost calm. Peter and the old man sat quietly and listened to a faint breeze blow past their ears. Suddenly Peter heard a noise that sounded like distant thunder. He looked toward the woodlot, and at first, he thought he saw a racing herd of deer. The animals came rushing out of the trees and were headed straight for the open gate. Peter felt a moment of panic when he realized that they weren't deer at all, but a herd of young steer. The two horsemen expertly turned the herd toward the field. They rode hard and separated one young bullock from the herd and chased him to the road. The bull ran through the gate and down the road in the direction of Grimard's farm, with the horsemen and dogs in pursuit. Peter and Mr. Brisson followed after they had closed the gate. The bull was skillfully chased right into the barn, and the men, satisfied with a good morning's work, went into the house for lunch.

After lunch Grimard gestured to Peter to hitch the strongest horses to the wagon. The bull was tied to the back of the wagon, and the plan was to lead the frightened beast to town while the horsemen followed. It seemed like a logical plan, but the young bullock dug his feet into the ground and refused to move. The horses strained to pull, but all that happened was that the wagon creaked and moaned as if it were going to come apart board by board. The bull began to bellow and froth at the mouth.

Mrs. Brisson ran out of the house shouting something and pointing to the animals. Peter didn't understand what she said, but as usual he felt sorry for any animal in distress. He'd never been able to watch a creature suffer in any way. The men weren't being cruel; they were just involved in a battle of wills and strength. Grimard untied the bull and set it free. The new plan was to chase the beast all the way to town. The bull seemed to sense what was in store for it and did all it could not to cooperate.

It's as if it knows it'll lose its freedom forever and wants to make the men pay for it somehow, Peter thought philosophically.

It took the men and horses an hour and a half to go six miles.

This is one job I never want, Peter thought. *The cattle dealers of the world are welcome to their work and will get no competition from me. I understand what they do, but I love freedom so much I can't watch while anything or anyone loses theirs.*

Chapter 50

Family and Flight

After the threshing was done, the other boys went to work and live on other farms, and Peter was left alone with the family. As the colder weather set in, he helped to store hay for the livestock and to bring in the remaining crops. With winter coming, the family told Peter that he could have a cot in the house and would no longer need to sleep in the bunkhouse. Peter felt highly complimented by their offer and was pleased that they liked and trusted him enough to let him live in their house. Peter liked the entire family.

He spent most of his time with the young farmer and greatly respected him. He seemed to genuinely love his work and showed deep concern for his animals, especially his horses. Another thing that Peter admired in Joseph Grimard was his fairness. Whenever Grimard had anything of great importance to discuss with Peter, especially his pay or the conditions of his work, he would take Peter to town to see Panko. The farmer explained things to Panko, and then the shopkeeper would carefully translate everything to Peter. Grimard had done this for all of his immigrant laborers. Peter appreciated the young farmer's understanding and care for justice and fairness.

If all Canadians are this way, Peter thought, *then, indeed, this is a wonderful country.*

Peter had always loved being around children and was fond of the two on the farm. Little Johnny was a smiling, energetic child. He was fairer than little Myhailo, but he had the same appealing charm of happy, inquisitive toddlerhood. Peter often watched the little boy play with his stuffed dog. Johnny liked to come over to Peter and talk while he showed him the fuzzy toy.

I wish I understood what he said to me, Peter thought. *Mama and Papa used to call me their scholar, but I feel so dumb! I can't even talk this new language as well as a two-year-old!*

The baby, with his smiles and coos, communicated very easily with Peter and seemed to understand Peter no matter what language he used. *At least I'm at the level of a six-month-old baby,* Peter thought, laughing.

Peter liked to watch the way Canadian parents raised their children and to see what it was like to have grandparents living with the family. He watched them all in the same fascinated way he had always watched life going on around him. In spite of the frustrations he felt, he also felt the familiar joy of learning new things.

They show me such trust and friendliness, he reflected often. *They never seem to forget that someone like me is lonely and far from home.* He always smiled at this thought and reminded himself to give thanks in his prayers each night.

One day Peter had just come into the farmyard by himself with a load of potatoes he had dug. He unloaded them and was about to return to the fields for more when Johnny ran out of the house and shouted to Peter. He held up some cookies and two pieces of candy and seemed to offer them to Peter.

"Cookies and candy," the child said, smiling.

Peter smiled back and said, "No. No, tank you." Peter's mouth watered at the thought of the sweet snack, but he had been taught that it was extremely bad manners to take anything from a little child, even if he seemed to offer it. Perhaps the child didn't mean to offer it at all, and to take it might be cruel.

Johnny didn't understand Peter's polite manners and was hurt that his friend didn't want the treats. His little face turned pink, and the boy burst into tears. He turned and ran toward the house and disappeared through the door.

Peter watched him run away and knew that he had hurt the boy's feelings. He felt terrible and sighed. *I could go after him, but how would I explain what I meant? No one can understand me either.* He shrugged his shoulders and began to climb onto the wagon.

"Petru!" Mrs. Brisson called from the door. Peter stepped down again and turned to see what she wanted. The woman came out leading the child by the hand and trying to comfort him as they walked.

"Petru, why didn't you take the cookies and candy from him?" She sounded irritated, and Johnny stood there looking up at Peter and sniffled.

Peter tried to formulate an answer. "Can't do it," he said, stumbling over the words. She looked puzzled. "No take cookie," he said, hoping to clarify his words by using gestures. "Johnny alone. No Mama here. No take cookie from boy alone. Not good. Not good to take."

His face pleaded with her to understand his inadequate words. He didn't want to offend anyone. She looked at him for a moment, and then her expression softened.

"I think I understand," she said. "It's all right, Petru. All right. You can take it." She nodded her head. "Johnny wants you to have them." She leaned over to comfort the boy. "He just didn't understand what you meant, dear. You know he doesn't understand our words all the time."

The little boy's face brightened. He held out the treats to Peter, and Peter felt that it would be proper to eat them right then and there. He bowed formally to the child and shook his hand while he thanked him. Then, while he ate them, Peter made appropriate sounds and patted his stomach to let Johnny know that the snack was delicious and very much appreciated. Johnny began to laugh, though his eyes were still tearful.

"See! Petru took them! He likes them!"

"Oh, yes! Petru likes zem very much!" Peter assured him.

Peter thanked the little boy once more and patted him on the head. The boy and his grandmother walked back to the house, and both Johnny and Peter did a lot of smiling and waving.

No doubt about it. These are good people. He hopped up on the wagon, sat down, and took the reins. He smiled to himself. *I'm very, very lucky.*

One day Grimard explained to Peter that they had to make a trip into town to see Panko. It sounded important, and Peter hoped that he hadn't done something wrong or that his job wasn't in danger. The family seemed friendly, and everything was fine, but he was a little worried. Life was slowing down, and there was little else to do than tend to animals and repair things in preparation for the winter. Peter feared losing his job.

Panko's store was a warm, friendly place, and Peter usually welcomed the chance to go there and talk to someone in his own language. Panko greeted them and asked if he could help with anything. Grimard began to explain something to Maxim, and Peter waited for the translation.

"Well, Petru," Maxim Panko began. "First, don't look so worried. Nothing is wrong. Mr. Grimard is very happy with your work. He says you work hard and learn quickly." Peter sighed with relief. "He came to discuss money."

Mr. Grimard explained more.

"He says that now that winter is almost here, he can't pay you more than the five dollars a month that the government gives you as a stipend for coming to Canada as a laborer. He can give you room and board in return for your help around the farm, but a regular wage will have to be suspended until field work begins in the spring. He wants you to stay on. He says you're a good worker, and his family likes you. What do you say?"

Peter smiled at the young farmer but felt sick inside. *I didn't think of this,* he thought. *I know the cycles of the year and how scarce farm money is at different times. I'm so happy with my new life here. I love farmwork, and the Grimard farm is a pleasure to work. But I have saved so little, and I owe Mama so much for my passage. Five dollars a month for all the winter months would leave almost nothing to send home! What can I do? Winter is almost here, and I don't even have a coat warm enough to hold off a prairie blizzard. And Mama? What of Mama and her big debt to the German?* He understood his employer's position and would have loved to stay in this place where he was happy and felt secure. But Peter knew he could not stay.

"Mr. Panko," Peter said, feeling his throat tighten. "Tell Mr. Grimard that I'm very sorry to have to say this. I have a huge debt to repay my mother. She borrowed the money for my passage and must pay it back with interest. She's a poor woman. I have to earn money to send to her." Peter paused. He regretted having to leave. "Tell him that he has shown me such kindness and patience! I didn't expect it in a foreign land. I'd greatly love to stay. He has a beautiful farm. It's a pleasure to work there. I understand his position and know that he also has debts."

Peter was saying so much that Panko motioned for him to stop while he translated. The farmer nodded, and his smile changed to a look of understanding. Peter went on.

"I regret to say that I'll have to leave. I don't know where to go. Maybe you can direct me to a city where I can find a job. I'll do anything."

Panko translated and then thought for a moment. "I was talking to another immigrant worker yesterday who wants to go to Toronto for work. There's a large Ukrainian community there. I can even give you some names. People who might help you. How does Toronto sound? It isn't the prairie. I'd feel strangled there in a city with all those people and buildings. But there might be work there. What do you say?"

"I'll go where I must. Thank you." Peter felt like crying.

"The worker is leaving in three days. Can you be ready?"

"Ask Mr. Grimard if I may leave then."

The young farmer looked like he understood, but he also seemed a little disappointed. He nodded, and the discussion ended after a few words about the cost of the ticket and the time of departure. Peter and Mr. Grimard drove back to the farm that day in silence.

Before supper that evening, Peter went out to stand by the fence to watch the sunset. He leaned on the rail and stared out at the fields beyond. The conversation at Panko's ran through his mind.

Oh God, I hate to leave. These are good people. I know it was

Mama's prayers and your kindness that brought me here. I could've been sent to work for some peculiar character like the moustache in Saskatoon. Now I have to get back on those long trains again. He sighed. *My duty to Mama isn't hard. I only wish I could fulfill my payments by staying here. But my wandering isn't done yet.*

He looked up and saw a small bird flying high in the air.

Ah, my little friend, he thought as it swooped by. *Did I ever tell you about the storks? They taught me the need to fly. I guess I flew a little too far, and now I have to retrace some of my path. I could have been so happy here. These were going to be my own steppes. The Ukraine I never got to see. Everywhere I looked, I saw my flag of blue over gold—the sky and the wheat. I came to an old friend here. I came to the land. It felt different in my fingers, and the color was different, but it is good soil to work. Now I go to a place called Toronto. A city. What's a farm boy going to do in a city?* He shuddered. *He'll do whatever he has to, I guess.*

He remembered the storks from that distant morning.

I thought I was like them, flying from one place to another. Free to glide on the wind and find a safe haven. Well, I found a haven here, but now I have to go on. I'm not as free as the birds. They aren't really immigrants. They own the lands they fly over and rest upon because their kind has owned them for centuries. They have no nationality except that of a continent or maybe even two. I'm an immigrant. I don't own the land I fly to. I won't go back and forth. I'm a seedling that needs to be transplanted, and I have to find a place to root before I run out of life. I don't know where I belong yet. I don't have a secret map in my head, like the birds, to show me the way. I have to find my way through wandering and seeking. So that's what it means to be an immigrant.

Peter stood still for a moment and watched the horizon and the sunset. It was magnificent. The bands of orange and pink and purple clouds flared like banners of fire across the pale sky. He said his night prayers while he watched. At the end he included a prayer of thanks. "Thank you for this safe haven. I hope you'll lead me to another one someday, somewhere."

A bright evening star began to twinkle above the horizon after the sun was gone. Peter remembered such a star back home in Opaka. Like an old friend, it cheered him a little. At least some things could be the same. There was comfort in that. He turned and walked toward the house lost in his thoughts.

I wonder if you can see stars in Toronto. All the buildings and the smoky air in cities. I wonder if the evening star shines there too.

The next three days went quickly. The Grimards and the Brissons were kind to Peter and let him know that they were sorry he was leaving. Mrs. Grimard cooked some of his favorite foods and did his laundry for him so that his clothes would be clean and fresh for the journey. They wished him well in his new work, whatever it might prove to be. Peter said good-bye to them with regret but with gratitude for all they had done for him. Mrs. Grimard packed him a huge lunch for the train. It was nothing like the meager packet he had received from the steamship company in Quebec. She even included some apple pie and a little packet of cookies and candy that were suggested by Johnny.

Joseph Grimard drove Peter to the station and waited with him for the train. The other boy who was to go to Toronto was already there when they arrived. Then it was time to go. So many thoughts had gone through Peter's mind in the last three days. There was so much he wanted to say. This young man's family was Peter's first real contact with the people of Canada. The experiences on the trains and in employment centers did not count. These were real Canadians. He was a stranger, a foreigner, and they had taken him in and made him feel welcome. They had put up with his first growing pains of learning about this new land with all the patience and kindness of a real family. He hated the fact that he couldn't express himself well enough to explain all his thoughts. The young farmer extended his hand to Peter. As Peter shook it, the young farmer smiled.

"Good-bye, Petru. Good luck to you."

Peter felt sad and said in the best English he could manage, "Tank you very much. For all you do for me."

His face explained what he meant and the sincerity he felt. Joseph Grimard nodded. Peter boarded the train with his suitcase and his lunch and waved good-bye as the train pulled out of Prud'homme.

Family and Flight

He sat by the window and looked at the fields. The sun was rising high in the sky, and he sat on the shaded side of the train. He saw his reflection in the window of the train as if he saw himself traveling and could sit back and watch his own adventure from a safe distance.

No, he thought. *I am the traveler. This is what I wanted. I've always had questions, and now I look for my own answers. Still, Mama, I wish you were here to answer my questions the way you and Papa did when I was little. But I'm not little anymore.* He looked out at the prairie that stretched to the horizon. The vast open prairie, like the world, was both frightening and exciting. *I wonder what will come, where God will point. I wonder, but I will not be afraid. I've been given a great gift. Freedom. To grow and to learn.* He looked at the grasses and the last few tenacious flowers bending in the wind. *The costs are so very high.* He looked at the prairie, but saw his family and Opaka. *With such a gift, I must cherish it and nurture it and try to be worthy of it all my life.*

Peter gazed at the images of his family and saw his own reflection as part of them. The train traveled on, and after a time he saw the smiling faces blend and become so like the blossoms of the field flowers that bent and endured in the harsh prairie winds.

Epilogue

There are many types of heroes. Mythical ones slay dragons. Others fight in wars or conquer vicious foes. Some face the despairs and losses and ironies of life head-on, and in spite of everything, they dare to believe in a dream. Life threw pain and obstacles in Peter's path, and too often good fortune eluded him, but at a very young age, he set his course and stayed on it for the rest of his life.

In Toronto, Peter found the people Panko had suggested. He worked as a busboy and then a short-order cook. A few years in the food-handling business taught him to be suspicious of restaurant food for the rest of his life. In time, he saved up enough to repay the money his mother had borrowed for his passage.

In his free time Peter joined a Ukrainian youth group. He became part of their dancing troupe and found he had real talent as a folk dancer. In 1933 he met Stephania Karman, a young Canadian-born girl of Ukrainian descent. Their dance instructor often paired them for special dances to be done by couples. They fell in love and were married in 1935.

In order to better support his wife, Peter looked for whatever work he could find that paid a little more money. He worked for a construction company and then later for a silversmith. Most jobs were temporary, and finally the frustration of not being able to find long-term employment caused Peter and Stephania to immigrate to America. On New Year's Eve of 1937, they went to Detroit, Michigan, to begin the new year and a new life in the United States.

Peter applied for his first citizenship papers as soon as it was possible. He found work with the Ford Motor Company on the assembly line. When the company began to do defense work, Peter was laid off because he was not yet a naturalized citizen. Peter was never drafted into the armed forces because he was just over the age limit. In 1943 he and Stephania became naturalized citizens of the

United States of America. His new citizenship gave him a deep sense of pride, but it did not automatically give him an easy life.

He entered an apprenticeship program to become a tool and die worker. Soon after he began, the program was dropped because new regulations stated that future apprentices could not train on the job and instead had to go for formal technical training. Because of the language barrier and the need to support his wife and himself, he sought other work. He worked with an electrical contractor and then in an auto body shop. Finally, he found employment with the Chrysler Corporation as a semiskilled laborer and stayed with that firm until he retired in 1975.

In 1941 Peter and his wife suffered the loss of their firstborn son because of complications in delivery. Fifteen months later, a daughter was born, and almost four years after that, a second daughter arrived.

Peter never really enjoyed his work or city living, but his sense of duty to his family dictated that he keep his factory position for the sake of even the tenuous job security the automotive industry offered. It was after work hours that he pursued his ideals of learning and patriotism. He became involved with the Ukrainian community in Detroit, and in his free time, he worked as the secretary of a branch of the fraternal insurance company known as the Ukrainian National Association. He served in that capacity for the rest of his life. He chose not to live in an ethnic Ukrainian neighborhood, but rather he and his wife raised their children in an area on the edge of Detroit where neighbors came from many ethnic backgrounds. He was an avid reader and not only studied classic novels, but also enriched himself in geography and history through reading and watching films and television. His love of nature and the soil was nurtured in his gardening and rare walks in the country. He and Stephania fostered the love of learning in their daughters, and both worked to see to it that in spite of the expense of higher education, both children went on to school. Their elder daughter became a registered dental hygienist, and the younger received her master's degree in physical geography and began a career as an interpretive naturalist for the State of Michigan.

Epilogue

Of Peter's immediate family in Opaka, the following is known:

Maryna died at the age of seventeen. Word of her death reached Peter on the day before his wedding.

Maria Fedyk died in the autumn of 1938. Three years before she died, she sent Stephania her treasured white wool shawl with the pink and red roses as her wedding gift.

Daria stayed married to Viktor Holkavich for the rest of her life. They had three more children in addition to little Marko. She passed away in 1965.

Myhal and his wife, Anna, had two children and spent their lives working the land and caring for their family and Maria Fedyk as she grew older. Myhal died in 1967.

Oleksa served in the Polish army in World War II. He was taken prisoner by the Germans, and while he was a prisoner of war (POW), he labored digging trenches during freezing, wet weather. It was believed that those conditions were the cause of a terminal bone marrow disease he developed later in life. After the war, before the delayed physical problems began, he immigrated to France with his village sweetheart. They married, had two children, and spent their lives working as tenant farmers. Oleksa died in 1960.

In 1971 Peter, Stephania, and their younger daughter traveled to Opaka. Peter visited his village for the first time in forty-three years. Of all of the family he had left behind, only Kashia was still alive. She had married, and she and her husband had three children. His other nieces and nephews were grown and living in the village, with families of their own. Ivan Soroka had also married and remained in Opaka as a farmer his entire life. One evening during Peter's trip, over rounds of vodka, Ivan and Peter recalled their escapades in Kazhanko's fields.

During the visit to Opaka, Peter's wife and daughter saw the poverty in the poorly developed area he proudly called his home village. Peter only saw how very far everything had progressed since his childhood and the war years.

In 1976 Peter and Stephania returned to Opaka for another brief visit. They left money there for Kashia's medical needs and to restore the deteriorating grave sites of Myhailo and Maria Fedyk.

Epilogue

Peter and his wife were looking forward to a happy retirement and the enjoyment of their grandchildren. He also began a hobby in woodcarving and found great pleasure in it. On February 5, 1978, Peter died suddenly of a massive heart attack. His sister Kashia died eight years later in Opaka after over a decade of chronic ill health.

Peter was my father. I am the daughter who traveled with him and my mother to Opaka. I saw the fields he explored as a child and the tree where he and his friends perched the farm wagon. When I was there, I began to understand the origins of my father's fierce patriotism and love of freedom. I understood what he left when he came to the West all alone. As a young boy, he faced the same trials as the rest of his family and his village, and yet it was his unique sensitivity and view of the world that made him so different from the rest of them. He had an overpowering dream, and he worked all his life to attain it. He never sought wealth, just a better life in a part of the world where he could be free. He dealt with whatever life sent to him, and he attained his dream. He never once forgot how precious it was. He never allowed himself to take it for granted.

His life and home were modest, but in comparison with what he left behind in Opaka, he lived in affluence. He took pride in all he did and gave it dignity because he believed in doing it as perfectly as possible. Whether he took great pains to make a mitered corner fit exactly in a carpentry project or simply polished the finish on his car, he did it with care and pride. He cherished and valued all he had—his freedom most of all.

Once, when I was little, he took me with him when he went to vote in a national election. No matter how tired he was after work, he never missed his chance to vote. In those days, there were no quick, efficient voting machines to speed the process. People waited for hours in long lines for the opportunity to mark their choices on paper ballots. The lines that day were incredibly long. It was early November, and we stood and waited in a drafty building until it was our turn to go into one of the dingy plywood voting booths. After an hour or so had passed, many of the people near us began to grumble and complain about the long wait and the cold. I remember that my father stood quietly and listened to them. I heard him sigh and felt him squeeze my hand gently. I glanced up to see his face, and he looked back at me with a serious, almost sad expression. “Little one,” he said, “they don’t know what they have.” But he did. He knew.

Glossary and Pronunciation Guide

NOTE: All letter o's are pronounced as the o in "for."

Baran *(bah RAHN):* a family name in the village; word means "sheep"

borscht *(BORE sh ch):* beet soup

Brama *(BRAH mah):* one of the village wardens; word means "gate"

bublichky *(BOO blich keh):* small buns or cookies

Bula *(BOO lah):* last name of man who acted as translator for Maria with the Prussians

Bura *(BOO rah):* one of the family milk cows; word means either "stormy" or "ruddy"

Chorney *(CHORE nee):* family name in village; word means "black"

Cyrillic *(seh RILL ik):* in reference to the alphabet invented by St. Cyril in the 800s. Alphabet used for writing Old Church Slavonic and for Ukrainian, Russian, and other Slavic languages.

Danzig *(DAHN tsig):* name of port on the Gulf of Danzig; now called Gdansk

Daria *(DAH ria):* Peter's half-sister

diak *(DYAHK):* man who assists the priest during religious ceremonies; the cantor

Fedyk *(FEH dik):* Peter's surname

Flis *(FLESS):* Maria's maiden name

Felzendorf *(FELL tsen dorf):* village near Opaka; an old German settlement

Galicia *(gah LEE tsee ah):* name of the region; crown colony of the Austro-Hungarian Empire

Gont *(GONT):* family name of kind neighbors next door to the Fedyks

Halychyna *(hah leh cheh NAH):* Ukrainian pronunciation of the region otherwise known as Galicia

Hershko *(hairsh KO):* Jewish grain dealer in Opaka; in English his name would be Hershel

Holkavich *(hol KAH vich):* family name of the man Daria married

holubchy *(HO loob chee):* stuffed cabbage rolls

hoopoe *(HOO po):* one of the birds native to Peter's region

icon *(I kon):* a sacred image, typically painted on a wooden panel and venerated by Eastern Christians, which attempts to portray the transfigured person or saint. In order to accomplish this, the artist does not attempt to show the third dimension and does not try to show real physical appearance, detail, or background; the artist uses blazing colors, a gold background, elaborate stylized clothing, and elongated features and eyes that gaze "beyond time." All this is done in an attempt to take the person viewing the icon beyond the present human state and to show humans what they are called to be. An icon is sometimes referred to as a "window of heaven."

iconostas *(ee KO no stahs):* the partition separating the area around the altar from the part of the church that holds the congregation. There are doors opening through it and icons suspended on it.

Irena *(ee REH nah):* Irene

Ivan *(ee VAHN):* John (Ukrainian)

Ivanchu *(ee VAHN choo):* diminutive of John; affectionate nickname; Johnny

Jaczko *(YAHSH ko),* **Janek** *(YAH nek),* **Janush** *(YAH noosh):* all are forms of John in Polish

Janko *(YAHN ko):* could be a form of John in Polish, but with the "ko" ending in this book, it is a Ukrainian surname; means "little John"

Janczura *(yahn CHOO rah):* Polish family name in village

Jordan *(yor DAHN):* literally Jordan (River); word used to name the holiday of Theophany (in Byzantine tradition) or Epiphany (in Western tradition)

Kazhanko *(ka ZHAHN ko):* family name in village

kasha *(KAH sha):* buckwheat groats

Kashia *(KAH shia):* short form or nickname for Katerina (Kathryn)

kistka *(KEEST kah):* stylus used to make Ukrainian Easter eggs

Knesh *(KNESH):* special bread made at Christmas

Kolada *(ko lah DAH):* a small bun, shared by the family at the beginning of Holy Supper

Komar *(ko MAHR):* surname of troublesome next-door neighbors

komora *(ko MO rah):* the main pantry; a room attached to the house, but entered by its own outside door

Koval *(ko VAHL):* a family name; the word means "smith"

Krashanka *(KRAH shahn kah):* a hard-boiled egg, dyed with non-toxic red dye made from onion skins

Krupka *(KROOP kah):* last name of one of the village wardens; word means one particle of buckwheat groats

Kucharski *(koo HAHR ski):* family name. If spelled with -ski ending, it is Polish; if spelled with -sky ending, it is Ukrainian.

kutia *(koo TYAH):* one of the traditional dishes at Holy Supper

Lubachiv *(loo bah CHEEV):* the closest large city to Opaka

Lukavich *(LOO kah vich):* a small village southeast of Opaka, near which the Prussians camped during the war

makivnek *(mah keev nek):* a poppy seed cake

Maryna *(mah REH nyah):* a form of Maria; first name of Peter's littlest sister

Maxim *(mah KSEM):* the name Max or Maximillian

Mlodzinski *(mlo DJEAN ski):* family name; the last name of Maria's first husband

Mooshka *(MOOSH kah):* the name of the little black dog who took Pundyk's place after he died; word means "little fly"

Myhailo *(meh HIGH lo):* Michael, Papa's name

Myhal *(meh HALL):* Michael or Mike, Peter's half-brother

Mykola *(meh KO lah):* is usually translated as a form of Nicholas

Oleksander *(o lehk SAHN dare):* Alexander, Peter's brother

Oleksa *(o LACK sah):* shortened form of Oleksander

Opaka *(o PAH kah):* name of Peter's village

Opshar *(op SHAR):* name of an area of fields, near the village

palamar *(pah lah MAHR):* the bell ringer at the church

pampushky *(pahm poosh KEH):* fried yeast buns, usually filled with prunes

Papa *(PAH pah):* word used as Dad or Daddy in English. Ukrainian children usually addressed their fathers as Tato (TAH to). Peter did, but in some parts of Ukraine, "Papa" was also used. "Papa" was used in this book because it is probably more familiar to readers of many nationalities.

Pan *(pahn):* Ukrainian word for "mister," "sir"

Panko *(pahn KO):* last name of Ukrainian shopkeeper in Prud'homme

Pashia *(PAH shia):* short form of the name Parascevia; Maria's sister, Peter's aunt

peech *(peech):* high shelf that extends from back of farmhouse stove to wall

perishkeh *(peh rheesh KEH):* dainty pastries made with prune and nut fillings

Petro *(pet RO):* Peter

Petrush *(pet ROOSH):* diminutive or affectionate nickname for Peter; also was shortened to Petru

pidpalkeh *(peed PAHL keh):* a large flat bread made on Generous Eve

Plashchenetsia *(plash cheh NET sia):* a tapestry showing the placing of Christ in the tomb, displayed in churches between Great Friday (Good Friday) and Easter Sunday

plishka *(PLEESH kah):* a small bird found in the region where Peter lived

prespa *(PRESS pah):* a long board placed on the ground on the sides of the house where water run-off from the roof strikes the ground, to prevent the formation of ruts in the soil

Pundyk *(POON dik):* the name of the family dog

pysanky *(peh sahn KEH):* Ukrainian Easter eggs

Roman *(ro MAHN):* the name Roman

Romko *(ROM ko):* the diminutive form of Roman

Shchedreh Vechir *(SH CHEH dray VEH cheer):* "Generous Eve," the day before Theophany (Epiphany)

slivovitz *(slee vo VEETS):* a strong brandy made from plums

Soroka *(so RO kah):* Ivan's last name; word means "blackbird"

Stash *(STASH):* Polish name; short form of Stanley

tetrapod *(TEH tro pod):* small table in front of iconostas. Ceremonies (weddings, baptisms, etc.) are conducted at this table. Table also holds icon of current feast day.

Tenuch *(teh NOOKH):* one of the village wardens

varenyky *(vah REH neh keh):* boiled dumplings filled with mashed potatoes, sauerkraut, or kasha

Vasyl *(vah SEHL):* the name Basil in Ukrainian

vooshka *(VOOSH kah):* tiny dumplings shaped like little triangles, filled with minced onion and mushroom mixture; word means "ears"

Voytek *(VOY tek):* Polish first name, translation unknown. Polish spelling is Woytek or Wojchiejc. Used "V" spelling for ease in pronunciation.

Vyhorova *(veh ho RO vah):* name of city near port where Peter embarked. In Polish the spelling is Wejherowo.

Vytol *(VEE tol):* Polish first name, translation unknown. Polish spelling is Wytol. Used "V" spelling for ease in pronunciation.

Zuravel *(zhoo rah VEL):* family name; Maria's sister's married name; the word means "crane"

zuruck *(tsoo RUK):* German word meaning "return" or "go back"